CW00970037

ADULTERER'S WIFE

ADULTERER'S WIFE

HOW TO THRIVE WHETHER YOU STAY OR NOT

C. J. GRACE

Jerome
Headlands
Press

Copyright © 2016 by C. J. Grace.

All rights reserved. No part of this book may be reproduced in any form or by any means, electronic or mechanical, including photocopying, recording or any storage and retrieval devices without permission in writing from the publisher, except in the case of brief quotations embodied in articles and review.

Published by Jerome Headlands Press, Inc.
Box 398
Hines, Oregon 97738
541-833-0080

Logo is a trademark of C. J. Grace.
Logo copyright © 2014 by C. J. Grace.
Logo concept by C. J. Grace, graphic design by James Ferrandini.
Cartoons copyright © 2016 by C. J. Grace.
Cartoon concepts by C. J. Grace, cartoon artwork by Aaron Austin.
Cover, interior design and print production by Lisa Petty, GirlVibe, Inc.
Editing by Diane Rapaport, Jerome Headlands Press, Inc.
Kindle formatting by Bookbaby.

PLEASE NOTE: Although every precaution has been taken to verify the accuracy of the information contained herein, the author and publisher assume no responsibility for any errors or omissions. No liability is assumed for damages that may result from the use of information contained within. The stories in this book have been substantially altered and fictionalized to protect identities, privacy and reputations. Any resemblance to actual people is coincidental and accidental. The information in this book is not intended in any way to be a substitute for medical, psychological or emotional counseling with a licensed physician or health care provider. This book is intended for mature readers as it contains profanity and some sexual content.

Any Internet references contained in this work are current at publication time, but the publisher cannot guarantee that a specific location will continue to be maintained.

Grace, C. J.
Adulterer's Wife: How to Thrive Whether You Stay or Not
1. Self-help. 2. Relationships. 3. Marriage. 4. Sex.
Library of Congress Control Number: 2016936002
ISBN 978-0-9618438-0-9
Manufactured in the United States of America
1 2 3 4 5 6 7 8 9 / 21 20 19 18 17 16

DEDICATION

I dedicate this book to all the women, both successful
and struggling, who have chosen to stay with adulterous husbands,
and to the brave souls who have shared their stories.

Help for the Horndog Blues

© 2016 C. J. Grace. Artwork by Aaron Austin, concepts by C. J. Grace.

Contents

ACKNOWLEDGMENTS

First, I want to thank all the women whose stories appear in this book. Next, I want to thank all the men I spoke to, especially those whose various forms of adultery provided me with fantastic fodder to include. I would not have had the imagination to make up some of the outrageous comments from philanderers that you will read in this book.

I am also grateful to my friends and family for all their suggestions and support: J. C. who encouraged me to write things down; P. T. who gave me useful feedback on early versions of the book and insisted that I have cartoons (even though she took a real dislike to some of the ones I planned to use); J. T. for numerous juicy tidbits and help with the later chapters; E. W. for his fascinating stories and endless support; C. T. for a reality check, incisive critiquing and valuable suggestions; and lastly my family members, most importantly the cat, for never-ending inspiration.

I also want to express my gratitude to Diane Rapaport of Jerome Headlands Press for marketing and publishing assistance, as well as developmental editing. I would groan at all the changes she wanted me to make, but once I had done them, I realized that she had helped me create a much better book.

Aaron Austin, a remarkably talented artist, deserves a big thank you for the fantastic cartoons he drew for me, bringing my ideas for humor to life more effectively than I ever could have imagined. Visit aaronaustin.net to see the range of his skills. I knew exactly what design I wanted for my cover, and graphic artist James Ferrandini took my poorly drawn sketch and turned it into something really sharp and eye-catching. Thank you, James—you are brilliant! Thank you also to Lisa Petty of GirlVibe, Inc. for book design and typesetting, a truly wonderful person to work with.

Without humor, a book about how to deal with an adulterous husband could be very dreary and depressing. I have been particularly inspired by the British comedy show, *Monty Python's Flying Circus* and its magnificent sense of the absurd. When I was a child, my parents, bless them, would let me stay up late to watch *Monty Python* on BBC1 TV. They even took me to see one of the episodes being filmed at Shepherd's Bush Theatre in

London—it included two seminal sketches: "The Dirty Hungarian Phrasebook" and "Mrs. Premise and Mrs. Conclusion Visit Jean Paul Sartre." I was in heaven! Those two sketches can be seen on YouTube and still make me laugh today. It is my belief that the seminal influence of *Monty Python* on comedy is like that of the Beatles on pop music. I should add that the American cable TV show *Penn and Teller: Bullshit!* and its fabulous fictionalizing was also a great source of ideas for this book. The program aired on the Showtime Channel from 2003 to 2010.

INTRODUCTION

Los Angeles, May 2013. I am attending a Kindle conference at a hotel near LAX airport. Participants in a long line wait to hear and critique the 30-second "elevator pitch" for my book—what I would say if I met someone influential in an elevator and only had as much time to talk to that person as it would take to reach his or her floor.

"I'm writing a self-help book for women whose husbands are unfaithful," I begin. The women to whom I pitch show considerable interest. A few admit that this is happening to them, and many more say they have a friend who really needs a book like that. Some of the men I talk to say they would buy the book for a friend. One or two even look pretty sheepish. Maybe these guys really mean that they would buy it for their wives. I continue my pitch. "If your husband is having affairs, how do you decide whether or not to stay with him? You might feel that your cornerstone has been kicked away and that you now have a gaping void in your life. How do you deal with the feelings of anger, loneliness, fear and betrayal? You could be swimming with dolphins in Hawaii, and yet your heart is filled with bitterness rather than joy. This book will give you tools not only to just survive but also to actually thrive within or without your marriage. You'll learn how to use the shock from your husband's actions to improve rather than diminish your life. Benefits you can achieve include increased self-reliance, joy and fulfillment; more adventure in your life; a new circle of friends; and psychological or even spiritual transformation. You'll be able to take back your power and gain both independence and peace of mind."

The response I got was overwhelmingly positive. "There's a huge market for this, and no-one is writing about it. It's a great subject." Were people telling me this just to keep me happy? All I can say is that I saw their lukewarm reception to a variety of other writing projects brought to them. Someone wanted to put a book together about how they had given up a big city job to run a New Age retreat center in the countryside. Another person wanted to write about tai chi. Someone even had a book about a topic related to mine—how to make your former boyfriend really sorry that he dumped you. But there was something about the subject I had chosen that seemed to touch a nerve and fill a need that set it apart from the others. It was not about taking revenge on an unfaithful husband; instead it was about how to empower the wife.

Back home, my book project languished for a few months. Then I began discussing the subject with various friends. I found that more and more of them would share stories of how they, or other people they knew, had dealt with unfaithful partners. As a former BBC radio journalist, I was used to interviewing people from all walks of life. Having lived on three continents, in Britain, America and China (where I worked for China Radio International in Beijing), I could attest to the fact that what one culture might take for granted as the norm or even sacrosanct might be seen as ridiculous or totally unacceptable to another. This was especially true as regards attitudes towards sex.

I found myself talking to women from several countries and all kinds of backgrounds, from the wealthy to the relatively poor. Each person provided new insights into how to cope with adultery. Yet despite the differences in background, there were many common themes. To protect the privacy of these women, all their names have been changed and in addition, stories have been combined, separated and somewhat altered.

I wrote this book specifically for the wives of adulterers rather than for the philanderers themselves. I am sure that some men will take a strong dislike to what I have written. They may prefer to keep their wives passively obedient rather than allowing them to take control of their lives. As far as adultery is concerned, there is somewhat of an "Old Boys Club" around the subject, with men covering for each other to hide the activity from the wives. New conquests may even be seen as a badge of honor.

Some of the people with whom I discussed this book wondered why I did not broaden its scope to include how husbands can cope with adulterous wives. I focused on helping cheated-upon wives rather than husbands for two reasons. First, despite the increased sexual liberation of women in the Western world, male adultery remains considerably more common than female adultery. Second, as a woman, I felt much more qualified to give a female rather than a male point of view on the subject. Nevertheless, I did talk to men—both adulterous and faithful—to get a more balanced outlook on infidelity.

One man described the anguish he had felt when the woman who was the love of his life began an affair—with another woman, no less, which he found to be a greater blow to his self-esteem than if she had cheated on him with another man. He asked me in a voice filled with regret, "Had I done such a lousy job of being her husband that it turned her off men for good?" I replied, "Of course not!" All I could do was tell him that the coping tools included in my book would most likely work just as well for men as they would for women.

The strategies I describe in the following chapters would also be valuable to women whose rival is not even a person at all. Men who work long hours or are frequently away on business can make their wives feel like virtual widows. Furthermore, many American males are sports nuts, obsessed with football, basketball and/or baseball. Watching the game takes precedence over everything else. Across the pond, many British men refuse to miss a single game, home or away, of the soccer team they support, leaving their wives alone for much of the time during the playing season. Similarly, there are guys who love to go away on fishing trips with their male buddies. In fact, in terms of participation rather than just watching matches, fishing is the most popular sport in the United Kingdom.

Aside from all the "sports widows" languishing out there, one woman described to me how she had become an "enlightenment widow." Her husband was frequently leaving her for trips to Japan to study with his Zen teacher. He insisted that he loved her deeply and wanted to stay married.

Sports Widows

© 2016 C. J. Grace. Artwork by Aaron Austin, concepts by C. J. Grace.

Of course, it was very convenient for him to have "little wife" keeping the home fires burning, managing everything while he was away. The bottom line was that, for good or ill, he put his quest for attaining enlightenment ahead of spending time with her. This particular woman was very supportive of his spiritual quest. "I'm not part of the 'Me Generation,' so it's not that I feel he always has to pay attention to me. But it can get lonely when he's away for long periods." She wanted to do whatever she could to keep the marriage going and was intrigued by the possibility that my book might have tools to help her.

This is not a book about couples therapy or how to reconcile with your husband. There are plenty of good resources already available on that subject, and I do not want to reinvent the wheel. Instead, I am writing about ways that you can feel more fulfilled and complete in yourself, whether or not you choose to stay with your adulterous husband. My aim is to give you some ideas that you can work with on your own, no partner required.

I hope that what I have written here will prevent women from following the extreme reaction that Angelika had to Stephan's infidelity. Her husband upped and left her for a younger woman. Although living apart from Angelika, Stephan chose to remain married to her, as it was more financially advantageous for him to do so. His wife floundered around for a year or two, trying all manner of New Age therapies to fill the aching void Stephan's departure had left in her life. Then she took her own life by swallowing an overdose of sleeping pills. Her 23-year-old daughter was devastated. What a tragic and unnecessary waste of a life! My choice would have been to divorce the bastard, move on and get my own life in order without him.

Originally, I had planned to give this book the subtitle *How to Thrive if You Choose to Stay*. However, friends of mine who worked in publishing told me this would limit the audience. They believed that some women would consider the idea of remaining with a philanderer to be a sign of weakness, and wives who wanted to leave their husbands would not think my book was relevant to them. Thus I broadened the subtitle to *How to Thrive Whether You Stay or Not*. My main aim—encouraging women to find ways to have a fulfilling life independently, without needing their husbands to feel complete—would be valuable whether or not the wife wanted to leave.

Plenty of books have been written about dealing with divorce, but how to continue to live with an adulterer has received far less attention.

This is despite the fact that many women do indeed stay with adulterous husbands and form a group that unfortunately receives scant support and little respect. They tend to be pigeonholed into the role of long-suffering wife or queen bitch—an object of pity or contempt. That is why, even though I did change my subtitle, I left the dedication as is to honor wives who decide to stay. If the husband dumps his mistress, it is easier for the two spouses to reconcile. Yet wives also choose the much tougher path of staying with habitual womanizers or men who will not give up their mistresses. Contrary to popular belief, this does not mean that these wives are sad, spineless examples of womanhood. Theresa, in her 90s when she told me her story, described her "until death do us part" marriage to a chronic philanderer in the 1940s. Extremely intelligent and fiercely independent, she was a tough cookie. After raising two daughters, Theresa became an attorney and later on a judge.

At first, I had wanted the main title of this book to be *The Philanderer's Wife,* but Katherine Trelawney had already nabbed it for a novel that she published in 2012. In addition, some of my journalist friends advised me against using "philanderer" in the title as they claimed some people were not familiar with the meaning of the term and might even confuse it with the word "philosopher." *Adulterer's Wife* was a second choice of title for me as "adulterer" has a much more judgmental, religious, "Ten Commandments" feel about it. You commit adultery, just as you would commit a crime, but you do not commit philandering. Philandering somehow sounds considerably more pleasant and romantic than adultery. A writer friend suggested naming my book *The Womanizer's Wife.* Despite the attractive alliteration, the word implies a lecherous, leering lout and I did not feel that it would be correct to define all adulterers as womanizers. *The Cheater's Wife* was another idea, but it begs the question, what kind of cheating? Perhaps he is a con man or cheating on his taxes. While writing this, the working title I used was *He Is a Fucker: How to Live with It.* However, much as I liked this name for the book, I knew that it might not be the best choice to grace a cover. Besides, there are many different meanings of the word "fucker," and it might not be clear to someone reading the title exactly what kind of fucker I was referring to.

As I have just been discussing fuckers, this is an appropriate time to warn you that the following pages are liberally sprinkled with salty language, profanities and politically incorrect views. For those of you with refined or conservative sensibilities who might be offended by this material, perhaps I shall bring out an F-word-free version of this book in the future. On second thought, scrap that idea—I will just stick with this version and assume that if you keep reading, my profanity does not bother you.

A female friend from my university days recommended that I include cartoons in this book to lighten up the subject a bit. I had never come up with ideas for cartoons before and did not think I knew anyone who would be able to draw them for me, so I thought her suggestion would never work. However, another friend—male, of course—lent me a 1971 book of cartoons from Playboy magazine entitled *Why Do I Get an Irresistible Urge to Laugh Every Time I Make Love?* (Playboy Press, 1971), which gave me a lot of inspiration. Then I found Aaron Austin, a gifted young artist who seemed almost telepathic in his ability to draw the pictures I had in my mind that I could only describe in words. Sadly though, my college friend was not impressed with my first batch of cartoon concepts for the book. They were all about sex, and she described them as "very explicit and crude and tending to emphasize relationships as being two-dimensional." My friend told me, "I was thinking of some more sensitive cartoons to highlight the broader aspects of a relationship. You have written so wisely about the other aspects—finance, self-confidence, children etc. I feel some of these should be represented too to give a rounder picture."

Aaron Austin had this to tell me about the cartoons he created for this book, "Humor is an important tool for defusing tension on difficult subjects and for dealing with life's challenges. Laughter has a way of cutting things down to size. Additionally, one cannot speak frankly about infidelity without speaking frankly about sex. I think a book for adults on the subject of adultery can't be shy about sex, and the cartoon ideas you gave me to work with are making honest statements on the subject that we can all laugh at. I think the cartoon idea about extra-terrestrial sex (see Chapter Nine) illustrates this point perfectly—we're discussing a biologically necessary activity common to all animals, and the crudeness of the subject is in the eye of the beholder."

Initially, aside from the sexual aspects of marriage and adultery, I was at a loss to come up with other humorous ideas that would work as cartoons. I admit it—I went for the low-hanging fruit, though later on in the writing process I did manage to develop some cartoon concepts that were not X-rated. Sadly, a few of the raunchiest cartoons did not survive final editing. Nevertheless, without sex, infidelity does not exist. So if you are an underage wife of an adulterer, you have never seen a naked body or you think you might be shocked at the sight of overly graphic graphics, stop now before you go too far…

Otherwise, whatever form of adultery, philandering, extramarital fucking or womanizing your spouse is committing, read on to find out how other women in similar circumstances have dealt with it, and what you can do to regain control of your life.

Have I been one of those women? You might very well think that; I could not possibly comment.

Chapter One

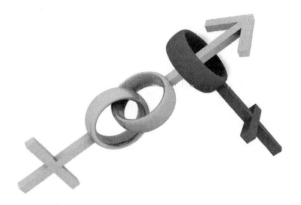

Discovery and Devastation

Completely out of the blue, you have been thrown into a deep, dark hole. After discovering his affair, the comfort and security that you took for granted has been replaced by an unrelenting feeling of dread in the pit of your stomach. He has made a mockery of the life you thought you had together—it now seems no more stable than a house of cards. The discovery of infidelity brings up an array of confusing, unpleasant feelings—anger, sadness, fear, jealousy, betrayal. There's a lot of shame attached to being the wife of an adulterer. It brings up all sorts of feelings about failure and lack of worth—common reasons for women rarely talking publicly about their husbands' infidelity.

No woman in any culture wants to be set aside for someone else. Wives of alcoholics can go to local Alcoholics Anonymous meetings to meet other women in similar situations and devise coping strategies. Various online support groups help people cope with an adulterous partner, such as beyondaffairs.com, survivinginfidelity.com or cheatingsupport.com, but local support groups with meetings that you can attend are few and far between. Yet infidelity is more common than alcoholism, and its effects can be equally devastating.

Phyllis was in a terrible state upon finding out about what her spouse was up to when he had claimed to be visiting his aged father in a retirement home. Up to that time, her husband had managed to hide the fact that his dad had actually died several months previously. Immediately after she found out about her father-in-law's death, Phyllis was distraught at her husband's betrayal and smashed into a couple of parked cars, driving away in a daze. Under normal circumstances, she would never have believed that she would be capable of doing a hit-and-run.

It is important to let yourself ride through the roller coaster of your negative emotions. Even if right now you think that you will never be free of them, over time they will most likely weaken, dissipate and change. Thus, it is important to make sure that you put off making any major decisions about how to deal with your marital relationship until you feel more on an even keel. The worst time for decision-making is when you are experiencing toxic emotions that are out of control.

In her seminal book, originally written in 1969, *On Death and Dying: What the Dying Have to Teach Doctors, Nurses, Clergy and Their Own Families* (Routledge, 2008), Elisabeth Kubler-Ross writes about the five stages of grieving experienced by the terminally ill:

1. Denial

2. Anger

3. Bargaining—trying to make a deal with God or some higher power to change things

4. Depression

5. Acceptance

Kubler-Ross developed this list from interviews with people who were dying. These stages may overlap, be combined, happen in a different sequence, or not occur at all. However, Kubler-Ross found that women were more likely than men to go through all five stages.

Many women grieving over infidelity go through this same cycle of feelings: first refusing to believe that their husband has been cheating; next becoming angry or depressed about it; then perhaps bargaining by trying to renegotiate the marital relationship in an attempt to reclaim their husband's affection. The final stage is to eventually come to terms with the situation in some fashion, whether the woman stays with her partner or separates from him.

Confronting Your Man

Perhaps deep down you were aware of your husband's infidelity, but you just didn't want to admit it or let him know you had suspicions. You may want to brush his philandering under the carpet and carry on as if nothing has changed. Some women can do this quite successfully for years on end; others find not telling their husbands what they know means that they are living an intolerable lie. Only you can decide which approach works for you. You may be able to keep quiet in the short term, but after a while you may feel compelled to confront your wayward spouse about his extramarital activities.

Many women spend little if any time working out the best way to tackle the confrontation. Understandably, they're just too damned mad to pussyfoot around. The tendency is to want to scream and shout, telling the scoundrel what a total and utter shit he is and perhaps booting him out of the house. There is a strong temptation to whack him in the face with a heavy object or destroy his prized possessions.

If you are so angry that you feel like you are going to explode when you confront your husband, you will react in a way that you are likely to later regret. You may be woefully unprepared for the slingshots that your spouse throws back and descend into an endless cycle of argument and acrimony from which there is no going back. Use some of the techniques described later in this chapter to help manage your fury. Before the confrontation occurs, try to take some time to carefully consider what results you want to accomplish that, in the long run, give you the most benefit.

Obvious Evidence

Sometimes a wife will have a nagging suspicion about her husband's infidelity and surreptitiously look at his texts, emails and credit card bills to check up on him. However, often the evidence of his affair is so obvious that you do not need to spy on him at all to see it. You just may not want to notice them. There are numerous signs of cheating. These include:

- You get an STD out of nowhere.

- You find condoms or Viagra in his suitcase.

- He is leaving for work earlier and/or returning later.

- He is taking more business trips.

- He will not let you get anywhere near his cell phone or computer, and they have become password-protected.

- He has set up a new email address, cell phone number and/or Skype account that you cannot access.

- He spends more time on social media.

- He becomes secretive about bank and credit card accounts.

- His attitude towards you changes, becoming more evasive and defensive.

- He is less interested in sex with you.

- He is frequently unreachable by phone.

- He is dressing better and taking more care over his grooming. God forbid he should scrape his new babe's delicate pudenda with jagged nails, or carve her shapely legs with serrated toenails, so they have all been cut short.

Alexandra didn't have to spy at all. Her husband, Jerome, had told her he would spend the whole day working on his computer in the local coffee shop. Then he totaled his car in a city that was a two-hour drive from home and was taken by ambulance to a nearby hospital. Alexandra rushed to see him. Jerome was evasive about what he was doing in a place two hours from where he was supposed to be. She initially thought this was caused by the shock of the accident. However, then she had to arrange for the car to be towed away and talk to the auto insurance company about the specifics of where and how the collision had happened. He had hit another vehicle while reversing out of the driveway of a woman he had dated prior to his marriage. It did not take Alexandra long to work out exactly what he had been doing there.

Excuses, Excuses

The excuses men give when confronted about cheating vary from extremely predictable to astonishingly off the wall. You might hope your husband says something like: "Yes, you're right to be upset. I'm so sorry for hurting you. I love you, not her. I'll never see her again. I'll do everything I can to make it up to you and save our marriage." Then he means what he says, follows up on his promise, and you live together in perfect harmony. Unfortunately, this is a very uncommon scenario.

When faced with the evidence of their adultery in such a way that they can no longer lie about it, here are some of the various scripts that cheaters have used. However absurd some of them might seem, none have been made up.

"I'm sorry. It was a mistake. I don't know what to say." What mistake is he sorry about—bonking the bimbo or the fact that you found out about it? In the 2013 movie, *The Wolf of Wall Street,* Leonardo DiCaprio, playing the title role, says something like this to his wife after she sees him canoodling with another woman in a limo. It is obvious he is only sorry about the fact that his infidelity has been discovered.

"I couldn't help it. It just happened." You have to feel sorry for the poor guy, ruled by his dick, with no free will in the matter at all.

"It's not what it looks like—I did not have sex with that woman." This is the kind of guy who, when he was in high school, told his teacher that the dog ate his homework, and the teacher didn't believe him either.

"She doesn't mean anything to me." So has he told the other woman that she is only a bit of fluff? Of course not! Or perhaps he is telling his floozy the same thing about you: "I'm only staying with my wife because of the kids. She doesn't mean anything to me anymore."

"It only happened once—I was drunk."

"She seduced me. It wasn't the other way round." Yeah, right—she just ripped the clothes clean off his back.

"I wasn't looking to fall in love with someone else."

"Don't worry—I'm not going to divorce you." What a relief!

"You're the one I really love, not her." Or "It doesn't mean I don't still love you."

"You just aren't enough for me." Obviously, he needs an assortment of willing females to feel truly complete. In terms of nurturing and emotional support, he is not enough for you either.

"I'm perfectly capable of being in love with two women at once." Yes, one for unbridled passion, and the other to make dinner, clean the toilet and do the bookkeeping.

"How can I choose between you and her? It would be like asking you to choose between our two children." This gem came from a dolt whose mistress was young enough to be his daughter, and he did not realize how inadvertently incestuous his comment sounded.

"I love you 100 percent. How could you expect me to love you more than that?" The trouble is that he is giving the mistress the same rap. He obviously inhabits an alternate universe with different mathematical rules where 100+100=100. This miracle man is also able to bend time and space in order to be in two places at the same time so that neither woman feels neglected.

"I really want to be with both of you." Just welcome her into the family. Yes, he really does want you to be a character from the HBO series, *Big Love*, that aired from 2006 to 2011. It was about the Henricksons, a polygamous family of fundamentalist Mormons in Utah. What a wonderful male fantasy to be Bill Henrickson with a bevy of adoring wives all living together in harmony!

"Don't you want me to be happy?" Well yes, asshole! But not by accepting the fact that you are sticking your dick in another woman.

"At my age, it's a gift to have fallen in love again." It may indeed be a gift for him—as long as the infatuation lasts—but no such thing for his wife.

"I did it out of kindness—she was feeling down and she needed some human affection." He really sees his dick as providing a public service.

"You're only upset because of your conditioning. You need to let go of having to be right all the time and find a way of being happy by accepting me as I am." Clearly the husband's conditioning does not fit well with that of his wife. Maybe she should accept him by finding a way of being happy with someone else with whom she does not have a conditioning mismatch.

"It's making me a better person so that I can be nicer and more loving to you." It is true that having great fucks can put your philandering husband in a good mood, but that does not necessarily translate into him treating you in a more considerate way.

"I reserve the right to fuck who I want, when I want. I don't believe in monogamy." What can I say that is positive about this horribly horny, humping husband? At least he is being honest. Grammatically incorrect, but honest. Perhaps the best reply a wife can give to this is, "Then I reserve the right to tell you to fuck off!"

"You shouldn't have kept pushing me to tell you what was going on— you were perfectly happy before." He is trying to place all the blame on you for finding out rather than taking any responsibility for his own behavior. You can imagine an ax-murderer telling his wife, "It's all your fault for discovering this—you really loved being with me before you knew!"

"The more love I give out, the more love I have for you. It will make me want to make love to you more, not less." Pure bullshit. If you show the slightest bit of dissatisfaction with the arrangement, he is likely to be less interested in sex with you. If you become as docile and submissive as the robot-like women in Ira Levin's book, *The Stepford Wives,* and do not criticize him at all, maybe he will be willing to have sex with you more or at least as frequently as before. However, there is a high chance that he might be giving you mercy fucks rather than anything based on mutual desire. You will know the difference and you will not like it. Of course, once you know that his dick is going into someone else, you may no longer be interested in sex with him anyway.

"We've had past lives together." This paraphrases what controversial Indian yoga guru, Bikram Choudhury, allegedly told one of several women who sued him for sexual misconduct. During a 2013 hearing for one of the lawsuits, Sarah Baughn claimed Bikram told her, "I'm completing karma with you," while pursuing her relentlessly and allegedly sexually assaulting her in 2008. (Her remark is quoted in the story, "Bikram Feels the Heat," written by Wallace Benjamin in the January 2014 issue of *Vanity Fair*). Choudhury has denied this and other claims of sexual assault. At the time of writing, the lawsuit has not yet been resolved.

Now I am not discussing whether past life karma does or does not exist, but how come cheaters come up with this line when they are having affairs with a pretty babe young enough to be their daughter? Why do we never hear about their need for some past-life nookie with the grandmotherly lady at the local post office or the overweight woman with a front tooth missing who bags their groceries at the supermarket?

Marital Damage Control for Dunces

© 2016 C. J. Grace. Artwork by Aaron Austin, concepts by C. J. Grace.

Interestingly, on the subject of karma and past lives, Tibetan Buddhist teachers will often tell you that everyone at some time or another has been your mother. They do this to make you aware of how you should be compassionate towards all sentient beings, whether or not you have any relationship at all with them in your present life. So that babe he is currently fucking was just as likely to be his mom as his girlfriend in a previous incarnation. Now that is a trifle twisted and incestuous!

Caught Cheating? Marital Damage Control for Dunces

You might assume that the dumb reactions men have when caught cheating means they deliberately want to end their marriages. More often than not, that is not the case. Here is advice for how men can exercise damage control and help stabilize their marriage. You are now reading the only part of this book specifically geared towards adulterous men, although my advice would be equally applicable for a wife caught cheating. "Caught Cheating? Marital Damage Control for Dunces" is also a page that you can find on my website, adultererswife.com, so you might want to print it out and leave it in a place where your husband will see it. Now you can give him some very specific guidelines to work with.

So listen up, philandering husbands! Unless you are absolutely sure you want to dump your wife and deal with most likely an acrimonious, expensive divorce, you need to invest your time in some serious damage control. Here are ten points to consider. Perhaps they will help you to salvage your marriage.

1. **Do not match her anger.** She is angry and probably rightly so. It may be a natural reaction for you to get upset and angry as she is pouring on the invective, a few words of which you may indeed find to be unjust. You may think that in some way she drove you into another woman's arms. You may also feel that she has been spying on you and thus be furious at her for invading your privacy. Think with your head rather basing your behavior on primitive emotions and your dick. Suck it up and stay contrite and friendly.

2. **Act immediately.** Do not wait for her needy and clingy phase to progress to self-reliance and independence. You may find that you

become quite irrelevant to her life. Take action before she no longer wants you around.

3. **Do not just say you love her—exhibit loving behavior.** Unless you back those words up with your actions, she will see them for what they are—hollow and meaningless. In his bestselling book, *The 5 Love Languages: The Secret to Love that Lasts* (Northfield Publishing, 2010), relationship counselor Gary Chapman describes five ways to make a partner feel loved:

   a. Saying words of affirmation that make her feel truly loved and appreciated.

   b. Spending quality time together.

   c. Giving her gifts.

   d. Providing acts of service—whatever it is that she would like you to do for her.

   e. Touching her affectionately. It is important to note that this physical touch can be either sexual or nonsexual. After find ing out about your infidelity, she may crave nonsexual hugs but be turned off by sexual caresses.

   Chapman claims that each person will have a specific preference and find one of these ways to be more important than the rest. It is up to you to find out how she responds to each of these five "love rewards" and use one or more of them to prove that you love her.

4. **Woo her back.** Think about your shared history together and remember what it was that you liked about her and enjoyed together. Remind her of that. Give her compliments that are genuine. Be romantic—groping at her while watching TV will not cut it. Spend some time paying attention to her alone. What if your wife no longer turns you on? Find other ways to make love to her if your erection isn't forthcoming and invest in a copy of Stella Resnick's excellent book, *The Heart of Desire: Keys to the Pleasures of Love* (John Wiley & Sons, 2012). She writes tellingly about long-term relationships that have turned celibate and how to bring back the sexual spark. Try to make love to your wife's whole body. Show her that you find her attractive rather than focusing on what your

wiener is doing. Turning her on might even turn you on. However, your wife may be so disgusted by the thought of where your dick has been that she recoils at your touch. You will have to woo her back gently, beginning with nonsexual physical affection, rather than expecting her to joyously and unreservedly welcome you into her bed.

5. **Be prepared to compromise.** Do not expect things to stay the same. She will not necessarily be happily providing you with all the wifely services you have been used to. She will be more likely to call you on your bullshit. She will expect you to prove you want to make things work by being more helpful and considerate than you were before. Step up to the plate if you want your marriage to survive. Be willing to go to counseling as this can help couples work together on repairing all aspects of their relationship.

6. **Focus on the mantra "I'm sorry. Please forgive me. I love you. Thank you for being my wife."** Think it, believe it, say it to her and use it to guide your actions.

7. **Do not tell her you love the other woman.** The classic question a wife will ask about your mistress is, "Do you love her?" Think very carefully about your answer to that question. You might believe that you love the other woman, but perhaps it is merely short-term infatuation. You are in lust rather than in love. Maybe you are having the best sex you have had for years and everything you do together is full of fun and laughter. Remember that you are still on best behavior with each other and that most affairs do not last more than two years. The more you get to know each other and the more the drudgery of daily life impinges on your relationship, the less fun it becomes. Telling your wife that you love both women equally will not cut it either. Who will come first for you? Will the interests of your spouse or your paramour prevail? In truth, the answer is obvious—your own interests will come first, won't they? However, what wife wants to have only 50 percent of their spouse's love and be second fiddle to the floozy? Get real—you would feel the same way if she told you she had a boyfriend that she loved as much as you.

8. **Dump the other woman.** You probably will not want to do that, but is she really worth destroying your marriage for? It is a rare wife that will knowingly put up with you keeping your floozy. The best way to preserve your marriage is to let go of the mistress.

9. **Open relationships open a Pandora's Box.** Despite the fact that you were having affairs first, you may find yourself consumed by jealousy if she follows suit. You may initially believe that she would never want to have another partner, even if you are philandering away, and maybe because of that you might tell her you would be fine with her having a lover too. But what if she finds one who is richer, better in bed, more attentive and/or less demanding than you? Just like you and your floozy, it will be all candy with no baggage. She may be the one saying *sayonara.*

10. **Remember that you and your wife are a team.** She is most likely very necessary for the smooth running of your life, even if you were the one who had to go to work every day while she stayed home. Appreciate your wife for what she has done for you. She has taken care of your home, your kids and maybe your business too. If you split up, it will be an almighty hassle. Most likely you will both be poorer and your standard of living will drop. If you own your home, you will probably have to sell it and move somewhere cheaper. Remember that you both have a lot to lose if the marriage fails.

All His Fault?

Taking a long hard, objective look at exactly why your husband is being unfaithful is likely to bring you well out of your comfort zone. You may think that you already know the reason why—it is totally his fault of course, the lousy shit! It is easy to put all the blame on him, but sometimes infidelity has more to do with the dynamic between the two of you that may or may not have unhealthy or dysfunctional aspects to it, and/or the force of circumstances. After the first few years of honeymoon are over, it is sad but true that marriage and great sex do not necessarily go together. Sebastian, a divorced man in his 60s who has been in a relationship with a married woman for several years, told me, "I had the absolute worst sex life while I was married, and now it's amazing!"

There are many reasons for adultery, but these are some of the more common ones:

- The boredom factor plays a big role in a husband's search for sex outside marriage. You will not like to hear this, but he could find sex with you dull after however many years you have been married. You may even be bonking each other regularly, but it is highly unlikely the spark you had earlier in the relationship still persists.

- Many men are drawn to forbidden fruit rather than what is always available. They want the excitement of exploring a new body that is not familiar enough for the sex to be predictable. Several men I spoke to believed that this was the number one reason why husbands have affairs. Couples who have been married a long time have to be willing to put effort into finding ways to keep their lovemaking fresh and alive.

- Because you have been taking care of the kids and house, and maybe also holding down a job or working in the family business, you may have become dreary and boring, not only to your husband, but to yourself. There is nothing new to talk about and little communication between you. Nothing seems exciting or interesting any more. Then on top of that, you feel sorry for yourself.

- A husband might begin having affairs as a reaction to finding out that his wife has been unfaithful, a situation sometimes known as a revenge fuck (although revenge may or may not be the true motive). That is what happened to Tom, who had been faithful to his wife for fifteen years, until she found herself a lover and made no secret about it. Tom began a relationship with a coworker that didn't last very long, but it opened the door to having one affair after another. Eventually the marriage failed. The two spouses began living very separate lives and simply grew too far apart.

- There may be other problems in the marriage, such as the partners no longer having sex. Celibacy in marriage is more common than you might think—more on that subject in Chapter Eight, "Sinking into Marital Celibacy."

- Men can become the equivalent of sports widows. Perhaps the wife has a job that involves long hours and has her traveling a lot. Maybe she has an intense interest in a cause that distances her from her husband. Jeremiah's wife, Sally, became heavily involved in radical feminism, to the extent that she did not seem to like men in general that much. She was constantly involved in demonstrations, protests, media events and planning sessions. Her activism began to take up most of her time and energy, and Jeremiah felt more and more excluded from her life. He filled the vacuum with an extramarital affair, finding himself a woman who did indeed like men.

• Now for a reason that you will find politically incorrect, but I will not sugarcoat it. I will put it in the third rather than the second person, so that you will not think I am talking about you. The wife may have become too fat, nagging or otherwise unattractive, at least in her husband's eyes. For example, what he considers to be nagging or meddling in his business might be what you are doing to try to avoid his asshole behavior affecting the family livelihood. Also maybe the husband has become fat and ugly too, but he still might be able to attract a woman on the side, especially if he has wealth and status.

• The unfaithful spouse may have a job, hobby or other interest that puts him in touch with a lot of other people in a close social environment and that takes him away from home for extended periods. He may spend the working week in one location, only coming home at weekends, or may travel a great deal. Remember the 2009 film *Up in the Air,* with George Clooney and Vera Farmiga? Their characters in the movie spend a great deal of time traveling in airplanes and have a torrid affair together, but Vera's character appears to be nonetheless happily married with kids. If two people are spending a lot of time working, studying or playing together, away from the family home—well, things happen.

Jerry was a chronic yet charming philanderer with the perfect job for his predilections—his company made custom closets, mainly for bedrooms. He would see each client twice—first to take measurements and then he would come to do the installation. Everything would take place in the bedroom, and most of the clients were women who were either single or whose husbands were away at work. Thus, Jerry had a steady supply of females to bonk, and after one installation was completed, he would happily move on to the next client.

- He may be in a position where many women make advances to him. Yes, seriously. Julio was a struggling actor whose wife had a steady well-paying job and supported him through many lean years in his career. Then he got a role in a TV sit-com that became quite successful. Now a minor celebrity, Julio was getting propositioned wherever he went. He eventually succumbed to temptation, and the result was not pretty. Once his wife found out, the relationship went downhill rapidly. She felt doubly betrayed, as she had financially supported him all those years. They stayed together for a couple of years but eventually had an acrimonious divorce.

- In sickness and in health? There is no doubt that the illness of a parent, spouse or child puts a tremendous strain on a marriage and can often lead to divorce, especially if the sick person is living in the family home. Most people are neither saints nor natural caregivers. Sometimes one spouse will begin an affair just to release some of the stress he or she is feeling, particularly if, due to ill health or because of fatigue from taking care of a sick family member, the other spouse is unable to have sex or has no libido. This is true for mental as well as physical illness. Clive's wife began behaving erratically and was diagnosed as bipolar. Although she was genuinely hell to live with, he decided to stay married until their two small kids had grown and were no longer living at home. However, he had no qualms about having affairs, some of which lasted for several years. When his youngest daughter went off to college, Clive divorced his wife and moved in with a woman with whom he was having a long-term relationship.

One of the saddest stories I came across concerned a famous New York doctor with a gorgeous wife, who helped him up the social ladder and was quite the hostess. Then she suffered a series of illnesses. Her physician husband could not take it and walked out on her in the middle of it all. The irony of this story is that his patients thought of him as extremely caring.

Revenge Is Not Sweet

When you discover your husband's affair, you might fantasize about cutting his dick off or maybe just kicking him hard in the goolies. You may imagine stabbing his floozy in the heart or punching her in the face. However, in most of the Western world, adultery is allowed, yet physically attacking your spouse or his mistress might cause you a few inconvenient legal problems.

In the movies, revenge is sweet. In real life, this is not necessarily the case. The desire for revenge can be a very toxic emotion that keeps you bound to all the negative effects you have suffered from his infidelity. Seeking vengeance can lead to endless hatred and bitterness—it never brings back what you have lost. It is very easy to smash something up, but it takes a lot longer to rebuild it. Out of revenge, you may do something you later sorely regret, but by then it may be too late to fix it.

I heard about a psychiatrist who was having an affair with a former patient. In a fit of rage upon finding out, his wife reported him to the medical board, and his license was taken away. This led to the loss of his practice and most of his income. The wife received a far lower alimony and divorce settlement than she would have been able to claim had she not turned her spouse in. Perhaps the man deserved losing his medical license for what he had done. Nevertheless, some might say that the psychiatrist's wife had cut off her nose to spite her face, acting out of revenge rather than good sense.

A famous aphorism from the New Testament illustrates the importance of forgiveness within Christianity: "Father, forgive them; for they know not what they do;" says Jesus while he is suffering on the Cross (Luke 23:34, King James version of *The Bible*). Quite an improvement on the "eye for an eye, a tooth for a tooth" revenge model from King Hammurabi's code of ancient Babylon. Nevertheless, "an affair for an affair" might actually be quite beneficial for some, but it might end up too much like hard work if you happen to have a horny goat of a husband who is out there bonking everything with boobs. If you had to keep up with all that fucking, you would feel like you were in a marathon race. In addition, bear in mind that revenge fucks do not tend to end well. If that is the main reason behind having extramarital sex with someone, rather than, say, you like him, find him attractive and enjoy his company, it is neither good for you nor fair to the guy.

The Dalai Lama is another spiritual leader who takes a strong stance against revenge. He advocates and genuinely practices compassion towards the Chinese who, for more than 50 years, have been persecuting people in Tibet and preventing them from freely practicing their religion.

If Jesus on the Cross and Tibetan monks tortured by the Chinese can forgive, how about trying to forgive your wayward spouse and his girlfriends? Even if you are an agnostic or an atheist, rolling your eyes at the mention of Jesus and religion, consider the value of trying to come to terms with your circumstances and finding a way to be at peace with yourself.

The bottom line is this: Why waste mental space thinking about how to take revenge on your husband and/or his mistress rather than putting your focus on making your source of happiness and fulfillment independent of the pair of them? The best revenge you can take is to move past the need for it. Easier said than done, of course, but it is still very much worth striving for.

According to Tibetan Buddhism, if you are guilty of sexual misconduct in your current life, in your next reincarnation you are likely to have a promiscuous, hostile and ugly spouse who also has committed sexual misconduct in a previous life. This rather bizarre belief appears in Patrul Rinpoche's otherwise excellent book about the Tibetan religion, *The Words of My Perfect Teacher,* (Harper Collins, 1994). Thus, as far as revenge is concerned, perhaps you can content yourself with the possibility that both your husband and his floozy will be unhappy and hideous to behold in their next lives. However, what Buddhists deem to be sexual misconduct varies considerably from one sect to another. Nevertheless, if there is a person you have come across who really looks like the back of a bus, now you have some idea of what he or she may have done to deserve it.

How Do You Deal with All the Negative Emotions?

It is easy to feel like a cartoon stereotype of the betrayed wife: anger and hatred towards your husband and the other woman; inadequacy, both sexual and psychological; fear and insecurity; and loss of trust. You may never have felt the slightest bit of jealousy towards anyone ever before, but now it arises in you unbidden whenever you think of your husband and his mistress. You may find yourself behaving in a way that you never had thought possible. Negative emotions can eat you alive and drive you insane.

In the beginning, you will find your mind turning to your husband's infidelity whatever you are doing. First thing in the morning; when you go to sleep at night; when you are doing your yoga practice; when you are driving; when you are working; even when you are out with friends. There is no doubt that the easiest thing to do is just to let your emotions take over, but this is the worst way to handle his infidelity. Keeping cool and taking a rational approach, although much more difficult to achieve, is worth the effort. It will serve you much better in the long run than allowing negative emotions to guide all your decision-making at this very critical period of your life. If at all possible, even if your husband and/or his girlfriend(s) are being absolute shits, take the high ground. Carefully look after your own interests and avoid an emotional meltdown at all costs.

If you feel mired in negative emotions, try to revitalize yourself by getting out of the house. Watch the ducks or the ocean waves, hear the birdsong and smell the flowers. Nature is a sanctuary. It might be a good idea to try to get out of the box you are trapped in—the one you live in every day—by doing something for someone else. You can start with random acts of kindness and perhaps then do some volunteering in your community. Supporting others helps you focus not on yourself and how pissed off you are, but on the other world that is out there. Knowing you have genuinely helped someone else does wonders for your self-esteem. Volunteering helps broaden your friendships and gives you a way to cultivate new connections.

Your husband's infidelity will most likely make you suffer shame and embarrassment. You may initially feel like a real failure. You have not been able to make the marriage work perfectly. You are not good enough, young enough, attractive enough or exciting enough to keep your husband's interest. You do not want to admit to anyone what has happened to your marriage. You feel a gaping void inside.

Then there is the fear. He has kicked out your cornerstone and your foundation feels really shaky. Is your home really your home anymore? Will you or he end up moving out? Perhaps right now he wants to stay, but later on is he going to leave you for her? Will you have to sell the house as part of a divorce settlement?

Sometimes your negative emotions may extend to others. You may suspect or actually discover that he has confided in a relative, friend, co-worker, client or employee. Perhaps the person was an enabler who helped him organize trysts and maintain the deceit, all at your expense. It will be difficult to be able to relate to that person in the same way, because he or she has betrayed you.

What should you do in a sticky situation like this? Even if deep down you might feel a strong sense of anger and betrayal towards a conspiratorial client, coworker or employee, it is best to keep a lid on your emotions in the workplace. Expressing them would be unprofessional and embarrassing to others. You are likely to be in a stronger position if you do not even let on that you are aware of what is going on. Willingly or unwillingly, that client, employee or coworker may be already on your husband's side. Whatever negative thoughts you may have about the person, it is imperative to behave as cordially as possible. If you lose it and rant at him or her, you can never take it back. It serves no useful purpose to make that person so uncomfortable that he no longer wants to be working with your husband.

Beware the downward spiral. If you let things slip and make a serious error in judgment in terms of your behavior or your actions, work hard to avoid becoming so disconcerted and out of touch with reason that you follow up with a series of even worse mistakes. Apologize and reverse decisions you have made, if appropriate. Try to maintain your mental clarity and sense of presence. Above all, acknowledge all those emotions coursing through you, but do not allow them to determine what you do and say.

If you have important decisions to make, postpone them if possible until you feel less emotionally raw. In addition, ensure that decision-making or important interactions with people are not taking place when you are tired or hungry. Under normal circumstances, you might be able to function quite effectively without having had enough sleep and/or having missed meals, but in your fragile emotional state, this may no longer be the case. You will increase the risk of making poor choices.

Josh Waitzkin, in *The Art of Learning: An Inner Journey to Optimal Performance* (Free Press, 2008), writes about witnessing a horrifying example of compounding errors. A woman listening to loud music on headphones and facing the wrong direction on a one-way Manhattan street walks into oncoming traffic and a cyclist bumps into her. She is unharmed, but rather than returning to the sidewalk, she turns to yell at the biker. A taxicab coming around the corner hits the woman from behind. She is sent flying into a lamppost, suffering serious injury.

You may also experience sexual revulsion towards your husband. Even if the lovemaking was fantastic with him before you discovered his infidelity, you may find that the thought of having sex with him now turns your stomach. Helen was never able to feel comfortable making love with her husband, Alfred, after she found out about his long-term affair with a co-worker. Sex had been an important part of the marital relationship. "I used to adore making love with Alfred. That was before I found out that he was also fucking Shirley. After that, if he tried to touch me, it felt like a cockroach was crawling on my skin." Helen spent a year trying to make the marriage work but eventually gave up and asked for a divorce.

Daphne, on the other hand, was initially disgusted with her spouse for having had a brief fling, and would not sleep with him for several months. However, after some time she relented and managed to reconcile with her husband. The wayward spouse has to be very patient and considerate to woo his wife back. Some couples find a marital guidance counselor can help them get back on track. If the husband dumps the other woman, there will be a greater possibility that over time his wife will be willing to sleep with him again. This is rarely the case if the other relationship continues.

Techniques to Tackle Toxic Emotions

Later chapters explain what you can do to find something to replace all those churning thoughts about his affair taking up mental space. In the meantime, here are four simple techniques you can try to deal with emotional spikes as soon as they happen rather than letting them fester. Your husband has pressed so many of your buttons that you simply want to explode. You want to avoid blowing up and reacting in a way that you might later regret—especially if you are both feeling stressed.

1. **Before you speak, slowly count to ten.** Do this even if you are as mad as hell or otherwise upset beyond belief and think you are going to lose it. You have heard this old chestnut numerous times already. The reason why is that if you actually do force yourself to do the counting, more often than not you'll have a lot more control over what will subsequently come out of your mouth.

2. **Focus on relaxing your breath.** When people are upset they hold their breath and tense up their bodies. Breathing becomes rapid and shallow. This can lead to a vicious cycle of your emotions making your body hurt, which in turn makes you feel worse, and causes your breathing to become even more jagged. Your emotions can literally make you sick. So see if you are holding your breath

or breathing in an irregular fashion. Try to relax your breathing, keeping the inhales and exhales even and natural. Make sure that you do not hold your breath.

3. **Notice where your body is tense and do your best to relax that area.** Perhaps it is your neck and shoulders or maybe your belly. Focusing on those areas and breathing into them will help you release the tension there. Now breathe into each tense spot at least three times, trying to feel the area, at the same time saying the mantra, "relax." You can say the word aloud or just repeat it silently in your head. Letting go of physical tension helps relax your emotions.

4. **Get the emotions out of your head and down into your feet.** Negative thoughts and/or emotions, and the energetic charge that accompanies them, become stuck in your head. For many, this causes a spike in blood pressure as well. You need to bring these toxic emotions down to your feet.

   To do this, focus, feel and breathe into the following areas in this sequence: top of the head, forehead, eyes, cheeks, jaw, throat, tops of the shoulders, breasts, belly, butt, thighs, knees and feet. As you do so, this will help you drop those emotions down from the top of your head, through your whole body, all the way down your feet into the ground below. You can do this standing or sitting and with eyes open or closed. Do whatever seems to work best for you. You can even practice this while engaged in an activity or while talking to someone. Maybe you will actually be able to feel all that nasty stuff sinking down your body, or perhaps you will just have to visualize it. Try to stay relaxed and do not force anything. You only need as much effort as you would use to look at the sky. You can practice this technique for as little as thirty seconds or as long as fifteen to twenty minutes.

Some men will react to you by simply mirroring your emotions. So if you get angry at him about his affairs, his defensiveness may manifest as anger towards you. You criticize him and then the tosspot will criticize you back. He will dig up all sorts of reasons why your actions and behavior have led to his infidelity. Whether or not you intend to stay with him, getting into this kind of escalating argument will not serve your interests. Furthermore, if you are constantly ranting at him, it will make you feel lousy and may prevent any possibility of reconciliation. Use the techniques in this section to try to dissipate your anger and defuse the situation. Even if you do not think reconciliation is what you want, you still need to be able have some sort of working relationship with your husband, whether or not he becomes your ex.

Nonviolent Communication

Developed by Marshall Rosenberg in the 1960s, Nonviolent Communication (NVC) techniques have been used worldwide in all kinds of settings including education, workplaces, hospitals, prisons and conflict zones. Indeed, a marriage torn apart by infidelity creates one hell of a conflict zone. According to Rosenberg, human beings tend to speak in terms of judgment and blame, disconnecting themselves from the feelings and needs of others. "It's not me, it's him/her that has to change" is what they proclaim.

The language of NVC is about learning to communicate with compassion towards oneself and others by developing empathy that leads to trust and nurture. To find out more about the technique, read Marshall Rosenberg's book, *Nonviolent Communication: A Language of Life* (PuddleDancer Press, 2003), In a nutshell, NVC follows a 4-step process based on Observation, Feeling, Need and Request:

- Make an objective observation of what your spouse has done in a neutral non-judgmental way.

- Describe the emotions that his actions or words have made you feel.

- Let him know a need you have that is not being met.

- Make a request to him to do something to meet that need. He then can do the same with you.

Many people have trained in NVC and found it to be extremely effective. However, some couples find it very hard to achieve its goals, particularly if only one of the two spouses is willing to use the technique.

This chapter has looked at how to mitigate the devastating cocktail of emotions that bubble to the surface when you initially discover your husband's infidelity. The next chapter describes how you can use all the crap that he has landed you in to spur you on to a more fulfilling existence than you had before. It can be a catalyst for positive change. No, it is not bullshit. You now have a golden opportunity to re-examine your circumstances to discover exactly how you want to live the rest of your life.

Chapter Two

How His Infidelity Can Transform You into a Happier Person

Can you turn lemons into lemonade? Most definitely. The point of this chapter is to give you some tools to catalyze a change for the better. If you take time and put in a bit of effort, you really can transform yourself into a more complete, mature, creative and joyful person. It is neither about revenge nor is it about showing your husband that you do not care about him anymore. Instead, it is about him no longer being the center of your universe, which he should never have been anyway. You are not doing this for him—it is for you alone.

Your life on this earth has no endpoint until you die. Some would say that to be fully alive, you need to continue to grow, change and work on new challenges. Yet a common belief is that all you need to do is get one thing sorted for everything to be wonderful. "I'll get married, then I'll be settled and have a happy life." "He'll dump the mistress, and we'll go back to loving each other." However, only fairy tales end with "and they both lived happily ever after." Real life is much more complicated.

Just believe in yourself and in your potential. Medical studies have shown that the placebo effect accounts for about 30 percent of healing for such conditions as pain, insomnia, depression, anxiety, bowel problems and urinary disorders. In other words, the power of belief alone can heal certain medical problems in almost a third of cases. Bruce Lipton's book, *The Biology of Belief: Unleashing the Power of Consciousness, Matter and Miracles* (Elite Press, 2005), describes groundbreaking scientific research that shows how your thoughts affect all the cells of your body. If you believe in yourself, you can achieve all kinds of positive changes in your life.

Your husband's infidelity should shock you into a very important realization. He is not your be-all and end-all. He is not the sole purpose of your life. You need to find a way to be complete in yourself, rather than needing him (or any other person) to feel complete. It is important to be able to gain happiness and fulfillment from activities that are not dependent on your husband. This is true for any relationship. If you were to leave your husband and make a new relationship, you still do not want to have a relationship based on need, so that you only feel complete with that person. You want to relate to the other person from a position of strength rather than from a needy feeling of being incomplete. That is how mature relationships can develop.

You may have spent a lot of your life ministering to your man and taking care of your children—even if the kids are now adults. Now it is time to minister to yourself. You have been given an opportunity (or what some might describe as a kick in the backside) to re-evaluate your life and reinvent yourself.

First, you must find a way to let go of the emotional pain that your husband's infidelity has caused you.

Use the Shock to Trigger Transformation

Personal transformation tends to be triggered by obstacles and adversity. If everything were on an even keel and hunky dory, why would you seek to make anything in your life different? As Malcolm Gladwell eloquently explains in his book, *David and Goliath: Underdogs, Misfits and the Art of Battling Giants* (Little, Brown and Company, 2013), adversity can either raise you up or smash you down. If you are trapped by constantly reliving the unpleasantness of something that happened in the past, such as how you were affected by finding out that your husband had a mistress, you cannot

Relaxation Therapy

© 2016 C. J. Grace. Artwork by Aaron Austin, concepts by C. J. Grace.

enjoy the present, and you certainly aren't living in it. You need to find a way to free yourself from the hold his infidelity has on you. Do you want to keep clinging to your emotional turmoil, or do you want to let it go? Hanging on to your anger will almost certainly fuck up the rest of your life.

The Buddhists emphasize the impermanence of life. Naked and alone you come into this world, naked and alone you pass out of it. Impermanence affects your life while you are alive, as well as when you die. Lovers, husbands, friends, good health and financial fortunes may come and go in ways that are quite unpredictable. You can never take for granted that everything in your life will stay the same. Buddhists and Taoists would advocate that you work towards maintaining an internal sense of stability, whatever changes are taking place in your external world. Or as a boxer would say, roll with the punches.

Relax, Damn It!

There is no doubt that your husband's infidelity will considerably increase your level of stress. Finding a way to deal with this will be crucial to regaining your peace of mind.

Husbands, whether philandering or faithful, often tell their wives that they need to relax. Sadly, the unsubtle ways they tend to do this are guaranteed to have the opposite effect:

- "Can't you just calm down?"

- "You're so tense—relax, OK?"

- "Lighten up."

- "Stop being so controlling—just let it go." His definition of controlling will be a tad subjective. What he really means is that you are dealing with something that he does not want you to deal with, or he does not like the way you are doing it. What he considers to be controlling behavior may depend on his mood and can vary from one day to the next.

- "You're being hyper. You need to relax."

- "You're so stressed out that it's making me stressed out too."

- "Take it easy, will you?"

Comments like these are generally delivered in an irritated tone with a sharp edge. They will usually make you feel more tension than you did before. For example, when you confront your husband about his infidelity, he might throw out an angry remark about your need to calm down. Is he simply criticizing you, or does he genuinely want you to relax? You will have to be the judge of that. At the very least, men making such comments are seriously clueless about human nature. Women tend to be less likely to yell at their husbands about their need to relax. This is probably because they have had to bring up kids, or even if they are childless, perhaps their childrearing behavior is genetically programmed. You cannot soothe a stressed-out child by shouting at him or her. Indeed, to reduce tension in both kids and adults, shows of affection, calming words and pleasant distractions will be considerably more effective than yelling at them. Massaging someone's neck, shoulders and back can calm that person down in a way that just telling them to relax never will.

Muttering Mantras

How do you get rid of tension and stay relaxed? Although massages and walks in nature help, mantras can be extremely useful. A mantra involves a phrase being repeated over and over again, with the aim of clearing the mind and developing meditative awareness. You can speak, whisper or silently hear the words in your head. Focusing your mind on the mantra can block out disturbing thoughts and prevent tension and unpleasant feelings from arising. Mantras are used extensively within Tibetan Buddhist and Indian meditation traditions. According to the Dalai Lama, practicing a mantra helps you transform your impure body, speech, and mind into the pure exalted body, speech, and mind of a Buddha.

Similarly, Catholics will repeat the "Hail Mary" prayer many times to help purify their thoughts and lead them to peace of mind.

Here are some examples of possible mantras you could use:

- The short version of the Green Tara mantra, *Om tare tuttare ture soha.* According to Tibetan Buddhism, Green Tara is an enlightened being and she provides humans with protection from worldly suffering. The translation of this Sanskrit phrase into English sounds fairly convoluted and certainly does not run off the tongue easily: "Essence of awakened body, speech and mind, quickly and boldly clear away the fear, distress and suffering of all beings, and have truth completely triumph over all negativity. May the meaning of this mantra take root in my mind."

- The most famous Tibetan Buddhist mantra, *Om mani padme hum,* relates to the Bodhisattva of Compassion. The literal meaning of the Sanskrit is, "Praise be to the jewel in the lotus."

- Any phrase you like, even "Abracadabra eeny meeny miney moe." It is best if the phrase has no real significance to you. You want to prevent the possibility of your thoughts getting stuck on the meaning and associations of the words that you are repeating.

You can repeat the mantra in your head if times are stressful, such as when your philandering husband, consciously or unconsciously, is making you feel tense; you are undergoing medical or dental treatment; or you are having a difficult time at work.

Let Go of Your Negative Emotions

Letting go of negativity is a key part of many of the world's spiritual traditions. You will find such techniques within Zen Buddhism, Tibetan Buddhism, Taoism, Christianity and various New Age movements. Christians might describe letting go as surrendering to Jesus or God. In Buddhism, the aim is to let go of attachment and aversion. The Taoists teach methods to dissolve negative energy blockages and find balance.

Joan Halifax, a Zen Buddhist teacher, emphasizes the importance of letting go when facing something that arouses even more negative emotions than infidelity: death and dying. Indeed, if you discover to your dismay that you are not the only emotional attachment that your husband has in his heart, you could feel that some aspects of the relationship you shared with him have died. In her book, *Being with Dying: Cultivating Compassion and Fearlessness in the Presence of Death* (Shambhala Publications, Inc., 2008), Halifax writes that letting go is not only to be done at the time of death. She asks readers to examine what they need to let go of to create a life "filled with meaning."

You do not have to subscribe to a spiritual tradition to let go. Marital counselors and psychotherapists offer their clients plenty of tools to do this. For example, psychologist and sex therapist, Stella Resnick, covers the subject in detail in her book, *The Pleasure Zone: Why We Resist Good Feelings & How to Let Go and Be Happy* (Conari Press, 1997).

A common simile used to describe how someone feels after hearing bad news is to say that it is like a punch to the gut. Among the cheated-upon women I spoke to, several commented upon getting an uneasy feeling in the pit of their stomach when they first began suspecting that adultery was going on. In Chinese and Indian meditation traditions, this area is considered a key energy center within the body. Known as the lower *dandian* in Chinese medicine and the *hara* in Indian Sanskrit, it is located about three fingers' widths below the navel in the center of the body. It is said to act as the body's brain and the governor of its health.

Another important energy center within these traditions is the *heart chakra* or middle *dandian*. It is located at the level of the physical heart, between and just below the breasts at the center of the body, or the solar plexus. This energy center is said to govern relationships and the emotions. Stella Resnick, in another of her books, *The Heart of Desire: Keys to the Pleasures of Love* (John Wiley & Sons, 2012), describes how to take inventory of different sensations in your body and notice areas where tension appears. According to Resnick, tension in the head may indicate mental stress; tightness in the throat could be anxiety or sadness; tension in the chest may also indicate sadness or anxiety, as well as fear; tightness in the solar plexus or belly could be guilt, anger or fear; and tension in the lower body and genital area may be a sign of shame.

Try this simple exercise to let go of whatever negative emotions you are experiencing:

1. Sit in a comfortable chair, close your eyes and relax, with your back relatively straight and a pillow for support if you need it.

2. Relax your breathing. You can do this by slowing it down a little and making it smooth and circular, especially in the transition between inhaling and exhaling. Try to avoid holding your breath at any point.

3. Take some time to try to recognize and become aware of the different emotions that are coursing through you. For example, you may feel anger, sadness, guilt, shame or disgust. Perhaps you will discover that certain things trigger particular emotions. Hearing music that you and your husband used to enjoy listening to together might

now make you feel extremely sad. The sight of his cell phone might make you feel angry as you remember all the incriminating text messages that you found to his mistress.

4. Look at how that emotion makes you feel and where in the body it appears to settle in or originate. Focus on a particular emotion, whichever one you feel the most strongly.

5. Now imagine that this emotion is concentrated in either the heart center or the *hara* in your belly, whichever place you can feel the most strongly. Focus on your feelings in that location. The emotion is like a hard dark ball of ice. Let it go by directing your intention upon slowly melting that ball of ice away. You can either imagine it dripping away down your body to the floor, or dissolving, vaporizing and dissipating outside your body, whichever feels the most comfortable. Do not force anything. Just try to maintain a relaxed focus on melting away that emotion.

6. When you end the practice, have a sense of dropping everything down your body through your feet into the ground.

7. If you get distracted by thoughts, try to let them go too. Go back to focusing on slow, relaxed breathing. Then try again to melt that hard block of emotion, so it dissipates either away from your body or down your body to below your feet.

8. You can focus on other emotions in later practice sessions. From one day to the next, different emotions may surface. This practice is easier if you work on one emotion at a time.

Some people have enormous difficulty letting go because deep down they want to hold on to their pain, disappointment, sadness or other negative emotions. A person may have become so used to those feelings that they are part of his or her identity, marking that individual out as a victim for all eternity. So it is important to ask yourself, "Do I really want to let this go, and if not, why not?" Make sure you are not just hanging onto the feeling of being right, fixating on thoughts such as, "I'm not the guilty party—he is," or "Yes, he really is a loathsome shit who has treated me appallingly." By letting those feelings go, you will leave space inside yourself to allow happiness to come back into your life.

Meditation, tai chi and yoga all have methods that may help people gain peace of mind and dissipate negative emotions. These disciplines have proved to be very useful for reducing stress and anxiety. Today, even a minor Internet or library search will lead you to many Western medical studies that will confirm their usefulness, such as those conducted by Harvard Medical School. You'll find classes in meditation, tai chi or yoga available in almost every small town in America. Trying them out can be a good way not only to improve your health and state of mind but also to meet new people at the same time.

Can't You Just Take Happy Pills to Feel Better?

If you are feeling like shit about your husband's infidelity, some might counsel you to take antidepressants. It is claimed they work by dealing with chemical imbalances in the brain. However, unless you sink into a clinical depression, feelings of anger and sadness are normal reactions to marital infidelity rather than signs of a chemical imbalance. It is up to you to take responsibility for finding a way to make your life happy and fulfilling rather than expecting the cure to come out of a bottle of pills.

Before deciding to get a prescription, take the time to read Peter Breggin's book, *The Antidepressant Fact Book: What Your Doctor Won't Tell You About Prozac, Zoloft, Paxil, Elexa and Luvox* (Da Capo Press, 2010). He describes some unpleasant side effects of SSRI (Selective Serotonin Reuptake Inhibitor) antidepressants, which are rarely publicized because the drug companies make billions of dollars ministering to human misery. According to Breggin, these drugs are heavily overprescribed.

There are numerous reports of people on these drugs developing violent and/or suicidal thoughts—although, who knows, maybe before taking any medication at all you already wanted to see both your deceitful dog of a husband and his witch of a floozy die a slow, nasty, painful death? Breggin gives the example of Eric Harris, one of the perpetrators of the Columbine High School Shooting in Colorado, who was taking Luvox for a year. Breggin also says that SSRIs may make you feel like one of those zombies in the 2012 black comedy, *Warm Bodies,* with psychotic tendencies, no libido, difficulty connecting emotionally and sexual dysfunction. The zombie protagonist in the movie, known as R, manages to come back to life by slowly falling in love with a warm-bodied human, Julie. You may not do so by continuing to take the prescription if you get side effects like these.

Get Out of Your Comfort Zone

Most likely you are stuck in a rut, particularly if you have been married a long time. You have made a habit of staying with what is comfortable and familiar. Once the cozy cocoon you have shared with your husband has been cracked open, it is time to take a step out into the unknown. Many people go through life reluctant to take up anything new or unfamiliar that arises. Without even thinking about it, "no" may be your default response. Now you have an opportunity to say "yes" rather than "no." Adventure beckons.

Getting out of your comfort zone can benefit you in various ways, such as:

• Broadening your horizons.

• Boosting your self-confidence.

• Giving you the opportunity to meet interesting new people.

Perhaps there is something that you were considering doing but decided against as you were not sure you could do it well enough—for example, a work project, taking up tango dancing or enrolling in a college course. Maybe you feel uncomfortable in new social situations with people you do not know. Whatever the activity is, try it now. You may be better at it than you think. It is never too late to have a go at something new. How about something really adventurous such as skydiving, doing voluntary work in Africa or learning an obscure language? You will never know if you will enjoy it if you do not have a try.

What you choose to do will be affected by your available income, your state of health and your age. A 50- or 60-year-old will not necessarily go for the same activity as a 30- or 40-year-old. However, some older folks end up doing astounding things. Remember how astronaut John Glenn went back into space a second time in 1998 at the ripe old age of 77? If you are middle-aged and still healthy, you most certainly still have the time and energy to reinvent yourself. Edith was clueless about how to look after her car and had left all the maintenance to her husband. When he left her for another woman, Edith's girlfriends taught her how to change a tire, use jumper cables and check the oil and water. She was proud to no longer feel helpless when little things went wrong with her vehicle.

You may have been at home raising the kids for a decade or two, and now you may want or need to find work after having been out of the job market for a long time. Take advantage of whatever training programs you can do to improve your skills, and network with friends, acquaintances and relatives to find job leads. Many positions, both part-time and full-time, are filled by connections, so taking advantage of those you know can be crucial in your search for employment. One route is by doing volunteer work at a nonprofit organization. Sometimes paid jobs open up at these organizations for which, as a volunteer, you may be in a good position to apply. Another possibility is to start your own business, if you have an entrepreneurial bent and there is a market for what you want to sell. The search for a way to earn money can be a challenge that takes you way out of your comfort zone.

I am not suggesting fast, radical changes, such as moving out of your house immediately, quitting your job and rushing off to live permanently in a completely new, unfamiliar place where you have no connections. You should not do anything to move so far out of your comfort zone that it puts your well-being or personal safety at risk. Do not underestimate the value of your sense of home and feeling settled. If you already have a routine that seems to work for you, maybe exercising every morning, and a particular kind of healthy diet you are used to, do not drop all of that. You have to find a balance between pushing the envelope yet fundamentally keeping your sense of stability. Before making any major changes in your life, wait till you have calmed down from hearing about your husband's infidelity, so that you can make rational rather than emotional choices. After some time has passed, you may indeed come to the conclusion that changing your job or where you live is the right thing to do. Such decisions should not be made in a hurry.

Find Your Passion

Just as you can have passion for a man, you can have passion for something you do—no male required—that intrigues you, lifts your mood and helps you feel good about yourself.

What are you passionate about? Think back to what you were good at or enjoyed doing at school or college. Maybe passion will arise from finding a cause that you really believe in, such as political activism, charity work or religion. Perhaps you will be propelled towards art, music, a foreign language, a particular sport or an obscure hobby. Maybe you have a novel that you have always wanted to write. You may well need to keep your day job to earn money, but that does not mean you have to let a new passion languish. Give yourself time to nurture it.

The anger and sadness from heartbreak can fuel bursts of great creativity. Former Genesis musician Phil Collins composed his first solo album, *Face Value,* while undergoing an acrimonious breakup and divorce. It was a runaway success and is considered to be some of the best material he has ever written. Painter Frida Kahlo had a troubled marriage to the famous Mexican artist Diego Rivera, and both partners had numerous affairs. The emotional upheaval she suffered was a major inspiration in her work.

Just to give you some ideas, here are some disparate activities people I know have become passionate about:

- Singing—Mary seemed quite mousy and introverted in her day job as a secretary, but was stunning and radiant when hired to perform for guests in her local restaurant. If you are not getting paid, you can still have a blast. There are karaoke bars all over the world where you will see the regulars really putting their heart and soul into their songs.

- Tango—insanely popular, but it should also be considered as a dangerous endurance sport, what with all those spiked heels flying around the crowded dance floor and dancers only stopping when their feet give out. One tango-obsessed friend of mine would go home and soak her feet in ice, only to happily return the next night.

- Salsa—the steps are a lot easier than tango. It is good for learning to let go of control and allowing your partner to lead your body wherever he wants it to go on the dance floor.

- Rifle shooting—just do not point it at your husband or his floozy!

- Volunteering in a children's hospital.

- Re-enacting famous battles—players really live the part and often become enthusiastic history buffs. It is definitely an environment to meet plenty of new people.

- Esperanto—it is so logically constructed that it takes less time to learn than most other languages, and there is a worldwide community of nerdy people speaking it that you will be able to join. Or maybe you would prefer to take up Klingon? Qapla'! Even Shakespeare's *Hamlet* has been translated into it—*The Klingon Hamlet: The Restored Klingon Version* (Pocket Books/Star Trek, 2000).

- Amateur dramatics—it is sad to say, but developing your acting skills is likely to be extremely relevant as regards effectively dealing with your husband and the other woman, especially if either one or both of them do not know that you are aware of the affair. Lights… camera…action!

- Riding in rodeos—not good if you have a bad back, but recommended if you want to get one.

- Flying an airplane—not a low-cost activity though, and you have to try not to fall out of the sky. If you do want to fall out of the sky, try skydiving, another popular sport.

- Making organic chocolates—Joy and her husband were both overweight and diabetic, but loved chocolate. Joy began making sugar-free confections that she and her husband could eat. All her friends loved them, so she ended up starting up a successful business selling the chocolates online.

- Collecting thimbles—yes, I really know someone who is passionate about thimbles.

Engaging in an activity you enjoy is likely to stimulate the pleasure centers of your brain and improve your mood. Becoming successful at something you initially found a little scary to do can do wonders for your self-esteem and make you feel on top of the world.

What if you find an activity that you are passionate about, but do not think you can do it well? How do you get good at anything? Practice, practice, practice. Persistence is more important than innate talent. Therefore, it damn well better be something you really are passionate about, otherwise you will not want to put in the work. If all you are doing is just going through the motions of an activity without any focus or effort, it is unlikely you will get any good at it.

Josh Waitzkin is a man who has worked hard to achieve excellence and win competitions in two disparate fields—chess and tai chi. His book, *The Art of Learning: An Inner Journey to Optimal Performance* (Free Press, 2008), offers many valuable insights into how to achieve success. He contrasts two different theories of intelligence: the "entity" view that a person is intrinsically talented or untalented at something versus the "incremental" approach that hard work and step-by-step learning leads to mastery. Waitzkin describes research showing that children taught to use the latter method tend to view a tough challenge as something that can be overcome if they put in enough effort, while those kids who believe that they are inherently smart or dumb at a particular subject may have learned to become helpless when faced with a difficult task.

In 2007, a study was published in *Child Development* journal entitled "Implicit Theories of Intelligence Predict Achievement Across Adolescent Transition: A Longitudinal Study and an Intervention." Co-author, Stanford University Psychology Professor Carol Dweck, has also written *Mindset: The New Psychology of Success* (Random House, 2007). According to Dweck, people with "growth" mindsets rather than "fixed" mindsets will tend to be happier, less stressed and more successful. Thus, if you cultivate a "growth" or "incremental" attitude towards learning how to do whatever you are passionate about, it will help you to overcome setbacks and improve your skills more effectively. Dealing with failure can be extremely beneficial in your learning process, making you stronger and showing you what you need to do to succeed. Learning how to cope with setbacks and failure will also be an extremely useful tool to help you move beyond your husband's infidelity, whether you want to continue your relationship with him or end the marriage.

Your passion will open the door for you to make new friends with like-minded people. It will offer you the opportunity to develop a social circle that is totally separate from that of your husband. Engaging in something that you are passionate about can give you a reason to get up in the morning and make you feel that you have a purpose in life.

Chapter Three

Five Things to Do
to Stop Feeling Like Shit

Wives and mothers can spend their entire lives ministering to their husbands and kids. They will put family needs ahead of their own. More often than not, they will be working full-time as well. Now it is time to look after your own interests and do whatever you can to make your life more fulfilling. You need to find out what you can do for yourself, not only to boost your self-confidence, but also to have something better than your husband's infidelity to think about. Forget about the past—learn to enjoy living in the present. It is important to remember that your husband is not responsible for your happiness. It is time for you to be in charge.

1. Find Confidants

Who are your dearest and closest friends that you can trust implicitly? They can become your confidants to whom you can safely vent, without their being judgmental. These friends will play a critical role as a sounding board to help you work out how to deal with your husband's infidelity and develop a course of action that works for you. A good confidant can also cheer you up, making you feel better about yourself and improving your self-esteem.

You have to choose very carefully to whom you are going to pour out your soul. You cannot just complain to everybody. If you make the wrong choices, you may find that your personal history will become a source of gossip and common knowledge to people that you do not want to know about it. Do not blab and blub your heart out to just anyone. You will want to confide in people who:

- Know you really well.
- Have your best interests at heart.
- Can give you useful advice.

You just need a few confidants—perhaps two to four people. If you can, choose at least one confidant who is male. He may give you some useful insights about your husband's behavior and how to deal with it. He will not simply give you the "Poor you, how awful—he's such a cad" response that you are likely to get from your female friends. You may not necessarily enjoy what he tells you, but he is likely to have a much more realistic idea of where your husband is coming from.

Amanda confided in Joel, who had been a friend of her husband, Peter, for decades, long before she had met him. Joel had helped Amanda get through the emotional morass of dealing with a serious illness a few years prior. As a result, she felt very comfortable talking to him about her husband's infidelity. Joel ended up showing himself to be strongly on her side as well as being monogamous by nature. He provided her with more useful advice about how to cope than all her other friends put together. His understanding of Peter's personality and character, drawn from years of experience, gave him a unique perspective as to how she should navigate her situation to get the best outcome.

Your closest confidant may be a marital counselor whom you are paying to see. If so, it is crucial to ensure that you go to someone who is appropriate for you and can genuinely help lift you out of the emotional quagmire into which your husband has dropped you. An unsuitable counselor can waste a lot of time and money.

If you have not decided whether to stay or leave the relationship, or want to maintain a decent relationship with your spouse if you do split, you do not want to mouth off about him and your private life to the wrong person. You may discover that some of what you have said has got

Channeling Your Anger

© 2016 C. J. Grace. Artwork by Aaron Austin, concepts by C. J. Grace.

back to your husband, maybe even in a garbled form that makes it sound worse than what you actually said. Being discreet is even more important if either one of you has any kind of public position. Perhaps he is some kind of minor celebrity, or you are a teacher in a local school with students in the community who look up to you as a role model. Maybe he is a local politician or doctor. Do not damage his or your reputation in the heat of the moment. If you do, be prepared to deal with all kinds of unpleasant repercussions. Neither of you are likely to come out smelling like roses.

Do not confide in people just because they are part of your social circle. You will find that some people will treat your relationship woes as fascinating gossip, even though they will not admit this to you. They will call you wanting to know all the latest details, commiserating with you about how terrible the man is, but they will not really understand what you are going through or offer any genuine support. They just want the latest episode of the soap opera that is your life.

At times feelings will just well up inside you and you will be bursting to talk to someone about it. However, remember that there is a fine line between venting as a release and continually obsessing in such a way that only serves to drag you down and make you feel depressed. Negativity breeds negativity.

Some psychotherapists advise those who are going through difficult times to write a journal about how they are feeling. Some people find journaling very helpful to express things they need to get off their chest that they would never be able to speak about to anyone. The journal becomes their closest confidant. However, other folks, especially if they're not too keen on writing in general, might find the idea of having to put their misery into words to be a dreary chore that would make them feel even worse. If you journal into a computer, give the file an innocuous sounding name—something boring and benign like "quilting notes" rather than "adultery journal." Password-protect the document so that no one else, especially your husband, can read it.

When you are socializing with friends, keep the focus off your miseries by asking them about what they are doing. Talk about any new activities you may have taken up rather than going on about how terrible your relationship is and how badly your husband has treated you. Do you want everyone to just see you as that poor woman with a cheating husband—an object of pity—or do you want people you hang out with to relate to a confident, engaging person who is not acting like a victim?

2. Cultivate Connections Both Old and New

Perhaps your whole social life has revolved around your husband and his circle of friends and work colleagues? Now you need to build your own community of people who are completely separate from any friendships you share with your husband. If you develop a new hobby or interest, friends are likely to arise from that. Internet sites such as meetup.com can be useful to find local people who share your interests. Even if you do want to find another partner, I would advocate checking out groups like this over online dating. They will give you the opportunity to do some sort of activity that you enjoy and at the same time make new male and female friends. If a relationship ensues with someone in the group, that is icing on the cake.

Sylvia always loved water sports and was fortunate enough to live in the Bahamas. Her husband was a habitual womanizer. A devout Catholic, Sylvia would never leave him. However, she knew that she needed to find other things in her life to make her happy. She decided to take up paddle-boarding and developed a completely new social circle. She became best friends with a born-again Christian and a staunch atheist, two men with whom she would have previously thought she had absolutely nothing in common.

Katerina was a rather shy woman who had always been in the shadow of her husband, Orlando. He had a larger-than-life personality and did not take criticism well. Devastated when she discovered his adultery, she took the advice of her best friend from high school and forced herself to go out and meet new people. Just before Katerina and Orlando were about to go to a social gathering, she voiced her unhappiness at his latest affair. "If you can't promise me that you'll stop complaining," he retorted, "you can go to the party on your own." Previously this not-so-subtle form of blackmail would have been effective, as she would never have felt comfortable going anywhere unaccompanied. Now she did not care and had made some new friends that she knew would be at the gathering. "I can't promise I'll stop. So if you don't want to go there with me, I'm perfectly happy going on my own." Shocked, he backed off immediately as he didn't want to miss the party and be left at home on his own.

Cultivating friendships with men is important. Your husband should not be the only man with whom you socialize. Even on a platonic level, relationships with men will be tend to be quite different from those you have with women, particularly as regards what you will talk about, the insights that you will exchange and the activities that you choose to do together.

When she was single, Meredith always found she got on better with men than women, and so most of her friends were male. However, after having had been married for more than 20 years, she had become so monogamous that she dropped all her male friends. She did not realize that she had done so until she took stock of her social circle after finding out that her husband was cheating. "I think what happened was that I felt I might be being unfaithful in principle, just because I was friends with a guy, without any sex happening." Meredith decided to stay with her husband, but she began developing friendships with various men who shared some of her interests. Some of them wanted to date her, but she was not comfortable with that and kept everything platonic.

Explore the possibility of reconnecting with friends you had before you were married, perhaps from high school, college days or previous jobs, including previous lovers. Some women with adulterous husbands, trying to rebuild their social circle, might say, "Leave no stone unturned!" Others might be extremely circumspect about linking up with people from their past, thinking that this might open up a whole new can of worms. The essential point is that you should try to reconnect with anyone you think you might still want to hang out with, whether a friend or a former lover. Social networking on the internet makes this much easier to do than it was in the past. You are likely to be able to track old friends down, for example, through Google searches, Facebook or LinkedIn.

Laughter Therapy

It is important to find people with whom you can have a good laugh. "Laughter is the best medicine," is more than just a trite cliché. Doctors claim laughing improves physical health and mental well-being. An Oxford University study done by evolutionary psychologist, Robin Dunbar, in 2011 showed that the physical act of laughing increased the body's production of endorphins. These brain chemicals are known for their feel-good effect. There is even a Laughter Yoga technique involving prolonged voluntary laughter that proponents claim provides the same benefits as natural laughter. However, to me forced laughter sounds like a lot more work and much less fun than spontaneous mirth. Smiling and laughing when you are around other people can improve your mood and reduce symptoms of depression.

Are you feeling so down that you cannot think of anything that will make you laugh or smile? Watching funny movies or comedy shows could improve your mood. Here are some of my favorites that you might like to consider seeing:

- *Monty Python and the Holy Grail* (1975)—this puts *Spamalot* to shame. I also love all the *Monty Python* TV shows.
- *A Fish Called Wanda* (1988).
- *The Blues Brothers* (1980).
- *Ghostbusters* (1984).
- *Dr. Strangelove or: How I Learned to Stop Worrying and Love the Bomb* (1964).
- *Young Frankenstein* (1974). As Igor says, "Walk this way." Maybe Igor was inspired by *Monty Python's* 1970 "Ministry of Silly Walks" sketch.
- *The first and the third Austin Powers movies: International Man of Mystery* (1997) and *Goldmember* (2002).
- *Bedazzled* (1967)—the original British version, of course, with Peter Cook and Dudley Moore.
- *Death at a Funeral* (2007)—the original British version, of course (am I repeating myself?).
- *Office Space* (1999). I never liked Mike Judge's *Beavis and Butthead* cartoons, but this parody he directed about cubicle life in an American software company had me in stitches, especially Milton, the guy obsessed with his missing stapler.
- *In Bruges* (2008).
- *Shaun of the Dead* (2004).

- *Tropic Thunder* (2008). Do not miss the previews of forthcoming movies at the beginning.

- TV cartoons such as: *South Park, Family Guy, American Dad, The Simpsons* and *Futurama*.

- Any clips of Robin Williams, the Irish comedian Dave Allen or the British comedians Mitchell and Webb that you can find on YouTube.

3. Love Your Body and Become Beautiful

"Ugly giant bags of mostly water." That is how human beings were described by one of the aliens on *Star Trek: The Next Generation* (yes, I admit it—I am a Trekkie).

Beauty may be in the eye of the beholder, but how beautiful you appear to be is strongly affected by your own attitude and self-esteem. Who do you think will tend to behave and carry herself in a more attractive way—someone who feels like shit or someone who feels on top of the world? Infidelity tends to make a woman feel ugly and unworthy. Wouldn't you prefer to feel more beautiful, both inside and out? Not for him, but for you.

There were two girls I knew at college. Claire was not particularly attractive—a bit plump and a very horsey face. Maria was drop-dead gorgeous—long blonde hair, blue eyes and a perfect figure. Nonetheless, Claire was the one who got all the best boyfriends. She had a fun-loving, sexy demeanor that guys found irresistible. Maria, in some respects, had allowed herself to become a prisoner of her supermodel looks. She could never believe that anyone wanted her for anything more than her body. Thus Maria could never be open and natural towards any of the boys who tried to date her. She did not feel she could trust them to like her for who she was. The particular face and body you happen to have are not everything. How you perceive yourself and the way you relate to people will strongly affect how you feel and how others treat you.

Ruby Norton was a famous stage and vaudeville performer of the early 20th century. For each of her six husbands, she would not take off her makeup or jewelry until she was sure that her mate was already asleep. She would arise half an hour before he would wake up to put her finery back on, so

Male Fantasy Sex

© 2016 C. J. Grace. Artwork by Aaron Austin, concepts by C. J. Grace.

Feminist Sex?

© 2016 C. J. Grace. Artwork by Aaron Austin, concepts by C. J. Grace.

that her man always saw her looking as perfect as possible. Ruby was a real beauty who knew how to make the best of herself with makeup, so that it was said that even in her 80s, at least by candlelight, she could pass for a woman in her 40s or 50s. Ruby clearly took looking attractive for each of her husbands to the ultimate extreme. However, it is far too common for women to take much less care over their appearance once they have been married for some time. The hunt is over, they have caught their prey, and they become bogged down in taking care of the family. Now is the time to take a long, hard look at yourself in the mirror and decide what you can do to make your appearance as fabulous as possible. At the very least, you will feel better about yourself and more confident.

It is understandable that some women will not want to put any effort into their appearance after having been betrayed by their husbands. They would rather crawl into a hole and hide, nursing their anger and sadness. A new client with beautiful long hair came into Lorraine's hairdressing salon demanding that she cut it all off. Lorraine told the woman that a very short hairstyle would not be a good idea and offered to trim and shape her hair instead. Lorraine persuaded the client to open up to her and found out that her husband had just dumped her for another woman, leaving her with the kids. The wife deliberately wanted to make herself look ugly. Who knows why? Perhaps it was punishment for her failed marriage. Fortunately, Lorraine prevented that. Soon after, the woman found a job after spending more than a decade as a housewife. She got on so well with her new boss that she eventually married him.

I know that in the first paragraph of this section I said that you should become beautiful for you, not for him, but now I am going to appear to contradict myself. In reality, becoming beautiful will help you be more appreciated by the men in your life, including your husband, whether or not he is your ex. Although it may not sound politically correct, males tend to be very visually orientated when looking for a mate. You may seek stability, companionship and the ability to provide, but he will tend to look at your body. That is unless you happen to be married to the man who mistook his wife for a hat. I kid you not—he was actually a real person suffering from visual agnosia, an impairment in the recognition of objects. He is one of several intriguing neurological case studies in *The Man Who Mistook His Wife for a Hat and other Clinical Tales* by Oliver Sacks (Summit

Books, 1985). Think about it—why are men attracted by the idea of women dressing up as schoolgirls or whores, when a woman does not need a man to look like a schoolboy, Captain America, Mr. Universe or anything like that? This is because women care far less about a man's appearance than men do about how a woman looks, at least in the initial stages.

The song "Keep Young and Beautiful," from the 1933 musical *Roman Scandals,* has lyrics that are delightfully politically incorrect according to modern sensibilities, particularly to women who are past their prime. The song reflects how many men think—they tend to find younger women more physically attractive than older ones. Nevertheless, whatever your age, there are many ways you can upgrade your appearance and find yourself receiving more male attention, which can be beneficial to your self-esteem, whether or not you want other men to make sexual advances towards you.

Consider doing such things as revamping your wardrobe, shaving your legs and armpits, manicuring your fingernails and toenails, wearing nail polish, pulling any stray hairs out of your chin, shaping your eyebrows and/ or putting on makeup. You may not have bothered to do any of this after having been married for several years. Of course, only deal with this stuff if you feel comfortable with it. For example, I personally hate nail varnish and would never put it on. I also dislike wearing makeup.

Magazines aimed towards women have thousands of suggestions for improving your appearance. If you want a cheap makeover, however, take the advice of one of my 60-year-old female friends. Go to the cosmetic counter of an upscale department store. Tell one of the women working there that you have been betrayed by your husband and ask her if she can help you find a new look to boost your morale. If she is not too busy, the salesperson will go all out and give you the full monty. "I was shocked at how glamorous and how much younger she made me look," my friend said. And yes, she did spend a fair amount of money on new cosmetics.

Less of You to Love?

If you have gained weight over the years, try to lose it. You will look and feel better, and the clothes you love to wear will make you feel more attrac-tive. Try to avoid mindless eating, especially when you are feeling down, unless you want to keep putting on the pounds.

There are many different ways to shed the pounds (or kilos, if your flab resides in Europe). Some methods are more successful than others. The best ones produce permanent changes in your diet, so that the lost weight does not return.

Some people have managed to lose weight by giving up wheat and flour products—read *Wheat Belly: Lose the Wheat, Lose the Weight, and Find Your Path Back to Health* by William Davis MD (Rodale, 2011).

Others have dropped their weight by cutting out carbohydrates, especially sugar, entirely. *Pure, White and Deadly: How Sugar is Killing Us and What We Can Do to Stop It* by John Yudkin (Penguin Books, 2013), originally published in 1972, makes a strong case for eliminating sugar.

Some low-carb advocates recommend the Paleolithic diet, based on the kinds of foods our Stone Age hunter-gatherer ancestors ate—mainly grass-fed meat; organic free-range eggs; wild fish; organic plants and fruit; and no GMOs (genetically modified organisms). The idea has become so mainstream that it has spawned numerous Paleo cookbooks. Is Stone Age food becoming the New Age diet? All I can say is that if this menu plan appeals to you, go ahead and eat like a caveman. It certainly would match the table manners of some males I have come across. Alternatively, you can go vegetarian or even vegan.

Still others have found the HCG (human chorionic gonadoprin) diet to be helpful. This approach involves restricting calories to fewer than 800 a day and often involves the injections of hormones. The diet was developed in the 1950s by Albert Simeons, a doctor from Rome, Italy, and is described in his manuscript, *Pounds and Inches: A New Approach to Obesity,* available free on many websites, such as http://hcgdietinfo.com/Dr-ATW-Simeons-Pounds-and-Inches.htm. Although there is considerable controversy over this weight-loss method, several friends of mine have used it very successfully.

For losing weight, a fascinating book about how to avoid overeating is worth looking at—*Mindless Eating: Why We Eat More than We Think* by Brian Wansink, PhD (Bantam Books, 2006). The author shows his sense of humor on the cover, which has a pitchfork and shovel on either side of the plate instead of a knife and fork.

Unfortunately, America is a country where people have become used to huge portions. In the entertainingly alarming 2004 documentary, *Supersize Me,* filmmaker Morgan Spurlock lives for one month entirely on fast food from McDonalds, eating the "Supersize" portions whenever McDonalds' staff offer it. The result? Spurlock's weight increased, while his energy level decreased. He was depressed more than usual. Medical tests showed a sharp decline in his health.

Supersizing fast food reminds me of a boy I once saw who was having a tantrum at Wendy's. He was furious with his mom because she had bought him a Biggie size of French fries instead of the Great Biggie size. Food items in America do not tend to be sold in small sizes, as the sellers do not think the public would want to buy them. Not even small eggs are sold in the supermarket— the smallest ones are called medium. It is only clothing that people like to buy in sizes described as small—if only they could fit into them.

Proponents of healthy eating advocate organic food produced without pesticides, herbicides or genetically modified organisms (GMOs) and avoiding processed foods at all costs. Deborah Koons Garcia's 2004 documentary film, *The Future of Food*, looks at many of these concerns. Poor quality nutrition can lead to health problems such as heart disease, diabetes, obesity and allergies. It is similar to the "garbage in garbage out" principle of computer science. Michael Pollan's book *In Defense of Food* (The Penguin Press, 2008) covers all these issues in detail.

Exercise for Health and Banishing the Blues

For losing weight, diet is more important than exercise. Heavy exercising can actually increase your appetite and make you eat more. However, exercise is vital for your health and well-being. One of the earliest studies to demonstrate this was conducted by Jeremy Morris, MD, the first director of the Medical Research Council's Social Medicine Unit in Britain. It looked at the health histories of 31,000 London Transport workers from 1949 to 1952. The study showed unequivocally that double-decker bus drivers, who sat all day long, had higher rates of heart disease than the conductors, who spent their whole working day walking around the bus and going up and down its stairs to collect the money for tickets.

Exercise can tone your body, boost your immune system, improve your mood and reduce depression, particularly if you do it outdoors. The sedentary life can lead to obesity, diabetes and cardiovascular problems. The trick is to find something you really enjoy doing, such as swimming, going to the gym, tai chi, yoga, running, hiking, tennis or even just walking the dog. It should not be something that ends up feeling like yet another chore you have to do. If you become physically fit, it will make you feel more attractive and comfortable in your own body.

Marie, one of the women I interviewed for this book, described a San Francisco seminar she attended in the 1970s where sex educator, Betty Dodson, taught women to feel more comfortable with their bodies. Dodson asked the 50 or so participants to remove all their clothes and stand in a circle. Then she asked them, "How do you feel about your body?" Marie was shocked that not one of the women was happy with her body. She told me, "Many of the women were drop-dead gorgeous, yet all I heard was I'm too fat; I'm too thin; my breasts are too big; my breasts are too small; I have too much flab on my stomach; my butt is too big. No one liked herself the way she was." Dodson pointed out that these women had self-esteem issues preventing them from feeling comfortable with their bodies. She urged the participants to exercise. Interestingly, Marie told me that the less physically active women in the group had a worse view of their bodies than those women who exercised regularly.

"You never make me feel attractive," complained Valerie to her husband, Jake. He replied, "That's not my job. It's just something in your own mind." Although there was some truth in his comment, his response was rather crass and disingenuous, especially given the fact that Valerie had recently discovered his affair with a much younger woman.

Having a husband who frequently compliments you on your appearance can be a wonderful boost to your self-esteem. Unfortunately, if his attentions are concentrated elsewhere, this is unlikely to happen. It is easy to fall into the trap of letting your self-image be determined by your cheating husband's attitude towards you. Rather than obsessing about whether or not you still love him or whether he loves you, try to shift your focus to loving your own body by taking good care of it, in terms of both diet and exercise. This is a key to developing both physical and psychological well-being.

The more you cultivate pleasurable pursuits that make you feel energized and fulfilled, the more interesting and attractive you are likely to seem to your husband, your friends and other men. You can kill two birds with one stone by finding aerobic activities, such as salsa dancing or group sports that not only exercise your body, but also allow you to meet new people and extend your circle of friends.

4. Be the Happy Hedonist

Many women, particularly if they are over 50, have been brought up to live according to the Protestant Ethic, emphasizing frugality and diligent hard work. They tend to avoid doing something purely for their own pleasure. Many mothers define themselves through sacrifice and the devotion of time and energy to their family.

Even if it may be totally out of character, you should become more hedonistic. Not in an extreme, damaging way or one that takes more out of your bank account than you can afford, but in a way that allows you to genuinely let go and enjoy life. Now is the time to widen the "feel-good" areas of your life. Accomplish something that you have always dreamed of doing. The more room you have for whatever activity, unconnected to your family, that gives you pleasure, the less room there is for negative mind states.

Retail Therapy

You may have been a very thrifty person, not wasting any money on leisure activities, clothes, shoes, jewelry, makeup or anything like that. No one can say that buying things is a guaranteed source of happiness, but after finding out about the scumbag's affair, a bit of retail therapy may be in order. If you have been married for a long time, your wardrobe may have become decidedly staid and frumpy. Do not break the bank, but take some time to buy some flattering new clothes. Melissa, egged on by her sister whom she had just told about her cheating husband, went a little crazy and spent $1,000 on swimsuits. Luckily, her husband never checked credit card bills. Her parents had a beach house in Florida, so Melissa had plenty of opportunities to wear the swimsuits, which made her look fabulous. Her extravagant purchases did wonders for her self-esteem.

You could get a new hairstyle or a makeup makeover. If you have only been cooking and eating what your husband likes, try indulging in food and treats you really enjoy eating (although not to such an extent that it makes you put on weight). Never had the time to go to the theater or to concerts you would have liked to attend? Just make the time to go. Want to go on a cruise? Save up and take a trip with a good friend.

Pamela contemplated suicide when she found out her husband had a mistress. Her best friend told her, "You still have your husband's credit cards, don't you? Why not take the trip of a lifetime first?" Pamela had never been outside North America. She decided to go to Paris and connect with Gerard, an old boyfriend from college days who lived there. They traveled around Europe together and had a wonderful time. Eventually she divorced her husband and moved to France to marry Gerard.

Intentional Incompetence

Does your competence at handling everything overload you and prevent you from having the time to engage in activities that you enjoy? You might benefit from investigating whether there are some areas in which you can become intentionally incompetent. Some men have widely cultivated this skill. They claim they are no good at cooking, cleaning, making tea, changing diapers, looking after the kids, dealing with repairmen, paying bills, you name it. This is especially galling when they come home from work, put their feet up and ask you to wait on them, even if you have a job too. If there is something you really dislike having to do, try to find a way to avoid it. For example, if he will not help you clean the house and you can afford it, pay a cleaner to come to your home—every two weeks, every week, twice a week—whatever works for you.

You might want to back off providing some of the things you do for your husband. For example, do you need to make him a cup of tea or coffee whenever he wants it? Tell him that you are tired or busy and show him how to do it himself. If he is pleading incompetence, recognize that it is intentional.

Many husbands are completely clueless about the effort their wives put into keeping everything together. They only notice when their better half overlooks something or makes a mistake, rather than the thousands of times that she is doing things right. If he is not even aware of a particular task you have been doing that you really dislike, this might give you the opportunity to take it off your shoulders and put it on his, or, if you have the money, to pay someone else to take it on.

Do not let him take your competence for granted. Take time to point out all the tasks you are performing. Tell him you are doing them and emphasize how busy you are. He may be totally ignorant of how much he needs your services. Because his mistress distracts him, he may be more oblivious than normal. Perhaps when he realizes how indispensable you are, he may leave his mistress rather than living in chaos.

5. Live in the Present

You never know if you are going to be given a tomorrow, so all you can do is make the most of today, even if on the face of it, you seem to have been given a poor deal.

A Tibetan Buddhist parable tells the story of a farmer who has managed to harvest a huge bag of grain from his normally meager land. He hangs the bag up in his tent. Before he goes off to sleep, he thinks about how he now can afford a wife, who will bear him fine sons to help him expand his farm and become wealthy. After the farmer is asleep, a mouse gnaws through the rope holding the bag of grain. It falls on the man's head, killing him. Everything he imagined about his future was in vain.

Learning how to live in the present is an important goal in Eastern religions. Buddhists talk about the importance of mindfulness—being fully aware of what you are doing right now rather than focusing on other things. After all, what is the point of doing anything if your mind is somewhere else? Unfortunately, whether or not their partners are having affairs, many people live their entire lives disengaged from the present, nostalgic about the past and worrying about the future. The Taoists believe that you are only truly alive when you are completely focused on the here and now. They advocate against being consumed by churning thoughts rather than engaging with what is actually happening in the present. Your mind can be your best friend or your worst enemy. The past is gone. It is water under the bridge, and you cannot change it. The amazing times you had with your husband when you thought you were the only one in his life cannot be repeated. The wrongs you believe he did to you in the past are gone. The future does not exist. It just consists of various ideas, imaginings and expectations you have in your mind. All you really have is the present, so enjoy it as best you can.

Of course, living in the present does not absolve you of having to plan for your future. Squirrels gather nuts to get them through the winter, even though it is unlikely that their tiny little squirrel minds are full of churning, worried thoughts about the future. The best way to proceed is to ensure that what you mindfully choose to do in the present works towards a lifestyle that would make you feel personally fulfilled in the future.

What Can You Do to Be More Aware of the Present?

Here is a very simple exercise to help you learn how to live in the present:

1. Set your alarm for how long you want to do the practice—any time from five minutes (which is a bit short but better than nothing) to half an hour or even an hour. You can build up to longer practice sessions as you get used to doing the exercise. Twenty minutes daily, or at least three times a week, is the amount of time that I would recommend—long enough to have an effect, but not too much out of your day, if you tend to have a busy schedule.

2. Sit in a comfortable chair that supports your back and keeps it relatively straight. Put a cushion behind your back if that will help to support it. You want to be comfortable, otherwise you will be focusing on how uncomfortable you feel rather than on doing the exercise.

3. Close your eyes and relax. Make sure you relax your face—in particular your eyes and behind your eyes, as well as your jaw. Try not to let your body slump, keeping your head, neck and back straight.

4. Breathe naturally, ensuring that you do not hold your breath, especially in the transition between breathing in and breathing out. Do not try to force anything.

5. Then count your breaths—each comprising of one inhale and one exhale. Try to stay aware of each breath. If you find that your thoughts have wandered, or you are not sure what number you have reached, start the count again. Count up to 20 breaths, and then whenever you have reached that number, begin another 20. If you feel even slightly that your mind is not focusing on counting your breaths, start again at breath number one. The goal is to let go of all those thoughts churning around in your head and just count your breaths. A good metaphor is to let your thoughts be like clouds passing through.

6. When the alarm goes—and I would strongly recommend using one with a fairly gentle sound that is not jarring—slowly open your eyes and give yourself a bit of time to get used to the normal world,

so that when you get on with next thing you have to do, you carry some of your relaxed focus with you.

Chocolate-flavored Mindfulness

Another way to learn to live in the present is to practice mindfulness. Try to make a habit of noticing whether you are focusing on whatever it is you are doing or whether your thoughts are taking you somewhere else. When you exercise, focus on making your movements efficient and relaxed. When you are out with a friend, try to put all your attention on that person. Try to be mindful when you are eating—slowly enjoy every mouthful.

Many schools in Britain have used chocolate to help kids learn how to focus on the present moment. If kids can do it, so can you. All you need to be able to do this exercise is one piece of chocolate candy, individually wrapped—perhaps a Hershey's Kiss, or if you are a little more sophisticated, a Lindt Lindor truffle. The exercise takes less than five minutes.

1. Sit comfortably in a chair and relax.

2. Put the chocolate in your open hand and pay close attention to how it is wrapped. Look at the color and shape. Notice how its weight feels on your palm. Feel the texture of the wrapper with your fingers. Imagine that this is the first time you have ever seen a chocolate like this.

3. Whenever your mind wanders, just be aware of this, let the thoughts drop away, and bring your focus back to the chocolate.

4. Now unwrap the chocolate, being mindful of exactly what your fingers and arms are doing in order to remove that packaging. Listen to the sounds of the chocolate being unwrapped.

5. Put the chocolate to your nose and slowly inhale. Notice how the chocolate smells. If you start feeling impatient, thinking about how you want to eat the chocolate, just be aware of those thoughts and bring your attention back to focusing on how the chocolate smells.

6. Maybe you will start salivating because you want to put that chocolate in your mouth. Perhaps some emotions will arise. Be aware of all these feelings.

7. Now put the piece of chocolate in your mouth and notice how it feels and tastes, but do not swallow any of it yet.

8. Leave it on your tongue and focus on how the chocolate feels.

9. Now move it around a little with your tongue. Become aware of how it tastes and how it feels on your tongue and the inside of your mouth. Notice how the consistency of the chocolate changes as it melts.

10. Notice the moment when you feel like you want to swallow the chocolate and then swallow it, focusing on all the sensations you have as it goes down your throat.

This exercise teaches you to be mindful of all five of your senses as you are eating the chocolate—sight, sound, smell, touch or feeling, and of course, taste. Now you can choose to no longer mindlessly gobble down candies without even tasting them—admit it, you have done that—we all have, especially when in a lousy mood.

Mindfully eating chocolate is just one small step on the path to living in the present. The more you practice mindfulness in all aspects of your daily life, the more you will be able stay in the present rather than drift somewhere else, and the more fully alive you will feel. It is a great state of mind to work towards.

Another great reason to mindfully eat chocolate: it increases your level of serotonin, a neurotransmitter with antidepressant properties. Eating chocolate also causes endorphins to be released, which can induce a feeling of well-being. Dark chocolate is preferable to milk as it has additional health benefits, particularly as regards the heart. It contains polyphenols that can lower blood pressure, and antioxidants that can boost your good cholesterol (HDL) levels. So have some guilt-free, dark-chocolate-flavored indulgence.

Multitasking Versus Being Present

The ability to multitask is highly valued in the workplace. Modern life constantly demands that people do multiple things at once—at the office, in transit and at home. This is especially true for mothers, whether they are working or staying at home caring for small children. In many ways,

Mrs. Allcock Multitasks at Home

Miss Jones Multitasks at the Office

multitasking prevents you from being truly present to the moment and remaining fully focused on what you are doing. Instead, it trains you to have a monkey mind that skips from one thought to another. If you want to live in the present and learn to enjoy it to the fullest, avoid multitasking wherever you can.

"The Myth of Multitasking" by Christine Rosen in the spring 2008 edition of *The New Atlantis* describes several studies on multitasking, including research showing that the brain cannot focus on multiple items at once, but instead moves very rapidly from one item to another, often struggling in the process. Switching from one mindset to another lowers productivity at work and impairs decision-making and short-term memory. As an aging baby boomer, I do not need anything to give me more senior moments. Multitasking can even cause weight gain. For example, eating lunch while playing a computer game will make you feel less full than if you focused solely on the meal. Multitasking can also encourage the mindless eating of more snack foods. Multitasking while driving can kill you. That is why many states in America ban using a cell phone while driving unless it is hands-free.

Your husband might make it very difficult for you to avoid multitasking. Denise describes a common scenario: "I'm trying to make dinner, with a fussy toddler grabbing my leg and demanding my attention. Then the phone goes and I have to deal with scheduling a repairman. And there's my husband, watching the game on the big screen in the living room, yelling at me to bring him a beer from the fridge. But God forbid I should ask him to do something at the same time as he's doing anything else, especially if it involves getting up from watching the game." However, at least this lazy lout is still being faithful to his wife.

Your husband's infidelity is likely to cause you emotional upheaval and churning thoughts as you try to work out how you are going to navigate through this difficult time. This situation can impair your mental clarity and focus. Thus, it is even more important to try to deal with one thing at a time, and go through what you need to do in a systematic and orderly fashion. Multitasking in your current frame of mind will make you even less able to get things done. Even though doing multiple things at once may be second nature to you, put some effort into recognizing its drawbacks when you are emotionally fragile, and try your best to finish one task completely before moving on to the next.

This chapter has looked at what you can do to stop feeling like crap and improve your mood. Now I am going to tell you what not to do. The following chapter covers some things that you should try your best to avoid doing if you want to try to keep your relationship with your husband as peaceful and harmonious as possible.

Chapter Four

Five Things to Avoid to Keep Your Life Peaceful

Do you want harmony or discord in your home? It is your choice. How you decide to behave towards your philandering partner will be a major factor. If you want to stay in your marriage, or you are not yet sure what course of action you want to take, it is important to try to create a peaceful atmosphere between you and your husband and steer your relationship back onto a course that works for you. Even if you know you want to end your marriage, you should try to avoid discord, particularly if you are trying to negotiate a divorce settlement that you will be happy with.

1. Do Not Drag Your Kids into a War Zone

If you and your former beloved are constantly fighting and criticizing each other in front of your children, you are effectively teaching your offspring to go out and have dysfunctional relationships when they grow up. Avoid behaving like the husband and wife in *The War of the Roses*, a 1989 comedy about an outrageously bitter divorce between Mr. and Mrs. Rose, played by Michael Douglas and Kathleen Turner.

Do whatever you can to avoid having toxic discussions with your spouse in front of your children. Even if he has behaved like a total shit, do not shame him in front of them and do not make negative comments to your kids about their father. If you do so, you are putting your offspring in the horrible position of having to choose sides. Why would you want to do that? Are you trying to take revenge on your husband by poisoning his relationship with his kids? This kind of behavior will not give you happiness and is likely to bring not only your husband but also your kids a bucket load of emotional misery. Furthermore, you may think you are turning the children away from their father, but you may find them withdrawing from you instead.

Ana Nogales, author of *Parents Who Cheat: How Children and Adults Are Affected when Their Parents Are Unfaithful* (Health Communications Inc., 2009), believes that most children are hurt by parental infidelity. They too tend to feel betrayed, just like the cheated-upon spouse. Her book looks at how parents facing an infidelity crisis can help their children cope. Marital problems can make kids feel invisible and abandoned. If you are overwhelmed by your own emotions towards your cheating spouse, you could find yourself giving less attention and affection to your children. In addition, if you and your husband have decided to separate, you will need to focus on the practical, legal and financial considerations of a breakup. This will drain even more of your time and energy. Thus, you have to make even more effort to ensure that your children do not get forgotten at this difficult time when they need your support more than ever.

If at all possible, you and your husband should present a united front and consistency in your interactions with your kids. Generally the younger your children, the more important it is to try to maintain a peaceful home and say as little as possible about your spouse's shortcomings. If your kids are very young, it is generally not a good idea to mention anything at all about their dad's philandering. It is essential that they should feel secure in their home rather than worrying that their dad might run off with another woman at any second, or that you might boot him out of the house. Adult children should be able to handle a lot more in that regard, but even they may feel extremely uncomfortable about hearing specific details. They will not want to get involved in any of the drama surrounding their father's infidelity. Obviously, compared to youngsters, adult children who have already moved out of the house will feel less fear and insecurity. Nevertheless, do not underestimate the painful emotions they are likely to experience from the conflict between you and your husband.

Depending on the specifics of your circumstances, you may find it useful to get counseling on how to approach your kids. At the very least, consult with a trusted friend or two before talking to your children about dad and his other woman or women. Be circumspect and take your time. Do not go off half-cocked just because you feel like shit about what he has done. Remember that once you say something, it cannot be taken back, so you had better be sure that whatever you tell your kids is what you would want them to remember when they get older. The point is not to vent or criticize but to inform, so that the kids can gain an understanding of what is going on between their parents in order to feel more, rather than less, secure.

Although it is much easier said than done, however wronged you feel by the man you married, he is still the father of your kids, and it will serve you better not to criticize him in their presence. Think whatever you like—just bite your lip and do not say it aloud. If you can do this, it might encourage him not to criticize you in their presence either.

2. Neither Be a Harpy nor a Stepford Wife

Whatever he has done, if you plan to stay with your husband, whether for the long term or the short term, you need him to continue to want to be with you. No man will find a needy, clinging and complaining woman attractive or pleasant to be around. Some adulterous husbands, guilty as hell though the selfish bastards are, will see the slightest bit of justified criticism from their wronged better halves as harpy-like behavior. You have become the bitch and the mistress is the sweet young babe. Unfortunately, the Catch-22 of your situation is that needy, insecure and complaining is most likely exactly how you felt upon finding out about his love affair, even if you had never been like that before and had never in a million years imagined that you might behave that way. Rather than continually express-ing those feelings to your husband, vent to other people that you can trust.

If you and your husband work together, particularly if you jointly own a business and have employees, the importance of not being a harpy extends to how you behave at work. You should try to be as professional as possible and avoid putting an employee in the middle of any conflict you may have with your husband.

What should you do to make your wandering spouse the happiest? Just put up with his affairs and shut up. In many ways he wants you to be a Stepford Wife. *The Stepford Wives* (Random House, 1972), a satirical thriller by Ira Levin, was made into a movie in 1975. The wives in the fictional town of Stepford, Connecticut are turned from being independently minded women into docile, submissive robots, happily attending to their husbands' every need and desire. The story became firmly embedded in American popular culture.

Your philandering partner wants a peaceful home, with you providing the same support and assistance as before. However, if you are bottling everything up, putting on a brave face while deep down you are in anguish, that is no life at all, and most likely you will make yourself ill. Instead, it is important to find other things in your life to make you happy, so that your state of mind is not dependent upon the quality of your husband's attitude and attention towards you. You need to find a way to keep smiling *inside,* rather than putting on a fake smile outside. Research has shown that just the physical act of smiling, even if you are not in the mood to do so, really does create a feeling of happiness, and conversely, frowning has a negative effect on how you feel. A study in 1989 by University of Michigan psychologist, Robert Zajonc, found that placing the muscles of the face into either a sad expression or a smile directly induced the specific emotions that these expressions represent.

Patricia was a very successful real estate agent who seemed to love life and have a perfect marriage. When she was diagnosed with a fast-growing form of breast cancer, her friends were surprised to discover that deep down, Patricia was torn apart by the fact that her husband of more than 20 years had a long-term relationship with a woman with whom he had reconnected at a high school reunion. Thankfully, the cancer proved to be a wake-up call for Patricia to get her life in order. Her close friends gave her a lot of support when she decided to get rid of her husband and focus on maintaining as healthy a lifestyle as possible. She became fascinated by nutrition, so she studied for a credential in the field. Patricia eventually changed careers and found a job as a nutritionist. Even though it paid less than selling real estate, she felt much more fulfilled.

In many respects, your relationship with your philandering husband may come down to a series of transactions of give and take and tit for tat, cold, calculating and mercenary though that analysis may sound. You have to find the balance between harpy and Stepford mode. If you stay in control and behave cordially rather than acting like an angry banshee, you will get brownie points and he is likely to reward you with a more pleasant and helpful attitude. However, those brownie points may not be redeemable later on—the slippery SOB may conveniently forget or belittle any compromises that you have already made in the past. If you want something in return for something you are about to do for his benefit, ask for it right away, if possible, in as neutral and unemotional a way as you are able to manage. A cynic or maybe a realist would say that you are only as good as your latest concession. Can you stomach staying in a "trading partner" marriage like this? If so, you have to find some way to let the affection and good feelings you used to have for each other back in.

3. Do Not Vent to Everyone

Venting is a double-edged sword. On the one hand, it can be a good way to let out and dissipate all the negative emotions that are welling up inside you, but it can also be a trap that gets you stuck in a loop of constantly thinking about how badly you have been treated. If you are continually churning negative emotions in your mind, it will eat away at your insides and make you even more miserable than you are already. Venting also can keep you in the victim role and make you an object of pity in the eyes of those to whom you vent. This may not be how you want to be perceived if you want people to enjoy your company and see you as complete rather than broken. Your marital woes will take over your friendships and prevent you being able to just go out and have fun with people.

What if your husband is a prominent member of the community, such as a politician, doctor, or some kind of celebrity? There will be a social stigma attached to "outing" his infidelity by venting to your friends. His position may bring you a considerable amount of wealth and status that you do not want to lose. Thus, you may find yourself subject to a code of silence to avoid damaging his reputation. You ensure that you never mention anything negative about him in public and may feel that you must be on your guard even when talking to close friends. You will have to decide if you are willing to pay the price of maintaining your position as his wife—living a lie in a flawed relationship and most likely having to put up with continued philandering. Infidelity often goes with the territory when a husband has a prominent position in his field. Even if the wife chooses divorce, her code of silence may continue. This is likely to be the case if she needs to rely on financial support from him and wants to prevent either of them from attracting negative media attention.

Remember that once you say something inappropriate to someone inappropriate, you can never take it back. It is best not to vent to:

- Friends of your husband, even if they are also your friends—do not test their loyalty to you versus him.

- Business associates of your husband—do not damage his reputation at work. Not only may the associate discuss your comments with your husband, but also the repercussions may have a negative effect on your joint finances.

- Your boss—venting may make you look very unprofessional and make him or her think that your negative emotions are affecting your ability to do a good job.

- A coworker, unless he or she also happens to be a really close friend.

- Any friends who like to gossip about others—your marriage will become the next hot topic.

It is important to have trusted confidants so that you are not tempted to blab about your woes to every acquaintance and at every social gathering. The previous chapter discussed how to find confidants to whom you can safely vent and also looked at how you can channel your anger and sadness by writing down your feelings in a journal. You can describe your deepest, darkest, rawest feelings in the privacy of your notebook or laptop.

Here are two other safe, yet effective, ways to vent:

- Buy a punching bag or go to a gym that has one. Alternatively, you can just punch a pillow.

- Go to a secluded place outdoors *where you are sure that no one will hear you* and then just scream away until the energy of your anger has dissipated. You can either yell complete gibberish with no words at all, or loudly shout about exactly how you feel and what you think about your husband and the other woman.

4. Neither Compete with nor Criticize the Other Woman

You will never be prettier, more exciting, more fun or more relaxing than the mistress, at least to your husband while the affair lasts. Although it is difficult not to compare yourself to her in all kinds of ways, competing with her is likely to end in pain and sorrow. Find something else to take up your mental space, rather than thinking about the mistress and why your husband is attracted to her rather than you. These thoughts can tear you apart.

Instead, be yourself as much as possible, and do not undervalue yourself. You have shared history with your husband, as well as skills and expertise that most likely up until now have allowed you and your husband to build a successful life together. She has no track record at all.

You can have whatever negative thoughts you want about the other woman, but avoid like the plague voicing those criticisms to your husband. Perhaps the other woman is nothing but a gold-digger, doing her best to pry him away from you so that she can have him and his assets all to herself. Maybe she is a really dumb bimbo or a totally naïve young girl, and you wonder what the hell she and your husband would have in common to be able to even have a conversation together (of course most of what they are doing with each other may not involve talking at all). However true to the floozy stereotype she is, your analysis of her character is not going to be well received. Your infatuated husband will hear it as strident complaining and the product of jealousy. You will make him rise to her defense and drive him right into her arms.

If you have been married a long time, and he is going out with a younger woman, most likely she is a sexier babe than you. In the same way, your husband is not as attractive, healthy and vibrant a hunk as he was when you first met him. But what is the point of comparisons like these? It is not as if there is anything you can do about it. The "Serenity Prayer," used

Comparisons: Young Sex Versus Old Sex

© 2016 C. J. Grace. Artwork by Aaron Austin, concepts by C. J. Grace.

by Alcoholics Anonymous and similar programs, provides good advice for women married to cheating husbands:

God, grant me the serenity to accept the things I cannot change,
The courage to change the things I can,
And wisdom to know the difference.

Colin had fallen in love with Jessica, who was less than half his age. His wife, Tina, was a highly educated university lecturer. Jessica had dropped out of college and drifted from one menial job to another. Deliberately sticking the knife in, Tina asked Colin, "If Jessica were your daughter, would you be happy with what she's done with her life?" If she had indeed been his daughter rather than his lover, Colin would have replied, "Of course not!" However, it was fairly predictable that hearing this pointed question did nothing to dampen Colin's ardor, and just made the jerk angry. He was clearly not in the mood to hear negative comments about the young girl who was giving him such an amazing time in bed.

It is important to maintain your self-respect and not be ruled by your emotions when dealing with the other woman. See Chapter Seven for some ideas about how to do that.

5. Avoid Spy Versus Spy

Remember those old black and white movies where the protagonist is a private detective? The sorrowful, angry wife, more often than not in her mink coat and perfect 1950s hairdo, would hand the guy a bundle of cash to find out the details of the woman that her husband was sleeping with. The grizzled gumshoe would go from one place to another, hanging around in train stations, hotel lobbies and restaurants to find evidence of the man's affair with his floozy. Nowadays, usually all you need to do is look at what is on his laptop or cell phone.

In the privacy-deficient Internet world in which we live, Microsoft, Facebook, Google, Skype, Apple, eBay, Amazon and LinkedIn, not to mention various other websites, know all our secrets. They have our email, voicemail, contact lists, comments, calendar and whereabouts, plus our buying history, photos, videos, opinions, likes and dislikes. We worry about the government or corporations grabbing all that data. Now we can use it ourselves to pry into our spouses' activities.

However, once you have discovered your husband's infidelity, how much more do you need to know? Spying on your husband is a double-edged sword. Are you spying to drive yourself crazy emotionally? Alternatively, are you looking for specific details on whether your husband has been spending family money on his mistress or seeking other information that might be pertinent if you choose to leave him?

If your husband thinks that you are checking up on him, there will be a mutual loss of trust that can be very damaging. He will most likely do whatever he can to make sure that you never again have any access to his phone or email communications, perhaps even getting himself another cell phone number and/or a new email address specifically for amorous use. Although in terms of infidelity, there is no doubt that your husband is the guilty party, as regards invading his privacy, he will start to look upon you as blameworthy too. You may have thought he was withdrawing from you before he felt you were spying on him. Now you will find that there is even more of a wall between you, as he looks for more and more ways to keep his activities hidden. So many barriers and so much ill feeling may arise that your marriage cannot survive.

Even if your spouse is unaware of your snooping, you may find that you get into a very negative cycle of addictive compulsion to continually look at his phone, surreptitiously reading his latest text or email to the other woman. Each communication will make you feel worse. That toxic telephone may literally deliver a sharp shot of pain to your gut every time you check it. Ask yourself this question: If you are already aware of the fact that the affair is going on, as well as the identity of the woman involved, does it really benefit your well-being to know the details of every single electronic interaction they have? If his infidelity has put you in a state of anguish, do you want to discover and endlessly analyze all the reasons for it, or do you want to find a way to get rid of your emotional pain?

It is important to mention that there may be circumstances when you need to gather as much information as possible about your husband's activities. This may be crucial because of the specific divorce laws in your area, for example, or if you are a victim of abuse, or involved in legal battles over family financial assets and/or custody of your children. You might also need to find out how much he is spending on his mistress so that this sum can be taken off his share of your joint assets when you divorce.

If you begin having a tit-for-tat affair yourself, you are in the same boat. Now he can take a peek at your phone or computer and find out all the details, unless you delete them or have passwords for everything. Just as you can spy on him, he can spy on you. How does that make you feel? How good are you at lying to cover up not only your spying on him but also your affair? Most likely you are a much poorer liar than your husband if he managed to keep his furtive fucking hidden for some time before you found out about it. If you want to stay married, it is critically important to be aware of the deleterious effect this "spy versus spy" mentality can have on the ability of each of you to successfully continue your relationship together.

CHAPTER FIVE

STAY OR GO?
PRACTICAL CONSIDERATIONS

How do you make one of the most difficult decisions of your life? If you have had a bereavement, most likely you were advised to go slowly, take your time and avoid any rash decisions. Finding out about your husband's affairs puts you in a very similar position, with much more complicated and conflicting emotions to deal with than the pure grief of losing a loved one. Stay put until your head clears enough for you to be certain that ending the marriage is what you really want. Remember that it is much harder to get back together after a split that you may come to regret than to part ways later when you are sure that you cannot make things work. This is especially true if the husband wants the marriage to continue. Few men want to break up their home, even when they have a mistress. If that is the case, you have some bargaining power to make changes for the better.

If you do think that you want to separate from your husband, it is much better to do so after you have given yourself time to get over both the initial shock and that feeling of being a vulnerable victim stuck in a black hole. When you have managed to build a bit of inner strength, you will be able to make much better choices. Also, if you tell him to leave right away, you are pushing him straight into the arms of the other woman so that they can walk into the sunset together. Do you really want to make it so easy for them to be a couple? What if the affair would otherwise have fizzled once the initial excitement had worn off? Sometimes the best decision to make is to be patient. As the ancient Chinese strategist and political philosopher Sunzi (also known as Sun Tzu), says in his famous book, *The Art of War* (Westview Press, 1994), "Move not unless you see an advantage."

That comfortable, secure feeling of intimate trust in your husband has been broken, but it was an illusion all along. You may have thought your husband was your best friend, who always had your best interests in mind, with whom you could be completely open and natural. Now you have to learn to play chess with him, and carefully consider the implications of what you say and how you behave towards him. It may not be in your nature to be guarded with someone who has been the love of your life, but now one wrong move could have dramatic consequences. It is tough not to be able to play it straight and be completely honest about how you feel. However, that may not be the best way to proceed, unless you want the marriage to collapse on you in a way that does not give you the best of a bad situation. At least outwardly, try to keep your anger and negative emotions in check when dealing with him. If you feel overwhelmed, try to step back and make a plan of action.

If you are deciding whether to stay, there are important questions to ask yourself that only you can answer. Often marriage counselors ask, "What did you like about him when you were first going out?" Do you still like those characteristics now? Is he kind to you? Do you like hanging out with him? Are you happier with him or without him? Are you just a doormat being taken advantage of? Can you go from being a victim of his philandering to taking control of your own life, not needing him to feel complete in yourself?

It is important to consider whether your husband treats you well and acts compassionately towards you. If not, why are you with him? Equally, if you want to stay with him despite his infidelity, you will need to be able to behave with decency towards him too. Bearing a permanent grudge against him will make the marriage untenable and bring you no happiness. Seeing a counselor may help you not only learn how to forgive him but also deal with your negative emotions and let them go.

The question, "Should I stay or should I go?" may not be the most appropriate one to ask yourself when deciding whether or not to stay with your philandering husband. If you want to end the relationship, it is much less of a wrench for you to make *him* leave the family home rather than you having to do so. Thus, a better question might be: "Should I stay or should *he* go?" This chapter covers some of the practical issues to consider:

- Is he abusive?
- What is the state of your finances?
- How will your children be affected?
- How does your religion view adultery and divorce?

The following chapter will look at the quality of your relationship and how much you are willing to compromise when determining whether or not to separate.

Is He Abusive?

One reason you should run to the nearest exit away from your marriage is if your husband is physically abusive and you fear for your safety. Perhaps he has a Jekyll and Hyde personality—usually sweet and loving, but every so often a terrifying monster. Do not get lulled into a false sense of security, even if he has been wonderful for quite some time. He may even be on best behavior if he thinks he might lose you, but he will never change. For whatever reason, that demon seed is deep within him, and you need to get yourself out of the firing line right now. You do not have to do it alone. Make sure that you take advantage of good friends and whatever resources for battered women you can find in your area to help you make a safe exit. Even if your religion says, "Till death us do part," you do not want that event to be hastened by a psychotic partner. Get the hell out as soon as you can.

There is a lot of truth in the proverb, "All is fair in love and war." When love goes sour, people can become their absolute nastiest. According to the saying, soldiers and those in love are not bound by the rules of fair play, and love gone bad can turn a peaceful home into a war zone. A spurned husband or wife, whether the adulterer or the partner who has been cheated-upon, may turn into a stalker, or become suicidal or even homicidal.

Andreas was a mild-mannered and much loved high school English teacher. He had to go on a three-week trip to Europe with his class and left his wife, Shirley, at home with a broken leg. Andreas enlisted his best friend Nick to look after her while he was gone and came back to find that they had fallen passionately in love. Shirley moved out and went to live with Nick. Andreas went crazy and started following the pair around, parking his car overnight outside Nick's apartment and staking them out. His soon-to-be ex-wife had to call the police to force him to go away and then go to court to get a restraining order.

Your husband may never have been abusive before, but now that you have called him out on his infidelity, and probably insulted the hell out of the contemptible creature, the gloves are off. You too may be behaving in an uncharacteristically unpleasant manner, so that the pair of you may be heaping all manner of abuse upon each other, verbally or even physically, creating an escalating vicious cycle. If you cannot stop doing that, it will be much better for your physical and mental health if you separate.

Should you leave him if he is psychologically abusive? That is much more of a gray area. What is psychological abuse? Only you can be the judge, perhaps with the help of a good relationship counselor. What one woman might consider no big deal might be intolerable to another. Are you thick-skinned or thin-skinned? For example, despite her best efforts to prevent it, Joanna's youngest son Oscar took relentless verbal abuse from his older brother, who took pains to belittle him in every way he could think of. The result was that Oscar was completely immune to bullying at school. "Is that the best they can do? It's nothing compared to what I got from my older brother."

Furthermore, what is seen as normal behavior from a husband in one country might be considered to be verbal abuse elsewhere. For example, according to cultural stereotypes, which may or may not be true, Italians and Greeks yell at each other but do not see it as a big deal, Brits keep a stiff upper lip and will not show their emotions, while it is believed that Americans are easy-going but talk excessively about their feelings and take them too seriously. Age can also be a factor. For example, an older wife brought up before the days of political correctness might accept behavior that a younger spouse would find intolerable.

What About Your Finances?

For richer for poorer? Although one of the main causes of divorce is financial instability, lack of money is also one of the main reasons couples stay together, even if unhappily married, especially if the economy is in poor shape. It is very common for people to stay married despite infidelity because to do otherwise would leave them both impoverished.

It is simple arithmetic—having half of the loaf may not be as bad as having no loaf at all, but you are getting a darn sight less bread than you would if you had the whole loaf. Generally, after a divorce, each partner ends up with a lot less than half the loaf. Having two separate homes costs much more than just maintaining one shared home. Property has to be sold quickly whether it is a good time to do so or not. You might have had a great mortgage on the house you want to keep, but you may lose it once you divorce and you could get a much worse deal when you refinance. Is your husband the main breadwinner? Have you given up your career to raise the kids and/or help manage his business? You can see why, more often than not, women suffer a sharp drop in their standard of living after separation.

Financial problems always create strain in a marriage. If the husband or the wife has lost a job, he or she may also lose self-esteem and become depressed. Alternatively, perhaps the wife is now earning more than her husband, contrary to the common expectation, even in the present day, that he should be the main breadwinner. Such circumstances may drive the spouses apart so that they seek solace in the arms of others, and often the end result is divorce.

Derek was trying to establish a career as a journalist. He earned very little at the beginning, while his wife had a decent salary as a computer programmer. She had a very public affair that almost destroyed the marriage. The couple managed to reconcile, but only once Derek's career took off, and he started to be well paid.

If you and your husband have no assets together, for example, you rent your home and have no joint savings, you may have little financial incentive to stay married. If you have a job with decent pay, you may be quite able to support yourself and have an acceptable standard of living without needing any financial help from your husband. However, if you are earning a lot more than him, he might be able to claim child support and/ or alimony from you in a divorce settlement, depending on the laws in your area. Conversely, if you have little work experience because you have stayed home looking after the kids while your husband brought home the bacon, you will have a strong financial incentive to keep the marriage going to maintain your existing standard of living.

Women of wealthy philandering husbands may stay in their marriages because they do not want to lose their extremely high standard of living. Maybe they had to sign a prenuptial agreement, or maybe they are too accustomed to all the luxury to want to split everything in two, even if in absolute terms, they would be able to retain a reasonable standard of living after the divorce settlement. If you are in this position, you have to ask yourself whether all that material comfort makes it worth staying with the fat cat fucker you chose to marry.

Spouses working together to run a family business makes for an especially sticky situation, especially if the business is not doing well financially, if the work is stressful and demanding, and/or if the husband and wife do not see eye-to-eye on how the organization should be run.

Many businesses spell out in advance what happens when one of the other spouses no longer wants to co-own it, whether or not they divorce. The state or country you live in will have laws about how businesses that are jointly owned should value and divide assets, including earnings that continue after an organization is dissolved.

If the business is successful, and you and your husband decide to separate, there will be a lot to weigh and consider. Do you want him to buy you out? Do you still want to have a continuing role in the business? How necessary are you to the organization functioning smoothly and remaining profitable? Do you want to disengage entirely? If so, can you avoid everything falling apart and find someone to replace what you do? Even if you decide to stay in the marriage, perhaps you might want to consider taking a step back from being heavily involved in the family business, particularly if you and your husband have been working very closely together.

Love, Lust and Litigation

This book does not cover the legal mechanics of divorce. There are plenty of resources in print and online to help you. For example, Nolo Press has

Asset Stripping

© 2016 C. J. Grace. Artwork by Aaron Austin, concepts by C. J. Grace.

a very detailed website on family law issues, http://www.divorcenet.com, that you can use to learn about some of the legal aspects of divorce, including the specific laws in the state where you live.

This section is about taking back control of your life by arming yourself with factual information, particularly with regard to your joint finances: bank balances, savings accounts, bills, credit card debts, insurance policies, stocks, pension plans, annuities, investments, long term care plans, loans, mortgages, etc. You need to know about all this, even if you did not have an adulterer as a husband and had absolutely no desire to split up with him. What if your husband were to become incapacitated or die suddenly? That would not be the best time to have to learn about your finances. You need to do it now. If you are considering divorce, this information will help you answer a very important question—are there enough joint assets to divide in two and still provide you with an acceptable standard of living?

If you are thinking about separating, it can be helpful to hire a lawyer for a few hours to learn the basics about divorce laws in your state or country and what you can expect financially. One of the first questions the lawyer is likely to ask is, "What is the state of your joint finances?" You may discover that you have quite unrealistic expectations of what you are entitled to if you do separate. You might think that once you have found out about your husband's infidelity, you can just boot the fucker out of the house and take him for all he is worth—unlikely in this age of "no-fault" divorces, at least in the United States.

Once you have some basic information, whether or not you decide to hire the lawyer later on, ask him or her, "What are the total fees that I am likely to see?" Be aware that divorce lawyers often make out bandits—the more acrimonious the split, the more lucrative it is for them. This is a compelling reason, if you and your husband separate, to do the best you can to keep things as harmonious as possible and decide how to divide your joint assets rather than letting dueling accountants and lawyers do it for you and drain the coffers dry in the process. You and your husband will still most likely need to have an attorney and/or accountant help draft the agreement.

If your breakup is acrimonious, and your husband is possibly hiding money and investments, a good lawyer can help ensure that you do not get shafted in the settlement. Ask divorced friends for their recommendations. If you can, get free consultations with your shortlist of possible attorneys before making your choice about which one to use. If you are out for revenge on the lousy cheat, you might want to get a lawyer who will take him to the cleaners, but bear in mind that these types of attorneys do not come cheap. Furthermore, taking a very aggressive stance will seriously affect your relationship with your ex and make things much more problematic as regards dealing with any children you have had together.

If you have cause to believe that remaining with your spouse puts you in danger, you may be able to legally force him to move out so that you can stay in the house on your own. Otherwise, more often than not, who stays in the family home is a question of negotiation, and one partner may have to buy the other out.

If you had assets of your own before you were married, you may not need to need to split those with your husband, unless you have put them in joint names. Unfortunately, it is a familiar tale that early on in the marriage, trusting, love-struck wives will do just that, sharing with their temporarily adoring husbands everything they previously owned individually, never considering that the perfect harmony they feel in their relationship could ever end. If all assets and bank accounts are in joint names, or worse, in your husband's name, if it is possible, consider setting up a bank account in your own name and building up the balance. It may be a good idea to have some money under your sole control.

His Babe-bonking Budget

If your husband has been having an affair, it is likely that his floozy has been the beneficiary of some of your joint income. Maybe only a little, maybe a lot. You might be able to find out about these expenditures by looking at his email, Amazon account, credit card purchases and/or bank statements. He may use business accounts for his trips and restaurant meals with her. He may even have bought her a car or rented accommodation for her. Instead of getting the security of a wedding ring, mistresses often receive lavish gifts—the stereotypical expensive jewelry and sexy clothing. Wealthy men setting their mistresses up in fancy apartments have been commonplace all over the world for centuries. However, if you can prove the douche bag has been spending a bucket load of money on the other woman, that amount might be taken out of his share of any divorce settlement.

That Bastard Grabbed Your Inheritance!

It is important to review whatever estate plan you and your husband have put in place. You should also to find out the laws governing inheritance in your state. Do you have wills or have you set up a living trust? It would be helpful to talk to a lawyer about how a possible divorce would affect them.

It is also important to find out if children from a previous relationship or a previous marriage might inherit some of your joint assets. These issues and others can be handled by such instruments as wills and trusts. Without these, dividing up an estate is much more problematic.

Does your husband's will exclude claims arising from illegitimate children? Men will tend to say they are sure that none of their extramarital girlfriends got pregnant. However, if this has happened, for a variety of reasons, the woman may not let the man know about it. As the story below shows, sometimes she may treat him as if he were one of those prize bulls that farmers use for insemination, but at least the sex is likely to be more satisfying for the human than for the bovine male.

Peter had a very brief affair with Sandy. It was clear that he would never leave his wife and their three kids for her. Sandy yearned for a child, and as Peter was a high-flyer—intelligent, good-looking, physically strong, creative and extremely financially successful—she believed that his genetic stock would produce high quality offspring. Since he did not want to father a child with her, she chose to get pregnant without his consent. Peter only found out that he had a daughter when she was 16, and Sandy wanted her sperm bank ex-lover to help pay for the girl to go to college.

You, as the wife, will be crystal clear as to whether or not you have any other kids outside your marriage, since you have had to pop all of them out yourself. Your husband can never be sure, and the more he has been playing the field bonking hundreds of babes, the more likely it is that he has spawned progeny all over the place.

Make sure inheritance documents do not contain language along the lines of "if we have other children, they will be entitled to an equal share to that of the children who have been named." This means that should one of his kids come out of the woodwork and make a claim on the estate, that child would get an equal share to those named in the will. If the illegitimate child is no longer living, his or her descendants could make a claim. Even if you, the wife, are clearly past childbearing age, the estate attorney may still have put this language in.

Lawyers can make a lot of money dealing with claims against an estate (much more than they earn from drafting the documents in the first place), so a cynical person might say that they can feather their nest very nicely by leaving that little bastard door wide open. You would think that a good attorney would actually ask you and your husband the question, "Do you want any other children apart from those you have named to have a claim on your estate?" However, the lawyer might not want to have to deal with opening a whole can of worms by asking this question. What if the wife and the husband have strongly different desires about how to deal with this issue? Maybe unbeknownst to the wife, he has fathered another child whom he wants to provide for in his will. Perhaps the estate attorney would be concerned about losing his or her clients to a divorce lawyer if the subject of other children is brought up when drafting inheritance documents, but to my mind, it is the only responsible thing to do.

If your husband does not know that you are aware of his affair or affairs, you may need to come up with some pretext or other to broach the subject of excluding other kids from your estate. If you know he had numerous partners prior to your marriage, you can always give that reason for adding the language to disinherit other kids. Alternatively, perhaps you can make up a story of a friend losing part of his inheritance to an illegitimate sibling.

To be iron-clad, your husband's will, and your joint living trust, if you have one, must include appropriate wording to specifically disinherit all other children and their descendants, except for the kids named and their descendants, provided that this is allowed in the location where you reside. If you are young enough to still get pregnant, then you would have to put in additional language to account for you and your husband having more children together. You should try to have all this done sooner rather than later. If for example, you or your husband has a serious health problem, or one of you is about to go in for potentially dangerous surgery, you will want to have the peace of mind that if one of you kicks the bucket, no lousy bastard can come on the scene to make a bad situation even worse.

Pauline's husband, Barry, had a brief affair with Nicola, who felt her biological clock ticking and deliberately stopped using contraceptives, unbeknownst to Barry. Once she got pregnant, Nicola broke off the affair and did not want Barry to have anything to do with raising the child. It was only ten years later that Nicola informed Barry about his son. Once he knew, he insisted upon giving Nicola and the boy considerable financial support, to the extent that his own children had to scale back their college choices in order for the family to be able to afford the fees. Pauline was furious, but could do nothing about it.

Imagine not only having to cope with the death of your philandering husband—with all the mixed feelings that would involve—and on top of that finding out not only that he had a kid with another woman, but also that the mother is suing his estate for a sizeable chunk. Aside from statutory child support requirements that may vary from state to state, try to make sure that you and your own children's inheritance is not at risk in this way. It is one thing for your husband to fuck you over by fucking others. It is quite another for him to fuck your kids over too by screwing with their financial future.

It is also important to ask an attorney what happens to the inheritance of the children you have had together if you and your husband divorce and he marries another woman. In addition, what might happen if he has another child with his new spouse?

When Estelle's father died he had a sizeable estate, but all of it went to his latest wife. There was nothing that Estelle could do about it. Thus, it is best to try to come to an agreement with your ex to protect the interests of your joint offspring in the event of his death. Perhaps he might be willing to write a will ensuring that the children will have an inheritance, or he could insist that his new partner signs a prenuptial agreement prior to tying the knot.

What About the Kids?

Sorry, all you hardworking single moms (or even dads), but a mountain of research shows that kids do much better when reared in two-parent homes, with both a mother and a father figure as role models. A large-scale study carried out in Sweden in 2003 and reported in *The Lancet* showed that children with single parents had increased risks of psychiatric disease, suicide or attempted suicide, injury, and addiction. A 2004 study carried out by the University of California, San Francisco and Princeton University showed that boys raised by single mothers were significantly more likely to be incarcerated in jail by the age of 30. Not to leave daughters out of the picture, a 2003 study by Bruce Ellis at the University of Arizona showed that about one-third of girls whose fathers left the home before they turned six became pregnant as teenagers, compared with just five percent of girls whose fathers were present throughout their childhood.

Unquestionably, staying together provides young kids with much more stability than making them split their time between two separate dwellings. It will be very hard to present a united front, and your kids may well try to play you off against each other to get what they want. More often than not, it is you, not your husband, who has done most of the actual rearing. He may be clueless about what is needed for your kids' classwork, extracurricular activities, meals or healthcare, not to mention any college, internship or job applications they may be trying to complete. Therefore, you can expect all kinds of screw-ups when it is his turn to take the children.

What if you and your man are really not getting on—constantly fighting and arguing? There may be no holds barred in what you are saying to each other and the kids are hearing everything. You cannot stand being with the lousy cheat—you hate him, but you have to stay together for the children. Well, in this case your kids may be living under such stress and disharmony in the marital home that it would be healthier for them if you actually did split up.

In her book, *Putting Children First: Proven Parenting Strategies for Helping Children Thrive Through Divorce* (Penguin Group, 2010), author JoAnne Pedro Carroll describes how when a marriage fails, the children will often refer to "my divorce," because the breakup is as much theirs as that of their parents. According to Pedro-Carroll, encouraging kids to talk about their feelings will calm them down and help them manage strong emotions. Otherwise, they will tend to stay silent, not wanting to rock the boat. If you split up with your husband, your children will need a lot of reassurance that both parents still love and care about them.

There are no hard and fast rules about what to tell your kids about your marital problems, except for the fact that you should do your absolute best to avoid bad-mouthing their dad in their presence. Do not try to make them have to choose sides. Children can become very insecure because they may pick up the negative emotions flying around between their parents and fear a breakup. Rather than ignoring the big elephant in the room that your kids cannot avoid being aware of, even if only subliminally, it may be best to acknowledge that mom and dad are going through some difficulties and are trying to work things out.

The degree to which your children figure in your decision to stay depends on their ages. If they are independent adults and live out of the marital home, whether or not you separate should be your decision rather than based on their needs. Alternatively, perhaps your grown children have never moved out. You may have wanted them to do so but have not yet managed to get them to leave. In this case, if you decide to boot your husband out of your life it may finally show you a way that you can kick your adult kids out of the house too.

If you have no children, your decision whether or not to continue the marriage will be easier as it can be based upon your needs alone. However, if you are childless but want to have children, the decision whether to stay may be determined by your age. A 12-year fertility study of 4,000 women led by Hospital Universitairo Quiron-Dexeus in Barcelona, Spain, was presented at the European Society of Human Reproduction's 2014 conference. The study showed a dramatic drop in fertility after age 35 with virtually no chance of conception once a woman reaches 44. Thus, a woman in her 20s might opt to split and hope to find another man to father her children, but if she is in her mid-30s or early 40s, she might decide to stay in the hope that she can get pregnant with her existing partner. Her biological clock might provide a strong incentive to make compromises with him. Alternatively, she might choose to leave and freeze some of her eggs to give herself more time to look for another long-term relationship.

Can Kids Cause Infidelity?

There is no doubt that the nature of your relationship with your husband changes dramatically once those little bundles of joy arrive. You cannot simply return them to the store if you are not completely satisfied, and it is most likely a 20-year commitment per kid.

You may be spending all your energy looking after the children so that you have none left for your husband. This is particularly likely to be the case if you are holding down a job as well. It is a rare husband who will pitch in to do anything close to half the work involved in childrearing.

When you have a baby in the house, you are the one who has to get up all through the night to breastfeed. You may be so worn out that your libido is completely flattened and sex is the last thing on your mind. Thus, your randy mate may go foraging in pastures new to find the oats he is not getting at home. There is no doubt that children can cause a lot of friction in a relationship, just as much as they can bring a couple closer together.

A husband may even become extremely jealous of the kids, resenting the love and attention you are giving them rather than him. His feelings may be primal, rather than from any part of his brain that is involved with rational thought. However, he will be likely to behave better than your typical alpha male gorilla that might kill a female's baby from another male in order to be able to mate with her. According to a book with a title that gives me a wry smile—*Demonic Males: Apes and the Origins of Human Violence* (Houghton Mifflin, 1996), by Richard Wrangham and Dale Peterson, infanticide is a common strategy among animals to accelerate the mother's sexual availability. Thankfully, biting the head off a woman's baby to be able to fuck her is not generally considered to be a successful strategy within human society.

Kids may cause infidelity both before and after they leave the marital home. Often monogamy ends once the nest is empty, which can lead to as much extramarital activity by the wife as by the husband. During the time that she has been rearing the children, she may have been starved of new connections, with a social life mainly composed of the mothers of her kids' friends. Once the children move out of the house, she has free time to take up a job, pursue interests or do volunteer work, for example, all of which put her in contact with potential lovers. If the husband has also spent a lot of time with the kids (bless him!), he too might now find other activities to fill it, such as bonking babes. Marriages can change a great deal when the kids have gone and it is just you two in the house. It can draw you closer or push you farther apart. You may no longer like being with each other in such close quarters without the kids acting as a buffer. There is also less guilt attached to adultery if the children are adults living out of the house, as they no longer figure that much in a parent's calculations about the logistics and possible repercussions of having an affair.

Rotten Role Models

Children are almost always psychologically affected by infidelity and divorce, and generally the younger they are the more profound the consequences tend to be. However, even if they are grown and no longer dependent on their parents, there are very likely to be emotional impacts.

Sometimes a parent will try to get a child on his or her side against the other parent and may even involve the kid in extramarital deception. This is especially common with adult children. Keith enlisted the help of his son to set up a new email account, so that he could communicate with his mistress. His wife, Winnie, discovered not only the affair but also that her son had known about it. She felt doubly betrayed and complained bitterly about the situation to her daughter. An acrimonious divorce ensued, resulting in the son being estranged from his mother and the daughter refusing to have anything to do with either her father or her brother. Infidelity had truly split the family in two.

Gabriel's father was a guitarist in a very successful rock band. Once he finished high school, he would tour with his dad and help the roadies. In his 40s and just out of drug rehab, Gabriel told me his story. "There were always parties after the shows, with loads of booze, drugs and pretty girls. Dad would get high and bonk his brains out. It made me feel very uncomfortable when I got home, and mom asked me how everything had gone. I couldn't be honest with her. It wasn't like I wasn't doing the same things as my dad. I ended up with a string of very unsatisfactory relationships with stunning-looking women and a serious drug habit. I wasted some of the best years of my life."

Rules of Religion

A woman's religious background, and that of her family, plays a huge role in her attitudes towards divorce and infidelity. Her beliefs might compel her to remain married. Even if a wife no longer believes in the faith she grew up with, her family may exert enormous pressure on her to toe the line. Parents from more traditional religious backgrounds tend to consider divorce a social stigma and a sign of failure in their childrearing. They are likely to strongly discourage a daughter from leaving her husband.

Many religions frown upon divorce and consider marriage to be a lifelong commitment, whatever happens. Said Sinead, who came from a staunch Irish Catholic family, "I wanted to leave Sean after I found out about his affair with a good friend of mine, but both my mother and my priest urged me to forgive him and keep the marriage intact at all costs. So I stayed. I'm not really happy with him, but I'm not happy with the alternative either."

Iona was in her 60s and lived in rural Scotland. Her husband drank heavily—not unusual in that location—and was a chronic philanderer. Brought up within the Church of Scotland, Iona was steeped in the Protestant tradition of diligence, working through obstacles and not giving up. "The young people today have unreasonable expectations about marriage," she bluntly asserted. "That's why there's so much divorce."

Eva and Peter were born-again Christians whose marriage was rocked by a brief relationship Peter had with another member of their Church. Peter begged for forgiveness, and the couple received a lot of counseling and support from their preacher to help them mend their relationship. "It's made our marriage stronger," declared Eva. "We both realized how much we loved and needed each other."

No religion offers a guarantee of ethical behavior. An atheist or agnostic is just as likely to be generous, kind and compassionate as someone who belongs to a particularly church. Many people completely ignore the ethical constraints of their particular faith when it comes to their personal lives, although they may judge others harshly. When former US President Bill Clinton faced impeachment for the Monica Lewinsky scandal, some of his harshest critics who professed to be staunch, upstanding Christians had had affairs themselves.

Ironically, the same religions that counsel against divorce also tend to consider adultery to be a terrible thing. So a cheated-upon woman may find herself between a rock and a hard place—there is no way that she can leave, yet the husband has betrayed not only the wife but also the religious tenets of her church, and the sacred vows he has made in the marriage ceremony. Furthermore, religious leaders will often have a double standard, being much more tolerant of male than of female infidelity.

The Mormons institutionalized male infidelity by adopting plural marriage, which allowed men to take as many wives as they wanted, but women were not accorded the same rights. The Mormon Church in Utah only agreed to renounce polygamy in 1890 as the US Congress would not otherwise allow Utah to gain statehood.

The Muslim religion also embraces polygamy. Islam allows a man to have four wives, whom he can beat, divorce and replace on almost any pretext. The wife is inferior to her husband and must submit to his will. In addition, he can possess additional women as sex slaves.

Ayesha was a shy Muslim girl who fell in love with a kind and gentle Nigerian Christian man, Jacob, with whom she worked at a hospital. They wanted to run away and elope, but Ayesha was convinced that her father and brothers would hunt them down and kill them both. Her family would never allow her to marry outside her religion. Instead, Ayesha submitted to an arranged marriage with a much older Pakistani man who treated her poorly and had several mistresses. Yet she knew that she could never leave him. As she talked about her life, Ayesha wore the required heavy Islamic scarf and complained about how uncomfortable it made her feel because it was a hot, humid day. "Divorce is not an option for women in my culture," she declared. The shocking aspect of this story is that it took place neither in the Middle East nor the Middle Ages, but in London, England, in 2014.

Does He Have a Guilty Conscience?

Some men feel guilty about their infidelity, others do not. This may be determined by a husband's religious background, how he currently feels about his wife, how good or bad he perceives their relationship to be, and/or his views on monogamy. Whether a man will suffer pangs of conscience for his actions will also be affected by his upbringing and the culture he comes from. For example, in Asia, rather than feeling the emotion of guilt, men worry about losing face.

Men who feel guilty about their adultery tend to be more altruistic and value their commitments. The affair may have just happened through force of circumstance, rather than because he was actively seeking an extramarital relationship. Men without guilt about their philandering generally do not take monogamy seriously. They are often out looking and open to the possibility of adding on another sexual commitment, however temporary.

However, if a husband feels bad about his infidelity, this does not guarantee that he will compensate by being extra nice to little wife holding the fort back home. As syndicated advice columnist Amy Alkon observes in *Good Manners for Nice People Who Sometimes Say F*ck* (St. Martin's Griffin, 2014), guilt may impel someone who has treated you badly to somehow blame you for what he did.

A habitual liar will be less likely to suffer remorse or feel guilty for unscrupulous behavior than someone who rarely lies. Yet in his own mind, a cheating husband may not be essentially dishonest. Nobody wants to admit to themselves that they might not be a good person. The man might see himself as the hero of his own story, as many of us do, and have convinced himself that his behavior is justified.

Other husbands may try to stay as close to the truth as possible—lying just enough to avoid their philandering being found out. They simply want as few hassles as possible. They neither want to deal the wife being upset about the infidelity nor risk losing the various services that she provides.

The popular stereotype is that women in general suffer more guilt over their perceived transgressions than do men, but this is not necessarily the case. Alicia came from a Catholic background, but she had no guilt whatsoever about having affairs with married men. She was a secretary for an insurance firm where the extremely well-paid salesmen loved to go out and have fun after finishing work at the office, as well as when they were away on business trips. Most of these salesmen were married, but nonetheless she dated many of them. Alicia adored staying in plush hotels, being taken out for fancy meals and receiving expensive gifts. "I don't care if they're already attached. That's between them and their wives. I don't want to marry any of them—I'm just enjoying having a great time."

Yvonne felt no guilt at all about being Sam's mistress, even though she knew that the affair had caused his wife much emotional anguish. Yet Yvonne was heartbroken when she discovered that sleazebag Sam had a third woman on the go.

Is It Best If He Confesses?

A husband will have a strong incentive to avoid telling his wife that he has been seeing another woman. He knows damn well that his spouse will be far less likely to selflessly minister to his needs once she is aware that his attentions have been focused elsewhere. Furthermore, he will not want to deal with a no-longer-loyal wife who is exceedingly upset and angry with him. Unless it seems that he will be discovered, his life will be much easier if he keeps his transgressions hidden.

Nevertheless, the Christian belief is that confession is good for the soul. Many times when a husband confesses to his wife about an affair that she knows nothing about, the main reason is to ease his conscience. He is attempting to make himself feel better, but in many cases, it puts an unnecessary burden on the marital relationship and his wife, making her feel insecure and unhappy, when she was fine before. If the affair is over, she has nothing more to worry about. If the affair is still going on, and the husband wants to continue it while still remaining married, confessing will make his wife have to choose between two unpleasant situations—divorce versus living with a philanderer.

One marital counselor I spoke to strongly advised against confession: "If the guy feels guilty, he's already punishing himself. He doesn't need the extra punishment of the marriage blowing up. He should keep his mouth shut and find another way of dealing with his guilt. Yes, he may have made a mistake, but life's not perfect. Honesty needs to be tempered with the practical in order to keep the marital relationship functioning as smoothly as possible."

Frank traveled all over Colorado selling and servicing office equipment. He loved his wife Jeannie and had no desire to leave her. They were married for twenty years. "In the early days, when I was a horny young buck full of testosterone, I would have affairs whenever the opportunity arose. In retrospect, I can see that I was a complete asshole. I felt very guilty about each affair afterwards, and it did affect my marriage. Although I never told Jeannie about the other women and stopped screwing around after the first few years of marriage, I always felt that my lies and deceit put a barrier between us."

Active deception always damages a relationship, according to Alex Comfort in *The Joy of Sex* (Crown Publishers, 2009). However, Comfort also mentions that sometimes confession itself is an act of aggression against the wife to help the husband avoid feelings of guilt, and this can also harm the relationship. Comfort's classic sex manual was originally published in 1972, but has been updated over the years and is still very relevant today.

Following the hacking of the extramarital dating website, ashleymadison. com, and the subsequent release of personal data on millions of their users in 2014, Elizabeth Bernstein wrote an article in *The Wall Street Journal* recommending that adulterers fess up (http://www.wsj.com/articles/after-ashley-madison-how-to-cope-with-infidelity-1441652059). She backs up this opinion with two studies. In a "Lust, Love and Loyalty" study of 30,000 cheaters carried out by television programs on MSNBC and iVillage in 2007, 45 percent of the men and 38 percent of the women surveyed said their spouses suspected or knew about the affair. 15 percent of the men and 11 percent of the women in the survey had chosen to confess of their own volition. Bernstein also mentions a small study of 115 participants published in April 2001 by the *Journal of Social and Personal Relationships*. It looks at the four ways an affair might be discovered and their impact on the survival of the marriage:

- The cheater confesses: 56.5 percent stay married.

- The spouse suspects an affair and forces the cheater to confess: 32 percent stay married.

- The spouse catches the cheater in the act: 17 percent stay married.

- A third party, often the mistress herself, tells the spouse about the infidelity: 14 percent stay married.

Of course, it does not take a rocket scientist to come up with the conclusion that being honest and contrite about infidelity will cause less damage to the marriage than being caught *in flagrante delicto*. However, Bernstein emphasizes that the affair must be ended before confessing, if the marriage is to have a chance of surviving.

Chapter Six

Stay or Go?
Relationship Issues

Now that you know he has been seeing someone else, do you still love him, even if you are mad as hell? Maybe you were not sure you loved him beforehand anyway. How do you cope with all the conflicting emotions arising from his behavior? Can you still love him if you hate him? What is the state of your relationship? Are you willing to compromise enough to make it continue to work?

This chapter will give you tools to help you assess how you feel about your marital relationship by looking at the shades of gray that often exist in the character of a cheating spouse and your attitude towards him. The goal is to help you begin unraveling the true nature of your feelings for your husband and navigate the tangled web of emotions that his infidelity has created.

Sadly, divorce is the most common outcome when you discover your man is having an affair. The loss of trust is too much to bear, so you give him the boot. He will go off and live with the other woman, and in many cases, after the initial glow has worn off and the dreary details of everyday life come back again, he may wonder if he made a big mistake to be with her. He may realize that you were the one he really loved all along, but by then there is too much water under the bridge, and you will not get back together. Alternatively, he may dump the woman he left you for and start seeing someone new, so that the cycle begins again.

Once you have found out about his extramarital activities, you cannot ever expect to go back to the feeling of a warm, intimate cocoon you thought was shared by only the two of you. Your love for him and your degree of loyalty and bonding towards him will never be quite the same. Complications and ambiguities will arise. You could find that your feelings about your marriage are inconsistent and conflicted, almost as if you are schizophrenic. One day it may feel as if things are more or less back to how they used to be, but on the next, you might feel quite separate from him rather than bonded. You may feel that he is not the soul mate he used to be, but instead a loathsome pain in the ass. This kind of ambiguity can occur frequently in long-term relationships, even when no infidelity has occurred.

When you first discover your husband's affair, you may react by becoming overly clingy and needy. However, after some time, you might find yourself pulling away from him, growing more emotionally distant. You may learn to become more independent and develop other friendships and activities to fill the vacuum the loss of his attention has left in your life. It will be difficult if not impossible to return to the easy intimacy and closeness you had before.

Your relationship can proceed in one of three ways:

- You stay together and he gives up the other woman (or women).

- You stay together and he continues to see her.

- You split up.

Obviously having him "ditch the bitch" is the best for you if you still want to stay with him. How can you achieve this? There is no guaranteed method. Nevertheless, I will tell you a couple of success stories.

Amy discovered her husband was having an affair with his secretary at work. Such a cliché, but that is because it happens so often. Amy cleared out the $50,000 nest egg that the couple had saved in a bank account and put it somewhere that only she had access to. Then she presented her husband with an ultimatum: either kiss the bitch or the cash goodbye. He chose to keep the cash and the couple stayed together. However, financial hardball with a man of a different personality might unleash a firestorm that you might wish you had never started. Who knows what kind of tit-for-tat game he might play? There might be so much acrimony that your marital relationship would be beyond repair.

Theresa, a university lecturer, found out that her spouse was fucking a pretty young thing with very little between the ears. She decided to hang in there and ride it out. Sure enough, within a year or so, the affair fizzled.

Yet, more often than not, getting a man to stop philandering is an uphill struggle. This is especially true if, for example, he travels a lot and fucking the locals has been his *modus operandi* for many years. Boy, those hotel rooms are a lot more fun with a bitch in the bed, especially in establishments where he just orders one up through room service. There are certain locations around the world where a man can indeed simply pay to play. Some guys may prefer this to a mistress because there is no emotional involvement.

If there is a new babe with whom your man is infatuated, everything is all new and shiny. She is the candy, a vacation from all the baggage at home. No responsibilities, no accountability. They will not be discussing the business, tax issues, problems with the kids or what needs to be repaired—all the dreary things that have to be taken care of when you are married. He will not dump her willingly.

You may have considerable leverage to get him to stop philandering. You give your husband a great deal that a mistress cannot ever provide. Through you he gets the familiarity, comfort, security and sanctuary of home. You may have spent much of the marriage managing your husband's life for him. Many wives take care of all the boring detail-oriented bits and pieces that, if ignored, would make everything fall apart. He may not even realize how important you are to the smooth running of his daily life and maybe his work too. Nonetheless, often the reason a man does not want to leave his wife is that he knows damn well how much more bothersome life would be if she were not doing all these things for him. The floozy may make him feel fantastic and be a fabulous fuck, but she would be a disaster at running his life for him. He really wants to have his cake and eat it too.

It is your decision how much of that managing you want to continue doing. If you are staying with him, you obviously do not want everything to come to a grinding halt, but you most definitely can scale back what you are doing for him somewhat, so that you have more time to do things that benefit your own life. Nevertheless, there are no guarantees that you will ever be able to stop him philandering if that seems to be his basic nature— if he gives up one woman, he may simply find another. He may even have several extramarital relationships going on at the same.

Try to look at yourself from your husband's viewpoint, and consider both the good and the bad. Most likely, there are reasons he has not left you apart from the convenience you provide and how useful you are to him. What are they? What has made you happy together and what has made you unhappy? What are the ways, before you found out about his philandering, that you shared enjoyment together? A walk? Swimming in the ocean? Going out for dinner? Enhance these activities. Insist upon them. Broaden the areas of pleasure that you had before you found out. You may have been blissfully happy with your husband until his affairs came to light. Then overnight, you became singularly unhappy. Carefully consider exactly how your perceptions changed when you found out.

If the marriage is to end, you should try to do it on your own terms. Obviously, it is best if divorce is either your decision or completely mutual rather than something foisted upon you by a jerk of a spouse who wants to replace you with a newer model. This is where some of the practical considerations covered in the previous chapter come in to play.

Do You Still Have a Good Relationship?

Adulterous marriages come in all sorts of shapes and sizes. Looking at some of these relationships, you might think, "Why on earth does the wife put up with it?" But, for whatever reasons, she does. The good, the bad and everything in between can be found in all marital relationships.

Anyone looking in from the outside might have a hard time believing why you have stayed in the marriage. Amazingly though, you may still have a good or even great relationship with your wandering spouse. Somehow it works. You may still share the same interests and enjoy each other's company. Especially if you have reared kids together and have been married for many years, you will have a huge amount of shared history, and there will be many things that only the two of you will be able to understand and have a good laugh over. You may feel fortunate that you have found a soul mate, even if he is clearly in some ways a deeply flawed individual. Come on, only in the movies can you find a completely perfect man. Despite all the odds, you still love him.

Some women are very tolerant of their spouse's philandering. Sharon had been married to Frank for three decades. Seven years older than he, she had lost all interest in sex and was quite happy without it. She knew he had affairs, but they had a tacit agreement not to talk about it. "I accept that he has certain needs that I'm not satisfying," she said, "but we're still best friends and we wouldn't want to be living with anyone else but each other."

One wife put it this way, "Am I OK with his affairs? Well, there are different levels of being OK with something. I just have to be pragmatic. I don't want to lose what's good in my marriage because I'm expecting it to be perfect all the time."

Bettina was going through a difficult time with her philandering husband and told her mother that she was considering divorce. "Mom told me an old story from China where a group of Chinese women recounted their tales of woe and put a pebble out on the table to represent those woes. When the women were asked to change pebbles, they all took their own pebble back. The moral of the story? Better the trouble you know than the one you don't. In the end, I decided that it was worth making an effort to keep my marriage intact."

A husband and a wife may have completely different opinions on what constitutes a good marriage, especially if he wants to keep having affairs and expects his spouse to simply put up with it and keep the home running smoothly. Many of the elements that might normally be considered essential to a good relationship, such as trust, a sense of security, being comfortable talking about innermost feelings, kindness, viewing your partner positively rather than with contempt, caring about each other, having fun together, finding each other sexually attractive, and admiring and respecting each other, are likely to be seriously impaired by the discovery of infidelity. Other aspects, such as being willing to compromise and forgive, having clear communication, accepting each other's flaws and allowing each other to grow and explore, may actually be strengthened by the couple working through their marital difficulties together.

Marital Counseling

This is not a book about marital counseling. However, it is worth mentioning that some couples dealing with infidelity find marital counseling to be invaluable. They may discover effective tools to repair their marriage with the help of an unbiased independent mediator who is knowledgeable about the dynamics of relationships.

Do not just pick a marital counselor at random from the phone book. It is best to get recommendations from people you trust who may have already been helped by counselors. Interview a few therapists before deciding which one to go for. It has to feel right. If a counselor is wrong for you, even if someone else found that person to be great, he or she may waste your time, drain your finances and make you feel worse rather than better. If the counselor is good, he or she will offer you professional expertise that you will not be able to get from your friends. The therapist should not only help you make much more informed decisions about what to do but also dramatically improve your state of mind.

If you and your husband are considering going for counseling together, the following points are important to bear in mind:

- Both husband and wife must be fully on board with the process, rather than one spouse dragging an unwilling partner to the sessions.

- Both parties must try to avoid getting sidetracked by the blame game and be prepared to compromise.

- The therapist not only has to be good but also must be a suitable match for both the husband and the wife. It will not work well if one partner really likes the counselor and the other partner is very lukewarm towards him or her.

You may not know whether you have a good marriage with your husband, or even what the necessary components of a good relationship might be. People do not tend to spend a long time analyzing the quality of the relationship before taking the plunge and tying the knot. They meet someone, fall madly in love, gloss over imperfections and they marry. An experienced marital counselor can help you take an objective look at the specifics of your marriage to determine its strengths and weaknesses.

Do not feel obliged to drag your husband along to counseling sessions. If you are trying to decide whether you want to stay in your marriage, seeing a therapist on your own may be the best route. This gives you a safe place to discuss your feelings towards your husband, the nature of your relationship with him, the specifics of his infidelity and most important, the outcome you would like to see. It is very likely that you will want to talk this over in private, without your husband present. If you are considering a split, you do not want him to be privy to your innermost feelings.

Joint counseling is best suited to couples who know that they want to try to stay together. The stronger their desire to do so and the more compromises they are willing to make, the more successful the counseling will be. If the relationship has gone really sour, then it may be a very appropriate time for the couple to honestly express their true feelings. There is nothing to lose. Often the husband does want the marriage to continue and therefore has an incentive to work at rebuilding the relationship. A good counselor can help to steer both partners towards a successful outcome for the marriage.

Alyssa wanted her husband Phil to see a therapist with her as she felt their marriage was on the rocks. He was extremely resistant to the suggestion, but she managed to drag him to counseling sessions. Alyssa explained, "Phil hated going, but eventually realized that the therapist was helping us to work through our problems in ways that we never would have come up with on our own."

Both Bob and Tracy had had affairs in the past and got over them, but now Tracy wanted to leave the marriage for good. Bob declared, "We went for counseling, but I found it useless and embarrassing. Tracy had fallen out of love with me and nothing could convince her to stay."

Your views on the value of counseling are likely to have been shaped by your culture and background. In her book, *Lust in Translation: Infidelity from Tokyo to Tennessee* (Penguin Books, 2007), Pamela Druckerman refers to the "marital-industrial complex" in America, where working with paid professional counselors over an extended period may often be seen as the only way to resolve marital difficulties. According to Druckerman, in most other countries, this is not the case. Many European couples would not be seen dead in a therapist's office.

Sherry comes from a working-class mining town in the North of England. She had this to say about counseling, "When I discovered my husband's affair, my friends really helped me get through it and find a way to reconcile with him. If it hadn't been for all their advice and support, I don't know what I'd have done. Never in a million years would I pay some stranger to listen to my troubles."

Whose Interests Come First?

In ancient Rome, there was the Latin adage *cui bono,* which means "to whose benefit?" The Romans would look at any situation in terms of who would have something to gain and who would be taken advantage of. In most cases, your philandering husband benefits from his mistress and not you, even if he tries to spin the situation to appear otherwise. Nevertheless, one valuable effect of his infidelity is that it may give you the freedom to change your life to something you find more fulfilling than what you are doing now, whether or not you choose to continue your marriage.

Generally, a wife expects honesty in her marital relationship. She assumes that her life partner will have her interests at heart and protect her back. However, once your man is unfaithful, whose interests will he look after? Yours, his own or those of his mistress? What are his priorities? Robin claimed he loved his wife, Stephanie, and wanted to grow old with her. However, he told her he was also in love with another woman, Jenny, with whom he insisted upon going off for a month-long exotic (or should I have said erotic?) vacation in Fiji. Stephanie was upset, but did not want to leave him. "What if I get sick or something?" she asked him, "Would you come back from your trip?" "Of course I would," was his response. Well as luck would have it, Stephanie came down with a serious viral infection and had to be hospitalized. When she phoned him from the hospital, Robin said how sorry he was that she was ill, but never once offered to come home. After she was discharged, she called him out on it. The callous cad said nonchalantly, "Oh, I had Jenny look at possible flights, but I decided by the time I got to you, it would either be too late or you'd already be getting better." From then on Stephanie knew that she could never rely on her husband or believe his promises. The marriage did not survive.

A promiscuous man may have a different view of marital commitment right from the start. Belinda discovered that her traveling salesman husband, Jeremy, had been away from home so much because he had a mistress in another state. Belinda told him sadly, "I don't feel married anymore." He coldly retorted, "I never felt married." To paraphrase, he had been having affairs throughout their relationship and never had any intention to be monogamous. This scoundrel of a husband had no concept of what his marriage vows really meant.

One reason why your husband may want to stay with you is that you are too competent for your own good. You provide too many useful services for him to ever consider divorcing you, but if he were thinking with his dick alone, he would be with her, not you. So he has an affair or two but remains married to you. The question is: Does he provide enough for you to want to stay with him? There are many superwomen who manage the house, kids and family business, not to mention all aspects of their husband's affairs. By that I do not mean organizing his extramarital bonking, but instead all the boring stuff such as healthcare, computer issues, bill paying, bookkeeping and so on. The problem is that even if these superwomen do leave their demanding, needy husbands, when they have another relationship they end up doing all that stuff for the new man too. Avoid that trap if you can.

You may now find yourself putting your own interests ahead of those of your philandering husband—both a good thing and a bad thing to do. For example, if you want your marriage to continue, do not jeopardize the smooth running of your life together by failing to take care of important issues that you had always looked after before, particularly if they could have a financial impact on the family. Marianne had always taken care of her husband's travel arrangements, despite having a full-time job as a bookkeeper. She managed to create an environment where everything ran smoothly. She discovered he had a mistress a month or so before he was due to leave for two-week computer training course, which would take place in the city where the other woman lived. The course was valuable for Nigel to attend and would most likely enable him to command a higher salary. Yet understandably, Marianne took a step back from organizing everything. She felt too angry and hurt to deal with the trip, so she let her adult daughter help Nigel with all the details and with packing his bags. This proved to be an unmitigated disaster. Nigel, always having relied on his wife to plan ahead, tried unsuccessfully to sort out several critical problems the day before travel. Then, when he arrived at the airport, he realized that he had left one of his bags behind, full of items that he needed for the course. Nigel laid heavy blame on his daughter for not having provided adequate support.

Clearly, without Marianne's organizational skills, his life was going to be considerably more inconvenient. The income stream they shared would most likely be negatively impacted.

Shades of Gray

Relationships are not black and white but rather come in shades of gray—and I am not referring to the sadomasochistic fiction series of the same name. Only in the movies are the characters either villains or heroes. In real life, people are neither but perhaps a mixture of the two. Even in marriages that are monogamous, there are likely to be times when one or both partners feel very ambivalent towards the other. They might wonder whether they still love their spouse or even like him or her anymore, especially if the couple is facing work stress, financial insecurity, illness or problems with the kids. When infidelity comes into the mix, such ambivalent feelings are amplified.

It is easy to demonize both your husband and the bitches in his extramarital stable. It is natural to see yourself as the pure, righteous, wronged victim. However, there are neither angels nor demons here. You are both simply human beings. Although in an objective way, your husband may indeed have treated you abysmally, you are not a completely innocent party. Yes, we know, compared to him, you are much more innocent, but in some way or another, you have chosen to participate in the dynamic that has brought you to this point.

Then, if you yourself have ever had an affair with a married man, even if only once, even if it was a long time ago, what does that make you? At the very least, you will have an inkling of what it is like to be in the other woman's shoes—the lack of stability, the stolen moments when he can get away, the secrecy, and so on. It may be sexy and exciting, but you do not have the comfort of living in your own home and planning your life together. Sounds like an even worse situation than the one you have.

Who is to blame? Well, we already know he is a total jerk, but what is the point of talking about it? Playing the blame game and dredging up the ancient history of how he treated you will not solve anything. Instead, it will make things worse and polarize the situation.

Remember that change is a part of life, however much you might want to avoid it, and you cannot predict where those changes will lead you. Maybe last year you had the best wedding anniversary ever, making love the whole day through. This year it is your anniversary and you are talking to friends about referrals for a divorce lawyer. Who can tell where you will be on the same date next year? Maybe you will have moved so far apart from each other that you both forget it was your anniversary and are both fucking other people.

"It was the best of times, it was the worst of times," is a famous quote from the beginning of the novel by Charles Dickens, *A Tale of Two Cities* (Dover Thrift Editions, 1999), which could be an accurate description of your marriage. Like many men, sometimes your husband can be wonderful, at other times he may be asinine. Is the balance between the two acceptable for you to want to continue living with him? Your relationship can go through periods of being great, good, mediocre and downright terrible, and not necessarily in that order. Over the course of just one day, it could be both amazing and horrible. Only you, in your heart of hearts, can know whether your marriage is working for you.

Tibetan Buddhists talk about the pitfalls of both positive and negative emotions, working towards overcoming attachment (to what you like or love) and aversion (to what you dislike or hate), as both are seen as causes of suffering and distractions from realizing enlightenment. The aim in this tradition is to attain wisdom and compassion for all sentient beings. Unconditional love—wouldn't it be great if you really could achieve it? If you have been a mother, try to remember the love you had for your children when they were babies, before they got older and any baggage developed between you and them. What you felt then was pure and uncomplicated. However, as for your relationship with your philandering husband, some days you will feel that you still love him no matter what, and other days you might wonder why the hell you are staying with him. Even if he were truly faithful, most likely there would be certain times when he would drive you nuts and you might ponder how great life might be on your own. So would you be happier living with him or without him? Take plenty of time to work out your answer to that question—it may be less straightforward than you initially might believe.

Heroes or Demons?

Modern media loves to build up all kinds of celebrities into champions and demonize adulterers. People in public life—rock stars, sportsmen, politicians—sometimes are portrayed as heroes and other times as villains. In reality, they are simply flawed human beings with varying amounts of good and bad qualities.

Former mayor of New York City, Rudy Giuliani, got into hot water for his affair with Judith Nathan, using public money to fund some of his secret trysts with her and to provide her with such items as a car and driver. He held a press conference in 2000 announcing his intention to divorce his wife, without having discussed the matter with her beforehand. As you might imagine, the split was exceedingly acrimonious. Yet Giuliani managed to redeem his media persona by the leadership role he played following the terrorist attacks on the World Trade Center in New York on September 11, 2001. *Time* magazine named him "Person of the Year" for his efforts. Nevertheless, some have claimed that Giuliani exaggerated his heroic image for political and financial gain.

The renowned Chinese dissident and conceptual artist, Ai Weiwei, has been willing to put his personal safety on the line to publicize government corruption and cover-ups in China. *Ai Weiwei: Never Sorry,* a documentary by Alison Klayman released in 2012, reveals that he is married but has a son by another woman who is much younger. On film, the artist says in a casual manner that he had recommended that the woman have an abortion. (Bear in mind that China's attitude towards abortion is at the opposite end of the spectrum to the religious right in America.) Since she wanted to keep the baby, he agreed to give her financial support and visit the child. Understandably, it seemed that his wife, Lu Qing, was not too happy about this situation, but a reliable source told me that she had been dating others too. Perhaps she started seeing other men as a reaction to the famous artist's peccadilloes. Some people might neither condone Ai Weiwei's affair nor like his conceptual art. Yet many believe that he has shown great courage and ingenuity in confronting the Chinese authorities about injustices.

Letters written by Albert Einstein to his stepdaughter, Margot, were publicly released in 2006. They revealed that he was a charismatic philanderer who thought nothing of writing to his second wife and stepdaughter back home about all his love affairs on the road and the numerous women who were chasing him. Does this mean that scientists should throw out all Einstein's theories on astrophysics? Of course not—the value and validity of his work has absolutely nothing to do with his personal life.

People can be very inconsistent in their attitudes towards adultery. When Vera told her aunt Mavis about her husband's infidelity, the aunt was shocked and refused to be on speaking terms with him ever again. This was despite the fact that Mavis had had several extramarital affairs of her own. Jerry's best friend Eric was quite a player and although married, would have sex wherever he could get it. Jerry simply accepted that was just the way Eric was. Yet when another of his friends confided in him about her husband's infidelity, he told her the man was a complete cad and not worth staying with. Upon hearing about the adulterous exploits of her best friend's husband, Sylvia declared darkly, "All men are cunts!" It was a confusing epithet to choose since this is the one piece of anatomy that no man possesses. Yet Sylvia herself had indulged in numerous relationships with married men.

Perhaps one of the most famous examples of a hypocritical attitude towards adultery was William Randolph Hearst, who openly kept actress Marion Davies as a mistress for many years. Yet he would not allow guests at his lavish parties to sleep with anyone except their spouse if they were staying overnight at his mansion. According to David Niven's fascinating and hilarious book about the early days of Hollywood, *Bring on the Empty Horses* (Coronet Books, 1976), if such a crime were committed, the offending lovers would receive a note with their breakfast advising them to leave the premises as quickly as possible. They would be banished forever from Hearst's gatherings.

Early Warning Signs

There are two major reasons for marital problems: first, a female's fantasy of thinking she can change her man and fix his failings; second, a man may have the opposite delusion. He thinks that his partner will never change, at least in terms of remaining as physically attractive and keen on sex as she was in the early days of the relationship. Yet the daily grind of dealing with the kids, home and perhaps a job too, will most likely dampen her ardor, and over the years, her body will lose its youthful beauty.

A woman may see something that she really does not like in her partner's behavior and truly believe she can alter that aspect of his character. Sometimes there are obvious clues before a woman gets married that her dearly beloved will be unfaithful. She may simply choose to ignore the signs, perhaps thinking that somehow or other the wedding vows will miraculously transform Mr. Libertine into Mr. Fidelity. "I should have known better—I should have seen it coming," is a common refrain you will hear from a woman leaving her husband, once she realizes that he will not change.

Cheryl married a flirtatious fellow, Kurt, who made no secret of having had numerous lovers before her. He promised undying loyalty and that he would never leave her. However, he also added, "The worst you could expect of me is that I might have a few bimbos here and there." Cheryl was happy to take his first statement on board, but was emotionally crushed when she found out, after being married to him for over a decade, that he actually did have a couple of bimbos on the go, and had done so for quite some time. Cheryl preferred monogamy, but her husband most certainly did not.

Wedding Woes

Walt has been a wedding videographer in Northern California for many years, and he reckons that, more often than not, he can tell which marriages will work out well and which ones will not. Despite the fact that it is supposed to be the best day of a couple's life, many people are at their worst during weddings—they are often highly emotional, stressed out and drunk. Walt has seen many brand-new spouses openly flirting with others—as many brides as grooms do so—sometimes indulging in kissing friends and coworkers who are guests in ways that definitely do not look platonic. After seeing the groom cozying up to another woman, his bride spent 45 minutes weeping in the basement of the building where her wedding had been held, delaying the first dance at the reception. Walt is paid by the hour for his videography services, so he was happy to oblige.

At one wedding reception dinner, the best man began his speech by asking the guests to look under their tables. There he had placed some recent photos of the bride that were very incriminating. The pictures showed her *in flagrante delicto* with another man. This story raises a number of issues.

If the best man thought that the groom should not have married the bride, why did he decide not to tell him before the wedding? How did this tosser get to be the best man when he was clearly the worst man for the future of the marriage? He was acting abominably towards both the bride and the groom. It is not known whether the bridegroom and the bride's father took the best man round the corner and thumped the shit out of him.

At another reception, behavior surfaced that was considerably worse than infidelity. The bride shoved cake into the groom's face, admittedly a tacky custom, but every so often newlyweds will do this to each other after cutting the cake. However, rather than responding by doing the same to the bride, the groom got angry and slapped her in the face, in full view of the horrified guests and the video camera. The bride was visibly shaken but tried to laugh it off. No wonder the woman was upset—she had just married a wife beater. If he could not even control his temper in public, what the hell was he likely to do to her in private? I just hope that she had the sense to ditch the brute. In fact, the company that Walt works for insists on getting the full payment at the wedding, even though it takes six months for the edited wedding DVD to be completed. The main reason for this is that sometimes the couples have already split up in that time, and then they do not want to pay for the video.

Wendy and Gordon had a registry office wedding in London, England. Recalls Wendy, "The registrar was a right old battle-axe who really didn't seem to like men at all. She didn't even want to let Gordon go off for a pee before the ceremony. Then during the wedding itself, when she got to the vow about fidelity, she glared at Gordon as if he were a serial killer beneath contempt. We both noticed how nastily she behaved towards him at that point. But in retrospect, now that I know that he was philandering all the way through our marriage, I'm wondering if there was something about Gordon's demeanor that made his unfaithful nature obvious to that registrar."

Julian's first marriage did not last long. At his wedding reception, he remembered being rather shocked at himself for looking at other women there and finding them attractive. Deep down he felt a strong urge to flee from the proceedings. Thankfully, when he got married for the second time, he did not find himself ogling other women at the wedding. At least at the time of writing this, Julian's second marriage seems very stable.

At a wedding reception in Glasgow, Scotland, the groom made the following announcement: "According to Scottish tradition, a marriage is not solid until consummated. I'd like to thank my best man for warming the bed for me." He then threw the champagne in his glass at the bride and stormed out. Apparently, most of the men continued enjoying the food and drink, while a group of inebriated women slugged it out in the parking lot.

Another wonderfully outrageous case of infidelity coming to light at a wedding occurred in Shenzhen, South China in November 2013 and was reported in newspapers all around the world. A pregnant mistress in a white wedding dress stormed into the ceremony, angry and apparently drunk—or perhaps she was just tired and emotional. Immortalized on video, she can be seen wrestling the bride to the ground as the groom tries to pull the pair apart (https://www.youtube.com/watch?v=renAtwvLPyA).

How Much Can You Compromise?

Every relationship demands compromise of one sort or another. What are you willing to put up with? How much tolerance do you have for your husband's infidelity? Only you know the answer. What is fine for one person might be purgatory for another.

Natasha was a cat lover, her husband, Les, was a dog lover. Natasha hated dogs, so she would joke about her relationship with him, telling friends, "I told him he could have me or a dog, and so far he's stuck with me." Her tune changed once she discovered his affairs: "I told him he could have me or a dog," she would say ruefully, "but now I've found out that he had me and a bitch all along."

Stay true to yourself. If you bottle up your feelings and put on a brave face, you may find yourself faking it all the way to the hospital. Negative emotions create all kinds of psychological and physical stress.

Elizabeth was the wife of former US Senator and presidential hopeful, John Edwards. She had to come to terms with the fact that her husband had been seeing a mistress for several years, fathering a baby girl with the woman. When the story became public knowledge, it was extremely politically damaging for the Edwards family. His wife, despite battling breast cancer at the time, appeared in various TV interviews, gracious and smiling, seeming to have come to terms with her husband's infidelity. However, according to various reports, her private attitude towards his behavior was quite different. In 2010, she died of cancer. Was her husband's infidelity connected to her cancer? Who can tell? Nevertheless dying of a broken heart is a common theme in the literature of all cultures and time periods.

One reason for the rise in divorces compared to previous generations is the increase in lifespan, so that "until death do us part" becomes a much longer period. In the past, you might have kicked the bucket before the relationship became intolerable. In addition, people of the baby boomer Beatles generation are less willing to admit that they are growing old. They do not want to sit in an armchair with hot milk and slippers—50 has become the new 30 and 60 the new 40. Thus, rather than making compromises to permanently settle down with one partner, they would be more likely to see themselves as eternally young and change out the old model for a newer one.

Your Book of Changes

According to the seminal Taoist text, the *I Ching (Book of Changes)*, everything changes. The Taoists have built a spiritual tradition around staying balanced amidst constant change. If you do not acknowledge that material existence is a continual succession of changes, they say, you are living in a fantasy world of stability. This fact becomes even more starkly obvious after a husband's infidelity is discovered. You do not want your marriage to change from the way it was before you knew, and most likely your husband does not really want to change how he was able to have his affair and have you too. However, accepting change is essential to be able to make compromises with each other to repair the marriage, if that is what you want to do. Most individuals will avoid dealing with change unless they absolutely have to. Generally, as people grow older they become more and more stuck in their ways and find it increasingly harder to cope with change.

When I was a child, my family kept a goldfish in a small bowl. We decided that he might be happier in a larger space with more interesting items to swim around, so we bought him a big rectangular tank. But the fish could not adjust to the new environment—he would not turn at the corners of the tank and kept bumping into the glass wall. We put the goldfish back into his little bowl and the tank sat unused in a closet. So, just like that goldfish, are you limiting yourself to what you are used to when there is a whole world out there to explore?

Great Expectations

© 2016 C. J. Grace. Artwork by Aaron Austin, concepts by C. J. Grace.

This cartoon was inspired by the 1999 South Park *"Chinpokomon" episode (Season 3, Episode 11), where the Japanese term* chinpoko *apparently means "small penis," and by my visit to the 2013* shunga *(Japanese erotic art) exhibition at the British Museum in London. I saw numerous paintings on display depicting samurai lovers sporting impossibly huge penises as wide as their partner's legs.*

One relationship counselor told me, "Insanity is doing the same thing over and over but expecting a different result. Learning to be flexible and being open to making changes in your behavior is the most effective path to improving the quality of your relationships and your life in general." He recommended self-reflection—observing one's own behavior and asking the question, "Is this really serving me well?" If not, you need to be willing to adjust what you are doing to allow yourself to achieve the results you want. A key part is to look at how your expectations can block your ability to change for the better.

Great Expectations

All relationships have their ups and downs, so if you want yours to be amazing all the time, there is no doubt that you have unreasonable expectations. Once you find out about his infidelity, you may have three very unrealistic beliefs:

• You can get your marriage back to how it was before.

• You can change him.

• You can stop his philandering.

Dream on. Maybe you can find an African witch doctor to fix everything for you, such as King Alli Chiwawula, "Herbalist and Mail Order" who advertised his services in the September 12, 2013 edition of *The Citizen* in South Africa, declaring that he could "Bring back lost lovers within same day, breaking up other relationships within 24 hours," as well as giving you "love power to control your lover from cheating and love you alone." However, if King Alli Chiwawula cannot help you, compromise of some form or another is essential in any long-term relationship, especially if infidelity comes into the mix. Expectations will play a key role in the decision of whether or not to divorce. In wealthier First World societies, particularly America, women have high standards as regards what they expect within a relationship. This is one of the reasons why the divorce rates are so high in the West.

In contrast, the traditional view of how life tended to be in China would be *chi ku,* literally translated as "to eat bitterness." (This is similar to the view in Tibetan Buddhism that worldly life and the continuous cycle of birth, death and rebirth—*samsara*—is characterized by suffering.) Thus, a Chinese wife would have far lower expectations about how she should be treated, and she would put up with behavior from her husband that would most likely send an American woman rushing to her divorce lawyer to take her wayward spouse for all he is worth.

Your attitude clearly depends on what you are used to and what you expect to be normal. To give an extreme example, some time ago I was watching a TV documentary and hearing the story of a woman from a war-torn country in Africa. She spoke about the anguish she had suffered seeing two of her children killed right in front of her. "Now I am fortunate to live in more peaceful times," she said through an interpreter. "My husband is a good man. He likes to see other women sometimes, but I don't mind. He provides for my family and never beats me. I have a happy life now."

There is a strong correlation between how much schooling a woman has had and the level of her expectations in a marital relationship. No doubt, men who want a more old-fashioned setup might bemoan the fact that all of us uppity Western women got the vote and an education.

One of the reasons Western men want to get themselves online or mail-order brides from Southeast Asia is that many regions there have a culture of female subservience to men. According to popular stereotypes, these Asian women expect to do all the cooking and cleaning, serving their husband hand and foot. They will also attend to all his sexual needs in a skillful fashion and are supposedly more tolerant of his infidelity, so long as he does not leave and is a good breadwinner for the family. In reality, however, the expectations of these mail-order wives once they come to America may be quite different from the stereotypes.

Sam earned a good living as a physical therapist and owned a comfortable house in Portland. He did not find the attitudes of American women he met to his tastes. He searched online to find an attractive Thai girl called Ratana, 25 years his junior, and brought her over to be his bride. Ratana's 11-year-old daughter, Mali, came too, and Sam adopted her. For many years, Ratana seemed like the perfect wife. However, when Mali finished college, all paid for by Sam, Ratana unceremoniously dumped him, making out quite well in the divorce settlement. It appeared that right from the start, she had no intention of staying with Sam once her financial needs were taken care of.

Ivana was an attractive Russian girl in her mid-20s. She had come to the United States as a mail-order bride and was already on her third marriage, moving up the economic ladder with each new union. Currently married to a corporate executive, she lived with him in a New York penthouse. This husband wanted more conversation and companionship from her than she was willing to give. "I already give him borscht and blowjobs," she complained to a friend, "What more can he expect from me?"

OK Before, Unacceptable Now?

Is your cup half full or half empty? Sometimes compromises you were quite happy to make before you knew about your husband's philandering become quite intolerable after you have found out about his other woman. The absolute loyalty that you may have had towards your husband despite his shortcomings will most likely have been shaken. Your expectations of what you should be doing for him and what you consider acceptable as regards his behavior will have changed.

Georgette's husband, Benito, had a very traditional attitude—he worked hard at his job in finance but did not lift a finger at home. Georgette served him all his meals, beautifully prepared, but he would only comment on them if there was something she had made that he did not like. She knew that Benito would never consider her cooking to be as good as the dishes his Italian mother made. Georgette would run his bath, making sure the water temperature was just right, and once Benito was in the tub, he would call his wife to turn off the faucets rather than do it himself. Even if the TV remote was closer to him than to his wife, he would still ask her to bring it to him. Benito would have the television on almost all the time, even while making love to his wife—the one time you might expect a woman to have her husband's undivided attention. Georgette was not over the moon about all these things, but they did not start to bother her deeply until she found out that Benito had been bonking his very pretty young secretary. Benito eventually gave up the secretary—she was not too bright and kept making mistakes at work so he persuaded her to take up a job at another company. However, Benito's wife found that she could no longer put up with his treatment of her and divorced him.

Barry was a computer consultant who loved food. The first Christmas he and his wife, Miranda, spent together was with the family of an old

Marital Counseling

© 2016 C. J. Grace. Artwork by Aaron Austin, concepts by C. J. Grace.

friend from Miranda's college days. There were more guests than originally expected, so when Barry looked at the rather small portion on his plate, to the shock of the hosts, he loudly blurted out the unforgettable line, "You would get more food at a Salvation Army soup kitchen!" Some months later, the couple went out for dinner at a Chinese restaurant with friends and the food was put in the center of the table to be shared. To Miranda's embarrassment, Barry quickly scarfed down most of the best dishes, without thinking of leaving much for the other diners. Miranda remedied this situation by only taking him to restaurants where everyone would have individual plates that were not shared. Then Miranda discovered that he was having an affair with one of his computer clients—the pretty young girl was clearly receiving one-on-one personal networking services. The result: Barry's behavior quirks that Miranda had initially found somewhat endearing now annoyed her intensely. She ended up leaving her husband for a cerebral fellow who appeared to be less driven by his appetites.

However, no longer tolerating your dearly beloved's character flaws after you have found out about his infidelity can be a double-edged sword if you want to stay in the marriage. On the one hand, calling him out on his crap may make him realize what he is doing and treat you better. On the other hand, it may either create more disharmony or make him feel like he has to walk on eggshells around you. He may conclude that he prefers being with his mistress, as she is not laying into him all the time—or at least, she is only doing that in the sexual sense.

Is Your Life Half Full or Half Empty?

Various people can attend the same event, and each one may have a totally different impression of it. One person may really enjoy it, another may be bored, and yet another may find it quite unpleasant. In effect, all the people attending are creating their own separate reality at the event within their own mind. Whatever mood and emotions you bring with you will affect how you experience any occasion. Some people suffer such anxiety over trivial things that it makes them physically ill, yet others may stay calm whatever chaos happens around them.

The concept of people creating their own reality is part of a Hawaiian spiritual tradition known as Ho'oponopono. This notion has also been embraced in various forms by some New Age therapists. According to

Ho'oponopono, you are 100 percent responsible for whatever occurs in your own life, including what happens to others with whom you interact. All that you perceive *is* created by your own mind. This hypothesis might be hard to swallow if you have just discovered that your husband has been cheating. Nevertheless, it is still true that you have made choices that have brought you to your current state.

Clinical psychologist Ihaleakala Hew Len is a proponent of Ho'ponopono. Some decades ago, he apparently managed to cure a whole ward of criminally insane inmates at Hawaii State Hospital. Rather than meeting with the inmates face-to-face, Len used a very simple technique from Ho'oponopono while looking over their files. "I just kept saying to myself, 'I'm sorry, please forgive me, thank you and I love you,' over and over again." The psychologist claimed that he was simply healing the part of himself that had created the inmates in his reality. The process involves empathy, focus and perseverance.

Perhaps you would like to try the same technique yourself while thinking about your husband and the other woman. They are unlikely to be crazy psychos like the folks Len had to deal with, so you might have an easier job reducing their toxic effect on your life. This technique might help you find an acceptable compromise that keeps your marriage alive.

Whatever your opinions about Ho'oponopono, bear in mind that much of what you see and feel is created by your own mind. Your particular belief systems are determined by such factors as your upbringing, education and/or religious faith. These influences will shape how you perceive events in your life (such as finding out about your husband's infidelity), and the emotions you feel when experiencing those events. I remember walking past a truck with a very shiny chrome bumper and noticing a quail getting very worked up fighting his own reflection in it. I watched him for more than 20 minutes and I do not know how much longer he continued the battle with his reflection. I found it very entertaining, but it was clearly an extremely unpleasant experience for the quail. He truly believed another bird was there. So take some time to consider exactly what you are really railing against and getting upset about. Is it just something of your own creation? A Tibetan Lama giving a talk about the nature of unhappiness came up with the following observation: "Poor people have physical suffering. Rich people have mental and emotional suffering."

What If the Other Woman Is a Man?

Staying with a husband who has been having affairs with men tends to involve even more compromises and soul-searching than remaining with a partner who has been seeing other women. Women who remain married to heterosexual unfaithful men often will often refuse to admit what has been happening even to close friends. These wives do not want to lose face or discuss negative, intensely personal feelings that they may have towards their husband. With homosexual infidelity, there may be even more shame and secrecy involved, particularly if the man has not come out of the closet. He may claim that he is bisexual, not gay, but a woman might still wonder if he had only been able to stomach having sex with her by fantasizing about being with another man. She may feel doubly betrayed—not only has he been unfaithful, but also he has not been honest with her about his sexuality.

Rugby is a very macho sport in the United Kingdom. When in August 2015, British Rugby League player Keegan Hirst became the first in the league to come out as gay, it was a big news item and he received over-whelming support. Married with two children, he had recently separated from his wife, Sara. He finally decided to come out of the closet, as he felt guilty that she blamed herself for the breakup of their marriage. Some might say that Sara was the one who needed more support. *The Daily Telegraph,* a national newspaper in Britain, on September 8, 2015 followed up the story with an anonymous article entitled "Why I stayed married to my gay husband." The woman had found out about her husband's orientation after discovering a postcard that he had received from a male lover. She writes, "While the husbands are praised for coming out, their wives are left more isolated than ever," and wonders why her husband has strung her along. "Was it all a lie? Was our marriage all a sham?" she asks herself. He claimed that he was bisexual rather than totally gay. The wife admitted that she was as attached to the lifestyle they had together as to the man himself, and stuck the marriage out for 15 years, until she finally got fed up and decided to divorce.

However, sometimes a woman will choose to marry a man who she knows is homosexual. The sexual aspect of the relationship may not be important to her. She may simply be looking for a good companion with whom to share her life.

The 2010 movie, *Beginners*, dramatizes the true story of director Mike Mills' parents. His mother knowingly married a gay man who, to his straight son's amazement, comes out of the closet once his wife dies. Christopher Plummer won an Oscar for his role as the husband, Oliver, at the end of his life. Although the film does not emphasize the male partners that he had while his wife was still alive, Mike Mills' father apparently was indeed having affairs with men while married.

Some wives find their husbands' affairs with men to be much less threatening than if they were with women. Kirstie's bisexual husband, Jeff, had occasional flings with men, but she knew that he did not want an open, 100-percent gay lifestyle, so she felt secure in her marriage. She still loved Jeff and believed that their relationship was worth holding on to. Other wives however, might find a husband's affair with a man rather than a woman to be a much greater blow to their self-esteem and feelings of femininity. Barbara was intensely hurt and disgusted when she discovered her husband's affair with another man who had been a long-time friend of the family. She could not bear the thought of ever having sex with her spouse again and filed for divorce right away.

If you are considering staying with a husband who also has male sexual partners, bear in mind that the risks of getting an STD such as HIV from him are amplified, especially if he is involved in anal sex. It is very important that he wears a condom to protect not just himself but you too. Even a heterosexual philanderer's anal play with a woman—you or a mistress—exciting though it may be, can be quite risky. One doctor friend of mine graphically illustrated this fact when he bemoaned the design of the female body, asking the question, "Why was a playground put right next to a toxic waste dump?"

As we have seen in this chapter, your feelings towards your husband can be complicated and variable. Although this may have been the case to some extent before you knew he was cheating, it is even more so now. It is crucial to take plenty of time to try to look as objectively as you can into the nature of your relationship with your husband to see if it can still work for you. Now that you have put your philandering partner under the microscope, are you ready to consider how to deal with the other woman? The next chapter includes suggestions about some ways to do that.

CHAPTER SEVEN

DEALING WITH THE OTHER WOMAN

Once you hear that your husband has a mistress, there is no doubt that she will start to invade your thoughts. It is a natural reaction to want to criticize or compete with her. However, there are many other ways to deal with a mistress that will serve your interests much more effectively.

Every situation is different. The woman may be in a different state or even another country, which means that you are unlikely to have to interact with her, unless you choose to make the effort to do so. Alternatively, she may live right in your community, so that you cannot avoid seeing her in the local supermarket, your kid's school or your husband's workplace. Do you try to ignore her? Do you face her down with a cold stare? Perhaps the best approach may be to greet her cordially in a business-like manner. Then there are other variables. Do you want her to know that you are aware of the affair? If not, you have to be able to treat her in exactly the same way as you did before you knew about it. You will certainly learn to hone your acting skills.

Take the High Ground

A very common reaction when you first find out about the other woman is to vehemently hate the husband-stealing bitch and to want all kinds of nasty things to happen to her. Admit it—you wanted her to crawl into a hole and die or get run over by a truck. You may even have fantasies about strangling or shooting her, just like a wronged woman would do in the movies. But think about it—how would you feel if you actually did kill her, or if she died in a car accident? Sure, she would no longer be there to fuck your husband, but you might be wracked with lifelong guilt, and you do not know how your husband will react to being without the woman that he seems to be in lust with. Of course, going to jail for killing her would definitely cramp your style and land you in a worse situation than you are already in. Perhaps you might want to consider other, less extreme options.

If you have not fantasized about killing her, perhaps you wanted to call her up or show up on her doorstep, swearing and screaming at her like an angry banshee, maybe even hitting her, telling her exactly what you think of her for fucking your husband. However, this will not give you the emotional peace you seek, and may even make her, rather than you, appear to be the wronged party. You do not want to look like an out-of-control, unpleasant caricature of a jealous wife, giving your husband more ammunition to back up why he wants to spend time with her rather than you.

Do not expect a mistress to care about the fact that the affair may seriously damage your husband's relationship with you. Quite the contrary—if this does happen, the mistress will see it as working to her advantage by making your husband feel emotionally closer to her.

Rather than demonizing the other woman, it can be more helpful to try to see her as a human being, albeit flawed, just like your husband, and attempt to understand her motivations. I am not saying that you have to be best buddies with her, all lovey-dovey and hugging each other, as if you were both in some New Age encounter group. Instead, if you do interact with the mistress, be cordial and stay in control—do not be ruled by your emotions. You should be careful what you choose to tell her about your own life, but being willing to have a conversation with the mistress might reveal a lot more about her and the nature of her relationship with your husband than he has been willing to share. How seriously does she take the affair? Does she want to have kids with him? Is she likely to pressure him to divorce you? How does she feel about any other women your husband might also be sleeping with? Is she jealous of them or of you? Remember that information is power.

Perhaps initially you felt like throwing the other woman under a train. However, remember that your promiscuous husband is equally responsible for the affair. Even so, you may find yourself being poisoned by all the negative emotions that the woman brings up in you, especially if she lives nearby, and every so often bumps into you at the supermarket or the movie theater. You could literally get a dagger-in-the-gut feeling whenever that happens. To dissipate these emotions, it can be very helpful to find a way to relate to her in a normal fashion. You may even want to tell the woman that you forgive her for what she has done. Most likely, she is expecting you to bite her head off, so she will be surprised to see you react in such a mature way.

Connie was married to a very successful singer and songwriter who had a predilection for European girls. He had his own record label and recording studio in Los Angeles. Aspiring musicians would come from all over the world to do internships at the studio, and Connie tried to be cordial to all of them, even to those she knew her husband was bonking. An Italian intern with whom her husband was having an affair naively told her "Oh, I love L.A! I'd really like to get a green card so I can stay and work here!" "So who are you planning to marry to get that green card?" thought Connie, "My husband?" Then the girl began gushing to Connie about how brilliant her husband was. "You have to separate the man from his music," replied Connie. "He's a flawed human being, just like you and I." At this point, the conversation slipped into farce. The girl, not that fluent in English, looked confused. Pointing to the ground she asked "Floor?" "No, flawed—F-L-A-W-E-D," Connie replied, spelling out the word. "Oh, now I understand," the girl replied, but in reality, she could still only see an idealized version of him as the perfect musical maestro.

Says Winnie, who had a long-term marriage to a chronic philanderer, "My mother always advised me to take the high ground and befriend the women that my husband was seeing. Often the other woman would begin to feel guilty. Sometimes that was enough to make her break off the liaison."

Diana is a spry old lady in her 80s from Maryland. She married Nathan in the mid-1950s and told me about a period where she had to spend several months out of state caring for her ailing father. She knew that Nathan had a mistress, Irene. At her husband's urging, she grudgingly agreed that Irene could stay in their house and cook and clean for him while Diana was away. Diana's best friend had counseled her to refuse Nathan's demands, exclaiming, "You're inviting a vampire into your home!" After her father passed away, Diana returned to a grime-encrusted bathroom that looked as if it hadn't been cleaned for months, and mice had been allowed to invade her pantry, so she had to throw away much of the food stored there. Clearly, Irene had paid more attention to Nathan's various personal needs than to the house. The couple stayed married—hey, it was the 1950s, so divorce was a much bigger deal, but although her husband had a string of mistresses, never again did Diana agree to let her husband have any of them stay in her house.

What if you cannot stomach the idea of being cordial or having anything at all to do with the home-breaking, gold-digging, bloodsucking, stinking whore because you hate her guts? I would recommend that you take the advice often attributed to the ancient Chinese military strategist Sunzi (also known as Sun Tzu), author of *The Art of War:* "Keep your friends close and your enemies closer." He may have lived back in the 6th century BC, yet many of his quotes are still relevant to modern life. However, some attribute this proverb to the the political philospher, Niccolo Machiavelli (1469–1527). To use a more contemporary American saying, "You can catch more flies with honey than with vinegar."

Villain or Victim?

Society likes to paint the mistress as an immoral floozy or a scarlet woman. She is the evil villain trying to pry that hapless, helpless husband away from his lawfully wedded wife. Some might believe that the mistress herself is being victimized in some respects. The following circumstances are reasons why this might be the case:

- He initiated the affair.

- He either never told her he was married or only mentioned it later on in the relationship.

- He may lie to her about the nature of his relationship with his wife. For example, he may say that they never have sex together or that he

SEVEN: DEALING WITH THE OTHER WOMAN

131

is only staying with her for the sake of their kids. Even if true, he still would have no desire to trade the lifestyle that he has with his wife.

- He may be having several affairs, yet she might believe that apart from his wife, she is the only other woman with whom he is intimate. Why should the mistress care about fidelity? Isn't that a contradiction in terms? Not necessarily.

  Phoebe had a long-term affair with Kenny, who referred to his wife as his "sister"—behind her back, of course—because their relationship had become celibate. Phoebe told him, "You can be unfaithful to your wife, but you damn well better not be unfaithful to me!"

  Anna would see her married boyfriend only about once every couple of months, but made it quite clear that, apart from his wife, he was to have sex with nobody else but her.

- She may be consumed by jealousy towards the wife and any other women he may be seeing. The mistress may also suffer from conflicted feelings as regards the husband and her relationship with him. She may go through similar negative emotions as the cheated-upon wife, but one difference is that she has chosen that path, whereas the wife has not. Logic would dictate that an adulterous man is very likely to continue to look at other women—after all, that was the basis upon which he met the mistress in the first place. Nevertheless, she will often erroneously assume that she occupies a special place in his heart and that he will no longer desire anyone new.

- He is in a position of power in relation to her, for example, boss versus secretary, teacher versus student, therapist versus client or influential older man versus young ingénue.

  Back in the early 1990s, Beatrice, a stunningly attractive and supremely competent secretary, applied for a position as personal assistant to the managing director of a well-known financial company in London. She was offered the job and a very generous salary, but her prospective boss, married of course, made it clear that providing him with sexual favors was part of the package. Beatrice turned down the offer.

- He never intends to leave his wife, so the affair does not have anywhere to go in the long-term as there isn't even the option of living together. She cannot build a home with him. Sometimes a woman will embark on a relationship with a married man wanting a no-strings-attached affair that boosts her self-esteem, safe from any complications or baggage. However, more often than not, over time the woman wants more. She falls in love with him. She wants the man to divorce his wife and marry her instead. She may hold these expectations even if the man tells her that he will never leave his wife. Usually, the mistress and the married man will have a very different set of expectations about where the affair will go.

- He will not want to have kids with her, which would be on the table in a committed relationship. If she wants to get pregnant, she will have to do it without his agreement. A love child is a double-edged sword for the mistress: it might make the husband closer to her or might drive him into an acrimonious parting. Most likely, she will end up as a single mother. Many men do not take kindly to being forced into fatherhood. Even if they eventually grow to have feelings for the child, they may harbor considerable resentment towards the mother.

  "What if I get pregnant?" Suzette asked her married lover. He bluntly replied, "That's what abortions are for." The following story, however, shows very different attitudes. Maria and her husband, Juan, had immigrated to California from El Salvador. She had two kids and a third on the way, so her unmarried sister, Valentina, came to live with them to help out. Within a few months, she was pregnant too, and Juan, a notorious womanizer, was the father. Valentina wanted to have an abortion, but Maria, a devout Catholic, put strong pressure on her to keep the child, and they all continued living together in a very small apartment.

- All she gains is temporary sexual pleasure, and it is on his schedule, not on hers.

- She cannot rely on him for financial support, which is taken for granted within a marriage.

- She cannot get emotional support from him whenever she needs it, something that would be normal within a full-time live-in relationship.

- The affair takes her out of circulation as regards being able to find an unattached long-term partner.

The excellent 2009 film, *An Education,* illustrates many of these points. Set in suburban London in 1961, it covers the relationship between a bright 16-year-old London girl, Jenny, who has aspirations of attending Oxford University, and David, a sophisticated older man. She has a fabulous time with him. He takes her to all kinds of cultural events and sweeps her off her feet on a romantic trip to Paris. David claims he wants to marry her but already has a wife. Jenny drops out of high school to be with David and puts her chance of attending Oxford in jeopardy. When Jenny finally meets David's wife, the long-suffering woman immediately asks if she is pregnant and makes it quite clear that David has had many affairs. Jenny drops him and manages to get her life back on track by reclaiming her dream of going to Oxford.

Many prisoners of war (POWs) in England during World War II were used for farm and factory labor. Mary was a young woman working in a hospital during that time. "You could always tell the difference between the Italian and the German POWs," she told me. "The Germans would look sullen and avoid eye contact. The Italians would be laughing and flirting with us local woman." Mary fell in love with Maurizio and dated him right through the remainder of the war until he got sent back to Italy. She realized she was pregnant just after Maurizio left, but he had said he would come back to marry her. He was the first man she had ever slept with. Months passed and she heard nothing from the man, so as she was Catholic just like Maurizio, she asked her local priest for help. He contacted the priest in Maurizio's village in Italy to find out what was going on. It turned out that Maurizio was already married and had several children. So Mary raised her son on her own and never had another relationship. Clearly, the force of circumstance during wartime increases the potential for adultery exponentially, for both married men going away to fight and the wives left behind.

The following wartime story is unusual because the couple concerned did not even know that they were committing adultery and there were no villains—they were simply victims of circumstance. Yacov and Ruth were Jewish war refugees who met and fell in love in a displaced persons' camp in Italy at the end of the Second World War. She became pregnant, and they were going to get married. Ruth's husband was missing and presumed dead, but shortly after the war ended, he reappeared. She went back to her husband, and her son Benjamin was brought up as his child. Heartbroken, Yacov eventually married another woman and had a son of his own, called David. Only once David reached maturity did he find out that Benjamin, whom he knew just as a friend of the family, was actually his half-brother.

Charles, a married man with two young children, lived in Seattle. His work as a political lobbyist frequently brought him to Washington D.C., where he had a long-term relationship with Sylvia, who was also married but no longer wanted to live with her husband. Charles was happy with the existing arrangement, but Sylvia wanted him to leave his family and live with her. Although he reckoned that he loved Sylvia, Charles refused to end his marriage, telling her that he did not want his kids to deal with their parents splitting up. He was shocked and hurt when Sylvia reacted by cutting off all communication with him, refusing to answer any of his phone calls. When, many years later, he told his wife about the affair, he described his refusal to leave her as a noble act. He said it had taken him many months to get over losing the other woman. However, had Sylvia not dumped him, Charles would have continued his relationship with her. Sylvia had realized that the whole relationship was on his terms and was not giving her what she needed. Her solution was to cut her losses and move on.

Alice married Dave, ten years her junior. He moved straight from his parents' house to the marital home. After two decades of marriage, she discovered he had been having an affair for several months. "I just wish he had been honest about it and told me," she said. Not that telling her would have made it any better. Alice did not want him to be with the other woman, but Dave claimed he loved both of them and not long after moved in with his mistress. Three years into the affair, Alice still loves Dave deeply and regularly sees him on "dates." Both husband and wife say they are not ready for divorce even though they no longer live together. Ironically, she is in the kind of unsatisfactory, partial relationship than you would expect a mistress to have. Dave says he loves Alice in a very spiritual way, and that the love he has for his new live-in partner is very earthy. Alice remains stuck in limbo and is profoundly depressed by the situation. Some might say it is time for her to let go of her selfish shit of a husband and get on with her life alone.

Similarly, you may find yourself in a situation where you will have to negotiate with your husband about when you can be with him, because he is scheduling you in to fit around his time with the other woman or women. Your status has become much closer to that of a mistress than of a wife. If this is the case, you have to think seriously about whether this is acceptable. Many women would consider such circumstances to be a travesty of a marriage, with the husband setting all the rules. Does he come to you when he needs you to get things done for him while going to her for all the fun stuff? Are you allowing your spouse to cement his relationship and build up shared history with the other woman while he grows more apart from you? If having an occasional husband works for you, so be it. However, if this is the case, you had better have some kind of activity you find fulfilling, whether it is a job, a hobby or volunteering that is independent from your part-time partner. You also need to have a very solid circle of friends and maybe even a lover of your own.

Perhaps the ultimate portrayal of the floozy as a victim, in terms of the price she pays, appears in the 1989 Woody Allen film *Crimes and Misdemeanors*. Judah is a respected ophthalmologist whose mistress, Dolores, upset that he will not leave his wife, threatens to tell her about the affair. Dolores also knows about some of Judah's dubious business dealings that he does not want to be publicly revealed. Judah's brother provides the solution to his problems—he arranges for a hit man to get rid of the bothersome bitch. After suffering pangs of conscience for a short while, Judah gets over it.

Is the mistress a victim or a villain? Just like any other person, the other woman will have good and bad qualities. The particular mix she has, and the specific circumstances of the affair, will determine whether she is fundamentally a fairly decent human being or a malicious character.

For more than two decades, Mariella had been married to Christopher, a very demanding and emotionally distant man. She had faithfully devoted her life to the needs of her family. Once their kids were grown, Christopher had a very public affair with Amy, a much younger woman. He flatly refused to give her up, expecting his wife to simply put up with it. Amy was the catalyst for her to take a very critical look at how her husband had treated her over the years. Mariella concluded that she was much better off without him. "I was devastated at the beginning and hated Amy's guts," Mariella told me, "But then I realized that she had given me a gift. I was able to leave my husband and have a much more satisfying relationship with someone else. I'm actually grateful to Amy. She's not a bad person, and I wish her the best of luck dealing with Christopher."

Often the philanderer is simply a horndog, out for sex wherever he can get it. "Of all the guys I've been out with, Jason is the only one who makes me feel unattractive," confided Jason's long-term mistress, Phoebe, to one of her friends. Despite claiming that he was deeply in love with Phoebe, Jason was always looking at other woman and was quite open about wanting to bed some of them.

Delia went on a vacation with her husband, Oswald, ostensibly to help the couple reconcile after she discovered that he was having an affair. She was sitting next to him on a tourist bus showing the local sights and realized that he was actually beginning to chat up the young blonde girl who was seated next to him on the other side. "You'd like to have had sex with her, wouldn't you?" Delia asked him later that day. "Sure," he admitted guilelessly, "She had an interesting vibe."

In many cases, the mistress will be merely a symptom, rather than a cause, of the problems in a wife's relationship with her husband. After reading this section, if you are still only able to see the other woman in a very negative light, ask yourself this: "Who is more of a villain, the mistress or the husband?" Remember that it is your husband, not his mistress, who took the marriage vow with you and promised to be faithful. Unless she also happens to be a close friend of yours, the lying and betrayal you have experienced come from your spouse and not his girlfriend.

Why Is He Fucking Someone Young Enough to Be His Daughter?

To steal Al Gore's catchphrase, here is an "inconvenient truth"—throughout history and right up to the present day, old men have been taking young women as sexual partners. Why? Because they can, and because young women are more attractive to them than older women. Many young girls are happy to find themselves a sugar daddy, and it is a stereotypical male fantasy to be one. He is old enough for her to be his daughter or even his granddaughter? Why should an old codger armed with his todger and little blue pills care about the age difference, if he can have great sex with her? (Todger is the British word for dick and to my ears, it sounds a lot less clunky.) Indeed, historically, young women would be preferred as they would be more likely to bear healthy children. In fact, wealthy old farts would take multiple nubile young wives, who were expected, upon pain of death, to be totally faithful.

In modern America, a rich man may be able to snag a younger woman who wants a sugar daddy. Alternatively, if he has neither the requisite wealth nor social status, and he is too old, fat or ugly to attract a sexy, young American girl, he can go to Thailand or the Philippines, where he will be in high demand. Women quickly lose their marriageable value in South East Asia, so a man from the United States would be a sought-after match as a good provider. The women may be in such dire economic straits that even a short-term fling with a Westerner is welcomed, as he is likely to shower them with gifts during the affair. "I'm invisible at home, but a god when I go to Asia," one overweight, balding guy in his 60s told me.

Modern males remain evolutionarily primed to want women who appear to be the best for breeding but who will not become pregnant with another man's child. *In The Evolution of Desire: Strategies of Human Mating* (Basic Books, 2003), evolutionary psychologist David M. Buss describes how males of all cultures desire attractive, young, eternally faithful wives. Buss bases this statement on a five-year study he and his colleagues carried out on how people choose a mate. The survey sampled 10,047 individuals from 37 different cultures from all parts of the globe.

Celebrities and politicians have no shortage of willing young babes to bed. At the time of writing, Russian president Vladimir Putin's long-term girlfriend, Alina Kabaeva, is 31 years his junior. As a former Olympic gymnast, she must be flexible enough to reach all the places that he is too old and creaky to reach. Rod Stewart's first child, Sarah Streeter, was eight years older than model Penny Lancaster, the woman he married in 2007. Celebs do love those models. Penny, his third wife, was 26 years younger. Comedian John Cleese complained that his third wife had ripped him off in an acrimonious, expensive divorce, but this did not appear to have put him off matrimony. Four years later, Cleese married Jennifer Wade, with whom he had an age gap of 31 years. Her parents were younger than their new son-in-law. However, the granddaddy of cradle snatching must be *Playboy* magazine founder, Hugh Hefner. In 2012, at the ripe old age of 86, he

A Most Unusual Mistress

© 2016 C. J. Grace. Artwork by Aaron Austin, concepts by C. J. Grace.

married 26-year-old model, Crystal Harris. Why would she wed someone 60 years older? Presumably because he is Hugh Hefner and rich as Croesus.

The ancient Chinese took the idea of old man/young woman couples one step farther. They believed such pairings were a good thing, as the old man would be able to gain *qi*—internal life-force energy—from a young girl by copulating with her. It was thought that he would not be able to obtain such *qi* from a woman of his own age. If the old man wanted to conserve his own energy, he could practice semen retention, developing techniques to reach orgasm without ejaculation. Thus, he could grab *qi* from his young sex partner and not have to give any back, which would do wonders for his longevity. In Taoist mythology, a man by the name of Peng Zi (also known as Peng Tzu or Peng Tsu) was credited with living to the age of 800. One of the factors attributed to reaching this ripe old age is that Peng Zi is said to have had sex three to five times a day with young women without giving up one drop of his precious sperm. He also would sleep in the same bed as young virgins, without having sex with them, to absorb their *qi*. So was the old goat an energy vampire? I will let you decide.

Some of these ancient Chinese practices still flourish in the Far East. Xiao Mei, who was in her 50s and lived in Taipei, Taiwan, was married to a 68-year-old man who subscribed to these Taoist beliefs. He actively sought out young women for sexual encounters and practiced semen retention. Xiao Mei had the dubious honor of being the oldest woman he was willing to fuck. Culturally conditioned to see her husband's behavior as acceptable, she was quite content to stay married to him, knowing that she would always retain the status of "Number One Wife." If she had been brought up in America or Europe, her reaction might well have been very different.

Rossini's opera, *The Barber of Seville,* is about Count Almaviva overcoming all kinds of obstacles to marry his true love, Rosina. Why do I mention this? Well, Mozart's work, *The Marriage of Figaro,* includes the same cast of characters but is set several years later. The count has now degenerated into a scheming old womanizer pursuing young Susanna, his wife's maid and the fiancée of his valet, Figaro. Susanna, Figaro and Rosina manage to outwit the count. This ending was revolutionary for its time as servants were not supposed to get the better of their masters. Susanna agrees to meet the count late at night in the garden, and the countess goes in her place. Miraculously, Rosina manages to regain the love of her wayward husband. Sadly, this is not a very realistic scenario.

Numerous modern movies depict a middle-aged or even senior-citizen hero and much younger heroine falling in love, with the fairy-tale ending of "living happily ever after." Literature throughout the ages also describes various versions of this story, such as Arthur Golden's *Memoirs of a Geisha,* Charlotte Bronte's *Jane Eyre,* Vladimir Nabokov's *Lolita* and Daphne du Maurier's *Rebecca.*

In reality, after time passes, the older man becomes more decrepit, while his wife is still in her prime. He may no longer be interested in sex or have become unable to perform the act. At this point, the wife becomes a strong candidate for having an affair or even for ditching her aging sugar daddy entirely to run off with a younger, healthier and sexier partner. Some older women who have experienced being replaced with a younger model might think that this serves the old plonker right.

The 2003 movie, *Something's Gotta Give,* was written and directed by Nancy Meyers, a woman in her 50s. The plot seems to be her perfect fantasy, given the frequency of aging Hollywood stars ditching their wives for girlfriends young enough to be their grandkids. Jack Nicolson is Harry, a record company owner in his 60s with a predilection for women less than half his age. After a heart attack brings him face to face with his own frailty and mortality, Harry finally realizes he might be better off with a more mature woman—an intelligent, attractive divorcee in her mid-50s, Erica, played by Diane Keaton. She is a successful playwright. A handsome ER doctor, called Julian, played by the dishy Keanu Reeves, treats Harry for his heart condition. Julian, who is in his mid-30s, is a fan of Erica's work and falls in love with her. Thus Erica, who has not had a sexual relationship since her divorce from a man who is, surprise, surprise, about to marry someone the same age as his daughter, now has two guys to choose from, one of whom is almost two decades younger. If only real life were like that.

Victor was in his 60s when he married Vanessa, a striking woman of 40 who had worked as a model. He had divorced his previous wife for her, a woman who when younger had been a head-turning beauty herself. The new marriage went very well for the first ten years or so. He was a wealthy man, so they had a very high standard of living and he was happy to help bring up a son Vanessa had from a previous relationship. However, when Victor reached his mid-70s, health problems started to develop. He began to look really old, so that his wife simply did not find him attractive any more. Instead, she would have strings of affairs with various younger men who helped to maintain the sumptuous country estate where the couple lived. Victor eventually found out about the affairs, but was so besotted with Vanessa that, amazingly, he was willing to stay with her, even if she wanted to continue seeing other men.

Even in medieval times, everyone was familiar with this kind of scenario. Just take a look at the "Merchant's Tale" in Chaucer's *Canterbury Tales.* Written in Middle English at the end of the 14th century, the story features a pretty young wife married to an old codger, and describes how she goes through all kinds of shenanigans to be able to have an affair with an attractive young squire.

Claude, a massage therapist from Phoenix with New Age sensibilities, was bemoaning the superficial values used when dating. "Men just go for the curves in a woman's body, and women are mainly concerned about the size of the man's wallet. I don't want to be a meal ticket anymore." However, despite the fact that Claude was in his mid-60s, he chose to date only women in their 30s and 40s. He had no interest at all in having a girlfriend closer to his own age.

Is a man leaving his wife for a younger woman a symptom of male menopause? Sometimes men go through a period of general dissatisfaction with life in middle age. They may begin questioning everything, getting depressed, quitting their jobs and dumping their wives for a newer model. Sometimes a man will regret this and later go back to his original partner. Some say these behavior changes are a manifestation of male menopause— also known as andropause—caused by age-related reductions in hormone levels. However, the existence of this as a general, widespread condition in older men does not seem to be as clear-cut as the existence of female menopause.

Should You Confront Her?

Your decision on whether or not to seek a confrontation with the mistress depends on the personalities involved, and more importantly on the strength of both your relationship with your husband and his relationship with the other woman. Unfortunately, there is no "one size fits all" answer. On the one hand, if the silly sod is totally besotted with her and she with him, you will have an exceedingly uphill struggle getting her to end the affair. You may end up confronting your way right out of the marriage. On the other hand, you may have a considerable amount of leverage—grown kids from your marriage might add their weight to a possible confrontation, or perhaps your husband may have health or financial issues that the woman is neither aware of nor equipped to deal with.

It is a good idea to discuss your options with trusted confidants and/or a trained counselor before confronting the other woman. You do not want to go off half-cocked, ruled by raging emotions. Instead, you need to take a rational approach by planning ahead so that you know what you are going to say. You want to sound cool, collected and confident. If deep down you do not feel that way, which under the circumstances is quite understandable, you have to get in touch with your inner actress.

Bess discovered her long-time spouse, Walter, whom she had nursed through serious illness, had for some time been having a torrid affair with Phyllis, a woman that he had met at an Argentine Tango workshop. Clearly some of the dance moves that he was doing were not what his wife had anticipated. Phyllis and Walter, both seniors, appeared to be madly in love with each other. He was about to leave his wife for her, but then Bess called Phyllis up and read her the riot act. From that point on, Phyllis refused to have any more contact with Walter, and the affair was over. Under different circumstances, confronting the other woman in this way could have had exactly the opposite result. It might not only have pissed the mistress off and strengthened her resolve to be with the husband, but also have made him angry with his wife for attacking the new love of his life. Marriage over.

Ariadne and Spiros had built a comfortable life together on the Greek island of Corfu. Their house had a gorgeous view of the sea and looking from the outside in, everything seemed to be idyllic. Not so. When Ariadne found out that her husband had been seeing another woman called Mira for quite some time, she not only gave him an ultimatum to stop seeing her, but also confronted Mira directly, threatening to make her life exceedingly difficult unless she gave up Spiros for good. Ariadne got what she wanted, but in a way that was a real Greek tragedy—Spiros dumped Mira, but Mira was so upset and so deeply in love with him that she committed suicide. Spiros was wracked with guilt for years afterwards, but continued to stay with his wife, and yes, he took another mistress later on. Something to do with Greek machismo, most likely. The other woman was quite high main-tenance. He was not particularly keen on her, but kept the affair going. You would have thought the tosspot would have learned his lesson.

A friend of mine who lived in a small Mexican town in the 1960s witnessed a dramatic confrontation. A butcher's wife saw her husband's mistress walking past his shop. Brandishing a meat cleaver, she ran out after the other woman. While the husband cowered behind the counter inside, the two women had a catfight on the street that the police had to break up. The mistress was never seen in town again, and the butcher and his wife remained together.

These days, I would not recommend the meat cleaver solution. It is better to try to obtain some insights into the background and character of other woman. This can enable you to work out how solid your husband's relationship is with her and get some ideas as to where it might go. Some wives might want to meet the mistress face-to-face, but others might find it too intolerably uncomfortable to be in the same room as her. However, understanding what the floozy wants out of her relationship with your husband and what he wants from her will give you valuable information. This will help you decide whether you want your marriage to continue and will steer you towards an appropriate course of action.

CHAPTER EIGHT

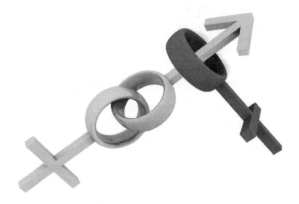

SINKING INTO MARITAL CELIBACY

Many women will keep their husband's adultery a shameful secret from their friends. Couples also are unlikely to discuss another common and embarrassing issue: they have a celibate marriage. Celibacy may be even more of a problem if it is one of the reasons why a husband has strayed. If you and your adulterous husband are no longer making love with each other, and you want to remain in the marriage, there are several questions to ask yourself. Do you want to stay celibate? Does your husband want to keep the marriage that way too? If he had been happy without any sex at all, he would not have been with another woman. If you do not want to have sex with your husband, do you really care if he gets it elsewhere?

More often than not, passion fizzles in long-term relationships, and the couple will have sex less and less frequently. Work, stress, health problems, lack of novelty and sexual boredom can contribute to this happening. Of course, rearing children can be a draining, tiring, 24/7 job for women, especially if they also work outside the home. It is no wonder that mothers may have little energy left for sex. If a man or a woman is not getting enough sleep and working too hard, it will dramatically diminish that person's sex drive. Hormonal imbalances can also have the same effect. Few couples, even if they are rutting like rabbits at the beginning of the relationship, seem to be able to avoid sinking into celibate marriages.

Roseanne, a stunningly attractive 30-year-old, works as a high-end call girl in Northern California. Most of her clients are married. According to what they tell her, many of them have not had sex with their spouses for at least five years. Men tend to become resentful, distant and less loving towards their wives if sex is rarely happening. Some might say that if you want a contented platonic relationship with a guy, you should live that way with your brother, not your husband.

The 2012 movie, *Hope Springs,* stars Meryl Streep and Tommy Lee Jones as a middle-aged couple who agree to attend a marriage counseling retreat to try to reclaim their lost sex life. They have been married for 30 years. The film eloquently shows how marital celibacy can happen. Once the initial luster of the relationship has worn off, the husband begins to solicit sex from his wife in a more "wham-bam-thank-you-ma'am" fashion. He is mainly concerned about getting his pole in the hole rather than anything else. He forgets about the romance, cuddling and foreplay that, earlier in their relationship, he would use to turn her on. Eventually the husband and wife stop having sex altogether. They do not even cuddle. Before you know it, the spouses are sleeping in separate rooms—something many wives do to avoid being kept awake by their husband's snoring.

In *Hope Springs,* the couple manages to make love again, but in real life, this is far less likely to happen. If the husband still wants to have sex and the wife does not, infidelity is only one of many problems that can arise. His resentment can manifest in all kinds of ways. For example, he might become grumpy, withdrawn, and/or emotionally distant towards her, especially if they are no longer having any physical contact at all. If they can agree to go to counseling together, as do the characters that Meryl Streep and Tommy Lee Jones play, the husband and wife have a shot at improving their relationship, even if they cannot reclaim all the passion that they may have had when they first got married.

One third of those polled in a 2014 British survey of people over 50 had sex less than once a year (maybe only a birthday fuck?) or not at all. The study of 1,837 men and women was commissioned by Relate, a provider of relationship support services in the UK, and *Mature Times,* a British newspaper geared towards people over 50. According to the study, many respondents rated affectionate behavior such as cuddling and kissing more important than actual intercourse. Of those in the 50-55 age range, 59 percent said sex had become less important to them, a figure which rose to a whopping 85 percent for those between ages 76-85. Sadly, many of the interviewees who were celibate also indicated they would like to have sex if they could (http://www.maturetimes.co.uk/more-kisses-cuddles-and-affection/).

According to Mariella Frostrup, "agony aunt" for *The Observer,* a national newspaper in Britain, many people over the age of 70 write to her for advice about what to do when their spouses stop having sex with them. Interviewed in *The Daily Telegraph,* on October 5, 2013, Frostrup described how seniors are devastated when this happens and contemplate divorce, because they believe sex is an essential part of their life (http://www.telegraph. co.uk/culture/tvandradio/bbc/10357341/Mariella-Frostrup-interview-Sexually-we-havent-moved-on-since-the-Fifties.html).

Donald and Marisa met in high school and got married right after graduating. They had been together for nearly 40 years, and he was unhappy with the fact that they rarely had sex any more. During marital counseling, Marisa told him that he no longer seemed to show any enjoyment of her body and would just briefly rub her nether regions a bit before ramming in his lubricant-slathered member. His clueless response: "I didn't think you liked foreplay." Thankfully, the counselor was able to help the couple reclaim their sex life.

Brenda enjoyed a wonderfully promiscuous social life at college and was bursting with sex appeal when she married fellow student Simon. Once she reached her 50s, however, she just could not be bothered with sex at all. Whether her husband wanted it or not, she simply was not interested.

Juliette was a child of the 1960s who had avidly subscribed to the hippie free-love lifestyle—sex and drugs and rock and roll. She had had a blast living in San Francisco during the Summer of Love. But guess what—now she is in her 60s and her marriage to John has been completely celibate for many years. "Of course we cuddle," she says, "And we do love each other, but I really can't get into the idea of sex anymore."

It can get boring fucking the same person for years on end. Couples need to put effort into keeping things interesting. Some maintain a romantic spark by planning time alone, going out for romantic dinners and injecting some unpredictability into their lovemaking. What is more of a turn on—a warm, candlelit bedroom and soft music, with your man telling you how attractive he finds you, or him groping you on the sofa in the living room while an action show blares on the TV? The answer seems obvious, yet many men are oblivious to the importance of creating a mood that makes a woman want to engage in lovemaking. Nevertheless, it is a very rare couple that can sustain the oomph and intensity of their early years together over the decades. In *The Heart of Desire: Keys to the Pleasures of Love* (John Wiley & Sons, 2013), Stella Resnick writes about how, over time, sexual desire is inhibited, as a husband and wife begin to treat each other like family rather than lovers. Her book describes various methods to keep romantic love alive within long-term relationships.

Over the years, Colin's wife, Rachel, grew less and less interested in sex. "Rachel became sexually dead to me. She seemed quite happy to be celibate and didn't want to do anything to bring back our sex life. This made me very sad, as I really liked to make love with her, but she just was not interested. I still found her physically attractive and loved her. But our relationship became more like brother and sister than husband and wife. It wasn't what I wanted. So now I have occasional affairs, but I'm still with Rachel as she's my best friend."

Emotional and Physical Reasons Why Sex Fizzles

You would think taking medicine to ease depression would make your sex life better not worse, but according to Peter Breggin, MD, it can be exactly the opposite. In *The Antidepressant Fact Book: What Your Doctor Won't Tell You About Prozac, Zoloft, Paxil, Celexa and Luvox* (Da Capo Press, 2001), Breggin describes how SSRIs (Selective Seratonin Reuptake Inhibitors) can diminish feelings of love or sexual desire, as well as causing impotence and the inability to climax.

Bill and Wilma had a great sex life, full of passion. However, after they had been married for several years, Bill dropped into a deep depression and was prescribed antidepressants. The medication brought him out of his dark moods, but it totally destroyed his libido and left him impotent. Wilma was very sad to find herself in a celibate marriage, making do with a few affairs here and there, but she would much rather have had sexual relations with her own husband.

However angry you are with that philandering fucker, do not wish for his dick to break and bend out of shape or for his balls to swell or shrivel up. All of these are actual medical problems. Should any man you are close to suffer any such symptoms, he will need to get himself checked out by a doctor. A man's testicles can indeed shrink into hard little marbles, a condition known as testicular atrophy. There are various possible causes for this, including aging, a testosterone imbalance, lifting weights, cancer or taking medications such as steroids—so ironically Mr. Universe can shrink his balls while he is building up his biceps. There are also some disorders that make the testicles swell up, which may cause considerable pain.

Peyronie's Disease is a condition affecting about one percent of men, where part of the erectile tissue of the shaft is damaged by internal scarring, resulting in a bend when the penis is erect. First described as a disorder by French surgeon François de la Peyronie in 1743, the severity of the condition varies and the causes are unclear. Some believe that the penile tissue is broken from vigorous sexual activity that bends the shaft in a direction in which it is not supposed to go. Another theory is that it is caused by medications such as blood pressure drugs and beta-blockers. President Bill Clinton's curved penis became public knowledge in the 1990s because of the sexual harassment lawsuit he faced from Paula Jones and from the Monica Lewinsky scandal. The media widely speculated that the "Clinton kink" was due to Peyronie's Disease. Prior to that time, few people had ever heard of the condition. Whatever the cause of Clinton's bent todger, it did not appear to affect his sex life.

One reason women go off sex is rarely spoken about. Childbirth, a hysterectomy and various other kinds of surgery can alter the position of organs in the pelvic area, damage the pelvic floor muscles and create a lot of scar tissue. Sexual intercourse may become painful, or it may feel as if there is an obstruction. This complaint is fairly common, yet women tend to simply put up with it, as they do not know that there are ways to dramatically improve the condition. Pelvic floor therapy can often help women resolve these issues. Unfortunately, few pelvic floor therapists practice in the United States. You might try searching the internet to see if there is one in your area. The American Physical Therapy Association website, http://www.apta.org, offers advice on pelvic pain and sometimes lists women's health practitioners. Good therapists are so sought-after that you may need to make appointments several months in advance. Vive la France! All women in that enlightened country are provided with free pelvic therapy, known as *la rééducation périnéale,* after they give birth.

Rita had found intercourse uncomfortable for many decades and rarely had sex with her husband. Then a new gynecologist recommended she see a pelvic floor therapist. She had torn badly while delivering her second child some 20 years or so earlier. As her water had broken the day before, labor was induced and she experienced much harsher contractions than with the birth of her first baby. For the first child, the doctor performed an episiotomy that healed quickly. For the second child, Rita's regular obstetrician was out of town and she had to make do with the doctor "on call." Rita felt that he should also have done an episiotomy to allow the baby to come out more easily rather than letting her tear. The pelvic floor therapist not only dealt with the scar tissue that had built up from the birth of her second child, but also showed Rita that her pelvic floor muscles were habitually tense and taught her how to relax them. Rita was able to reclaim her sex life and get orgasms again. "My therapist is a *fucking* miracle worker!" she exclaimed, with appropriate emphasis on the word "fucking."

Then there is the C-word, possibly the scariest condition of all. Some of the treatments for prostate cancer may leave a man impotent and incontinent. Then there is testicular cancer for which cyclist Lance Armstrong had to endure multiple surgeries and arduous chemotherapy treatments. He had an advanced form that had metastasized and spread to his lymph nodes, lungs and brain. Whether they afflict a man or a woman, most forms of cancer and their resulting treatments will tend to squash his or her libido.

John Edwards found his political career in ruins after news broke of a long-term extramarital affair. He fathered a child with Rielle Hunter, a filmmaker working on his presidential campaign. For two years or so he denied paternity, but eventually admitted that he was the father. The situation was further muddied by claims that Edwards had knowingly used campaign funds to support Hunter and the baby girl, but he was acquitted of these allegations in court. As mentioned previously, his wife Elizabeth was suffering from breast cancer, which, although in remission for some time, led to her death in 2010. Although most people in America looked upon John Edward's behavior as unequivocally appalling, Rhiannon, a breast cancer survivor, has a very different take on the issue, which many would find quite politically incorrect. She was married to Phil, and one of the reasons that they were drawn together was because they had extremely strong sex drives and enjoyed a lot of passionate lovemaking. However, once Rhiannon was diagnosed with cancer and had to undergo radiation and chemotherapy, her desire for sex completely disappeared. Her husband did what he could to support her but was completely stressed out. So she actively encouraged him to have an affair with a mutual friend, and it did wonders for his state of mind, releasing a lot of his tension. "You're doing a John Edwards on me," she would joke to Phil. "Well at least I don't have a love child!" he would retort. Thankfully, Rhiannon's desire for sex returned not too long after her treatment was over, and Phil was happy to give up his affair.

Too Fat for Sex?

Sometimes men and women are in marriages where sex has become just too uncomfortable. Hip problems, joint injuries or various health issues may cause this, or it may be due to obesity. Advance warning: I am now going to be politically incorrect. These days calling someone fat is almost like using the N-word. I could borrow the wonderful euphemisms that were used to describe the Botswanan detective Precious Ramotswe in the *No. 1 Ladies' Detective Agency* (Anchor Books, 2003)—people with "generous proportions" or who are "traditionally built"—but I have chosen to be more direct. If you are offended, then ignore this section. As one lady bluntly told me, referring to her dearly beloved in rather harsh terms, "If you can't see your own dick when you look down, you're too fat!"

If your man has bulked out while you have stayed fairly slim, it can be very uncomfortable making love in the missionary position. As he is pounding on you, you may feel squashed to bits, as if he is the big hammer, and you are the little nail. It may even be hard to breathe. Cowgirl position will not work well either if you are trying to straddle legs as wide as tree trunks. If you could not do the splits in your high school gym class, you certainly will not be able to do them now. Then, if has a huge wobbly belly, his little pecker may be completely hidden underneath it and not very accessible. And the fatter he has become, the sweatier he gets from the exertion of fucking. Not a very romantic situation. The bottom line? You and your porky partner are moving towards a celibate marriage. If you are chubby too, maybe you will not feel so squashed when he is on top, but it still will be difficult to find comfortable positions, and your wobbly belly will block access to your nether regions, just as his does. If one spouse has gained a lot of weight, oftentimes their partner will seek sex elsewhere.

One slim, single friend of mine declared uncharitably, "I never date fat men. They're sweaty, smelly, and they snore!" Indeed, however overweight a person may be, he or she will tend to be considerably less attracted to a fat person than to someone who is slender. Ralph was a corpulent corporate executive who would not tolerate any negative comments about his weight. He railed on about society's prejudice against fat people. Married with three kids, Ralph was a notorious womanizer and would only hit on girls with perfect figures. He was never interested in women of generous proportions.

Celibacy, Infidelity and the Viagra Effect

Before 2000, it was often the husband who steered a marriage into celibacy. "I only comes 'ere 'cos I can't get it up no longer," a grizzled old fellow in the audience at a strip club in Somerset, England, once told me sadly, in his broad West Country accent. (You might ask, what was I doing in a strip club? No, I was not on stage. I was covering a story for BBC Radio.) The old geezer was bemoaning the fact that aging is not kind to todgers. In addition, the increasing use of maintenance prescription drugs also can play havoc with a man's ability to have erections as well as dampening his libido. Today, erectile dysfunction (ED) drugs, such as Viagra or Cialis, enable men to be able to get it up, however ancient they happen to be.

These days, more often than not, the woman tends to go off sex before the man. Before you throw stones at a husband for having an extramarital affair, a factor to consider is whether or not his wife is having sex with him. The marriage may be completely celibate. Alternatively, she may be having sex with her husband only occasionally, more to keep him happy than because she is into it herself. He will not appreciate having to make

The Viagra Effect

© 2016 C. J. Grace. Artwork by Aaron Austin, concepts by C. J. Grace.

do with a "mercy fuck." If he is not getting fed at home, he is likely to find himself a take-out. A celibate marriage gives the partner with more libido a reason to seek sex elsewhere.

Nevertheless, sometimes ED drugs can rekindle passion between a husband and wife even after adultery. They can transform him from Mr. Flaccid to Mr. Stallion. He may need less stimulation to become erect— perhaps now he can perform for his wife rather than only for a buxom young floozy. He can keep going considerably longer and give his wife more time to achieve an orgasm. He can be more confident in the bedroom. It is as if the wife has found herself a younger, more virile partner.

Increased life expectancy and better health when older in developed nations has led to more later-in-life affairs and divorces. According to projections from the UK's Office for National Statistics, up to two-thirds of British babies born in 2013 may live to 100, giving those boys many more years for philandering, because an elderly man no longer has to make do with a flaccid penis. The advent of Viagra, Cialis and related ED drugs can enable hoary old codgers to keep fucking until it is time for them to kick the bucket.

You may be in one of the many marriages where over the years you have lost interest in sex. You may feel quite happy that your man is gaining these services elsewhere and no longer bothering you for them. In this case, his philandering may be no big deal or even have become a positive aspect of the marriage. ED drugs have allowed men to resume an active sex life that may have been stalled for years. No doubt, many wives are appalled by rather than delighted at having to minister to their husband's reclaimed tumescence. ED drugs can allow a man to have a big erection as solid as a broomstick, as well as dramatically cutting the time between climaxing and getting another hard-on. He can also keep going for perhaps as long as two hours, when before he might have been finished in less than twenty minutes. All this can take quite a toll on the vagina, especially for older women who have lost a lot of their natural lubrication. Of course, it is not just wives who complain about the Viagra effect—hookers all over the world do so too, as they have to work harder with each man and can see fewer clients in a day.

Janine's middle-aged, computer salesman husband, Jeremy, traveled a great deal, and the couple virtually never had sex any longer. Janine realized that he was being unfaithful when she found packets of Cialis in his suitcase. She knew that Jeremy had never used the stuff with her, and therefore was only taking it to have sex with another woman. Just before Jeremy left for his next trip, Janine took her revenge by removing the packets from his travel bag. Then, when Janine herself began an affair with an older man, she gave the Cialis to him.

I have heard that in Britain, among City of London gentlemen, ED drugs are currently referred to as "poker pills." However, in America, "poker pills" are ADD drugs or herbal supplements used by poker players to improve their concentration and stamina. No wonder George Bernard Shaw declared, "England and America are two countries separated by the same language." He himself was neither English nor American but Irish. Nevertheless, many men are very embarrassed about their ED issues, and either use poker pills in secret without telling their partners, or are too ashamed to even obtain them in the first place. In such cases, a wife who lets her husband know that she is fine with him using such drugs can make him feel much more relaxed about having chemically-induced boners. A less-inhibited older gentleman from Britain had this to say about using ED drugs with his partner: "Well, why wouldn't I? It's only good manners."

CHAPTER NINE

RETHINKING SEX AFTER ADULTERY

Finding out about your husband's infidelity is likely to shock you into re-examining your sexual relationship with him, as well as your attitudes towards your own sexuality, and sex in general. Just as they say that money, or the love of it, is the root of all evil, sex is at the root of all affairs.

Yet some wives feel very jealous if a husband has a strong emotional connection with another woman when no sex is involved, but he could just as well have a really close bond with a male friend. Neither of these situations constitutes infidelity, even if your husband is spending a lot of time with that person. However, if his relationship with another woman is extremely flirtatious and stops just short of sexual activity, does that mean he is cheating on you? I would still say no, but it is much more of a gray area and creates a situation that many wives would not tolerate.

Nevertheless, an affair involving both sex and a strong emotional connection is likely to be far more devastating to the wife than if the husband only wants sex from the other woman and nothing else. Deirdre's venture capitalist husband was always eying up attractive women and had had several no-strings-attached affairs. Yet Deirdre was proud to be his wife, secure in

In a Far Away Galaxy

© 2016 C. J. Grace. Artwork by Aaron Austin, concepts by C. J. Grace.

Shock! Horror! Obscene public display of eating offends couples enjoying some open-air sex.

the knowledge that she was the only woman he truly loved, and that he would never leave her. "Yes, he's looking at all these pretty women," she said, "but I'm the one he's chosen to stay with for the long haul."

Morality Minefield

A person's morality as regards sex, love, relationships and affairs is not something absolute or true across all cultures, but is very much a product of the specific values and beliefs of his or her family background, where that person comes from, and one particular point in time. Furthermore, a society's views on sex and infidelity may vary enormously according to gender and social status. A woman's sexual activity may be judged much more harshly than that of a man, and the wealthy and famous may be held to different standards than ordinary people. If you are trying to pick up the pieces after discovering your husband's philandering, you are likely to find yourself much more aware of how these attitudes percolate through the media, and of how much they vary from one country to another. Yet no matter what stance a culture takes on adultery, the fact remains that a woman tends to be deeply wounded by her husband's infidelity, and her feelings are rarely part of public discussion. Rather than being given support, wives of philanderers, whether they stay or leave, are often intensely isolated.

Almost all cultures on planet earth have rules and taboos about sexual behavior to define what is acceptable. However, I would not be surprised if somewhere in a far away galaxy there are some space aliens for whom copulating, urinating and defecating in public are perfectly normal activities, yet eating in public is taboo. In this society, meals are consumed in private, and if done in the company of another, there would have to be a very close relationship between those two individuals. Public eating would be considered disgusting and obscene. Such aliens would find earthlings' attitudes towards food and sex to be very strange indeed.

Culture Clashes

In the British Isles, Victorian attitudes towards sex, particularly as regards any desire for it exhibited by women rather than men, were exceedingly draconian. The Catholics were just as bad, as reflected in the treatment of unfortunate young Irish women who got pregnant and had nobody to turn to except for the Church. Based on actual events, the 2013 film, *Philomena,* tells the heartrending story of a pregnant Irish girl taken in by a convent and forced to be a slave laborer there. Her son was given up for adoption against her will. The nuns believed that Philomena deserved this treatment as penance for her fornication. Philomena's baby was born, not back in Victorian times, but in 1952. Over the years, she tried to make the nuns tell her where her child had been placed, but they refused to give her any information. Fifty years later, with the help of an investigative journalist, she finally discovered the truth of what had happened.

Thank God, or at least Jesus and Jehovah, that Jews and Christians, even though some of them might believe every word of the Bible is true, have cherry-picked and modernized it enough to believe that stoning to death is no longer an appropriate punishment for adultery. As Jesus so aptly said in the New Testament when an adulterous woman was brought to him facing death by stoning, "Let he who is without sin cast the first stone." Jesus forgave the woman and prevented her execution.

Sadly, this is not the prevailing view in many Islamic countries that are living in the Dark Ages in the 21st century. In Saudi Arabia, Sudan, Iran, Iraq, Indonesia, Brunei, Yemen, Nigeria, Mali, Pakistan, Afghanistan and Somalia, the stoning of adulterers and their lovers has been taking place right up to the present day. Muslim women, even if they are only adulterers because they have been raped, are far more likely to suffer this fate than Muslim men. Make no mistake—stoning is one of the slowest and most painful forms of execution, and is in effect an extreme form of torture. There is no reference to stoning in the Koran—instead it appears in later Hadith literature, which is based on oral reports of the deeds and sayings of Muhammad, some of which are quite controversial and contradictory.

Modern-day America has very schizophrenic attitudes towards sex, sometimes taking it far too seriously and at other times not seriously enough. On one hand, sex is used to sell any kind of product you can imagine, and children watch many of these advertisements. In 2010, a nine-year-old got into trouble for loudly singing the Viagra jingle in the school playground and did not understand what the fuss was about. Fairly explicit advertisements for erectile dysfunction drugs appear frequently on prime time TV, including during telecasts of NFL games. In addition, young girls' fashions make them look more and more like kid versions of streetwalkers.

Yet God forbid anyone should see a woman's breast, let alone a penis, on broadcast TV, except on cable channels. However, scenes of violence and torture are quite acceptable. I have to say that I for one would much prefer to see an attractive naked guy on screen, proudly erect todger and all, rather than a clothed man getting his head blown off, even if he did have a handsome face before it was shot to bits. Most adults are familiar with what human bodies look like naked, but thankfully, most Westerners have not had to witness human carnage. Which of the two is the more offensive, do you think? In Europe, naked bosoms abound—in the cinema, on TV and on many of the beaches. Nakedness is not a big deal in many European countries.

When the Monica Lewinsky scandal broke and President Clinton faced impeachment in 1998 for getting a blowjob from an intern, people in China and Europe were baffled by the controversy. What difference did it make if he was married or not? What on earth did it have to do with his ability to govern America? The Chinese took it for granted that a powerful man would have liaisons with many women—although these days, the Chinese government frequently uses sex scandals to discredit opponents.

Folks that I spoke to from France were beside themselves with scorn and ridicule at the fuss over Clinton's extramarital activities. "We wouldn't trust a candidate for President of France if he *hadn't* had an affair or two," one middle-aged French lady declared, "There would have to be something wrong with him if he'd never had a mistress." Indeed many French presidents have had affairs, and journalists there have chosen to keep the details private. Francois Mitterrand was President of France from 1981 to 1995. When he died in 1996, invited to the funeral by his wife were his mistress and her daughter that Mitterrand had fathered. The next president, Jacques Chirac, who held office from 1995 to 2007, confessed publicly at the end of his presidency, "There have been many women I have loved a lot, as discreetly as possible." According to his former chauffeur, Jeane-Claude Laumond, so many sexy babes were streaming in and out of Chirac's office in the 1980s and 1990s, when he was mayor of Paris before becoming president, that females working there gave Chirac the nickname *trois minutes douche comprise,* which means "three minutes, shower included." Indeed, France has had a long-standing tradition of the *cinq à sept*—the five to seven o'clock tryst that a man has with his mistress after work before going home for dinner with his wife. Undoubtedly, two hours with your paramour would be considerably more satisfying than Chirac's presidential three minutes.

It was very much contrary to Gallic custom that, in January 2014, a special edition of the French celebrity magazine, *Closer,* covered in lurid detail French President François Hollande's affair with an actress. His first lady was a live-in partner, not even a wife. The public's increasingly voracious appetite for scandal, passing it on in tweets and blogs, have led to more and more of this kind of muckraking and yellow journalism.

Most French believe that what a man does in the bedroom is his private affair and should neither be legislated nor reported upon, no matter what public office he may hold. Moreover, the French media are subject to strict privacy laws that are more restrictive than most other Western countries. BBC correspondent, Adam Gopnik, describes the French view on sex and privacy as follows (see http://www.bbc.co.uk/news/magazine-25756961): "Sex with children or by force is wrong, and the rest is just the human comedy, unfolding, as it will. Puritanism is a sin against human nature, and the worst of it is that puritanism is the most leering and prurient of world views. Far from wanting to keep sex in the private sphere, the puritans can't wait to drag it out in public."

America had different views on philandering politicians in the 1960s. President John F. Kennedy (JFK) made Clinton look like a complete amateur. JFK is on record for having said, "If I don't have sex every day, I get a headache." JFK had many affairs, most notably with Marilyn Monroe. His 1,000-day presidency was apparently noteworthy for its 1,000 nights of romantic trysts. At that time, no journalist would have been crass enough to report any of them in the newspapers. It would have been seen as an outrageous invasion of his privacy. Indeed, if anyone in the media sought to get JFK out of office for having affairs or make him publicly answer questions about them (as Clinton was made to do on prime time TV), the journalists would have been seen as ridiculous. At the time of Clinton's sex scandal in 1998, I heard some people claim that since the beginning of the 20th century, the only US president who had not had an affair was Richard Nixon, and thus Tricky Dick was the only US president morally suitable for the job.

If you are a powerful enough man, even being a cripple in a wheelchair will not prevent you from having mistresses. The 2012 movie, *Hyde Park on Hudson,* tells the story of a love affair between President Franklin D. Roosevelt (FDR) and Margaret "Daisy" Suckley, who was a distant cousin. The film was based on diaries that Daisy had written that was found after her death. Crippled with polio from the age of 39, FDR was President of the United States from 1933 to 1945. FDR also had a long-term affair with Lucy Mercer, his wife's social secretary. In her book, *FDR and Lucy: Lovers and Friends* (Routledge, 2004), Resa Willis writes that his wife, Eleanor, felt betrayed, not only by her husband, but also by this woman that she had regarded warmly, as well as by friends and family who had encouraged FDR's affair. When she first found out about it, Eleanor wrote in a letter to a close friend, "I have the memory of an elephant. I can forgive, but I cannot forget." Yet one factor that would not have helped her husband stay monogamous was that Eleanor hated sexual intercourse. In the book, *Franklin D. Roosevelt and the Making of Modern America,* (Longman Publishing, 2006), Allan M Winkler writes that Eleanor described sex as "an ordeal to be endured." Nevertheless, she had six children—although that alone might give some women an aversion to sex. FDR also apparently had a 20-year relationship with Marguerite "Missy" LeHand, his private secretary. She was obviously providing private services over and above the call of duty. Despite what Eleanor had told her close friend in that letter, it seems that she was unable to forgive FDR for all his affairs, as the couple led very separate lives, remaining married in name only and staying together for political reasons. Nevertheless, for the work he did while in office, bonking aside, many consider FDR to be one of the top three American presidents, alongside Abraham Lincoln and George Washington.

Journalist Pam Druckerman took an international tour for a humorous look at exactly how and why spouses of various nationalities cheat. She wrote about her findings in *Lust in Translation: Infidelity from Tokyo to Tennessee* (Penguin Books, 2007). What inspired her to write the book? While working as a correspondent for *The Wall Street Journal* in Latin America, she found that married men were continually making advances, not only to her but also to many of her female friends. One Argentinian businessman was baffled by the fact that she was offended by his actions. He believed that he was simply offering her an opportunity for great pleasure. Druckerman interviewed psychologists, counselors and adulterers from around the world. She concluded that Americans, whether the cheaters or the cheated-upon, were the least skilled in handling affairs and had the worst outcomes.

According to a study of attitudes in 39 different countries conducted by the Pew Research Center in 2014, the French were the most likely to accept rather than condemn marital infidelity. In France just under half of those polled—49 percent—agreed with the statement: "Married people having an affair is morally unacceptable." Of the Brits surveyed, 76 percent agreed, as did a whopping 84 percent of Americans. Yanks showed more intolerance of infidelity than any other Western country in the survey. Unsurprisingly, more than 90 percent of those surveyed in Muslim nations such as Egypt, Pakistan and Turkey, found extramarital affairs morally unacceptable. Remember, however, many men in these countries avoid adultery by having more than one wife, and Islamic societies are generally much more tolerant of male rather than female infidelity (http://www. pewresearch.org/fact-tank/2014/01/14/french-more-accepting-of-infidelity-than-people- in-other-countries/).

Double Standards

Sexism around the subject of infidelity is deeply entrenched in cultures past and present worldwide. More often than not, societies expect women to put up with unfaithful spouses and remain loyal to them. Male infidelity is considered quite natural. The husband may view any negative reactions by his wife towards his adultery as unreasonable jealousy. According to the old adage, "Hell hath no fury like a woman scorned." What about male jealousy? Why isn't it "Hell hath no fury like a *man* scorned?" In many countries, men refer to a man with an adulterous wife with such insults as "cuckold" in English, *cornuto* in Italian and *cornudo* in Spanish. The Italians even give a man the "sign of the horns" gesture—the index and little finger point upward with the rest of the hand in a fist. The insult and gesture reflect social acceptance for the man to defend his honor. The unfaithful woman may suffer beatings or worse. History is littered with the corpses of women who have paid for adultery with their lives, yet in the majority of cases, this has been seen as a totally appropriate way for a man to act.

No abusive words exist to describe a woman whose husband is an adulterer, the implication being that it is normal and acceptable for this to happen. Instead, there are various derogatory terms that can apply to any wife, such as "ball and chain," "old lady" or the Cockney rhyming slang "trouble and strife." The sentiment embodied in these expressions is that she is an old nag restricting her husband's freedom.

Most cultures in the past and in Third World countries today are much more forgiving of male adultery than they are of females doing the same thing. In many case adulterous males would be admired for their prowess, while women might be killed for the same activity. Thus, for example, in Fin-de-Siecle Paris, around the dawn of the 20th century, a husband might get off scot free if he murdered his adulterous wife as a *crime passionnel* (crime of passion).

During Victorian times in Britain, a woman would surrender all her rights to her husband once she got married. In his book, *At Home: A Short History of Private Life* (Doubleday, 2010), Bill Bryson describes how 19th century divorce law was overwhelmingly biased against women. A man could divorce his wife if she was unfaithful. A woman would have to prove her husband committed a much more major offense, such as incest or bestiality to be granted a divorce. A divorced woman would usually lose custody of the children and all her property.

In olden times and in cultures that still have arranged marriages, the wife would be chosen for her status and family connections. These same cultures condone men who see women outside the marriage for sexual enjoyment, and maybe also for love. There would be no expectation that the husband would love or have his best sex with his wife. These are modern expectations of the Western world, which, looking at the course of history, are extremely recent, just as are women's rights.

In the past, it was customary that leaders would rule by violence and physical strength. Some might say that in a land of plenty, civilization is a thin veneer covering man's brutish nature. It is even harder to maintain in less developed areas where resources are scarce.

Two seminal psychology experiments illustrate exactly how thin that veneer is, even in the so-called civilized country of America. In an experiment on obedience to authority begun in 1961 by Yale psychology professor Stanley Milgram, students were persuaded to give what they believed were painful, dangerous electric shocks to a person supposedly participating in a research project on learning. The 1971 Stanford Prison Experiment arbitrarily divided students into prisoners and guards (see http://www.prisonexp.org/). The "guards" became increasingly sadistic and psychologically abusive to the "prisoners," many of whom passively accepted it. Two prisoners quit the experiment early and it was abruptly aborted on the sixth day.

What's Love Got to Do with It?

Sex and love are not the same thing, and men tend to find it much easier than women to separate the two. Women often confuse great sex with being in love. This is part of their cultural conditioning—females are not supposed to enjoy no-strings-attached fucking. They are meant to go for emotional connection, committed relationships and having children. Males are much less likely to assume that they love a woman just because they have a fantastic time bonking her. Some guys look at it in as mundane a fashion as wanting to try different flavors of ice cream. They see an attractive woman and want to find out what she is like in bed. They do not need to love her, or even be interested in her conversation. They just want the sex. They may not want a long-term relationship at all because of all the obligations and burdens upon them that will ensue. Men can be natural hedonists, enjoying sex with multiple partners, no strings attached. Men and women in sexual relationships may have a huge disparity in expectations.

Sex alone is not necessarily the basis for a long-term relationship, however passionate it may be. Even if the emotional feelings of the man and the woman are powerful, there has to be a deeper foundation, or the relationship will eventually crash.

Can you truly love more than one sexual partner at the same time? Men are more likely to claim they can do so than women. You might want to differentiate between the more passionate, all-consuming nature of being *in love*—somewhat ephemeral, not necessarily long lasting and hard to maintain with multiple partners—and the love for a partner whom you have known for a long time as an imperfect human being and not some idealized mental construct. The 2013 romantic comedy-drama, *Her,* puts a unique twist on this concept. This science fiction movie describes how Samantha, an artificial intelligence within a computer operating system, falls in love with more than 600 human users, outdoing even the most chronic philanderer. However, can a computer program's actions really be considered infidelity? If your husband wants you to stay with him despite his infidelity— and maybe he does not want to stop bonking others on the side—he will probably be quick to insist that he still loves you. Does he mean it? You will have to be the judge of that. A cynic might say that the rogue loves you like a comfortable old shoe, whereas the floozy is a passionate vacation away from the drudgery of normal life. Nevertheless, if you have been taking the love within your marital relationship for granted, the heartbreak you feel at his infidelity may give you valuable insights about what love really means to you, and what you need to have a fulfilling relationship.

Sexual Regret

Even today, men still tend to be ruled by their evolutionary imperative to spread their seed far and wide in as many sexual encounters as possible, while women, biologically designed to invest years of time and energy raising offspring, are much less keen on casual affairs. A study on sexual regret by researchers at the University of California Los Angeles (UCLA) and the University of Texas at Austin was published in 2013. It concluded that the three most common regrets about sex for men all pertained to missed opportunities for fucking: being too shy to proposition a potential partner, not being sexually adventurous when young, and not being sexually adventurous when single. In contrast, the three main regrets that women reported were all about engaging in sexual activity when they wished that they had not: losing their virginity to the wrong person, cheating on a present or past partner, and moving too fast sexually.

Sometimes a man divorces his wife for another woman, only to discover, after some time has passed, that he sorely regrets having left his spouse. Martin, a piano teacher in Austin, Texas, did not want to suffer that kind of regret. However, rather than having a lover himself, it was his wife who regularly slept with other men, even though Martin remained faithful to her. Why did he put up with it? "Sometimes to keep someone special, who brings a lot into your life, you have to make exceptions," he explained, adding, "As regards relationships, there's a fallacious belief, especially among men that 'I can always get this again.' I don't subscribe to that idea."

Love Versus Lust, Romance Versus Commitment

People of both sexes have widely divergent views on the importance or even the existence of romance. One polyamorous husband, Sydney, who had studied advanced Tantric sexual practices in India, proclaimed, "There is no such thing as romance, only karma." Without his wife's knowledge, Sydney had numerous affairs, yet his marriage became virtually celibate after only five years or so. Arthur was at the opposite side of the spectrum, declaring,

New Year's Resolutions

© 2016 C. J. Grace. Artwork by Aaron Austin, concepts by C. J. Grace.

"Without romance, what else is there in life?" This man was able to keep his wife happy sexually throughout a 22-year marriage. Why? Because he was willing to take the time to create the right mood, work out ways to keep things varied and unpredictable, and really listen to how his partner was responding so that he could adjust accordingly to maximize her pleasure. Arthur needed no knowledge of Tantric techniques to do this.

Rajas in India trained extensively in techniques from the Kama Sutra. Yet these Indian monarchs and princes often found that the sex became very ho hum. Apparently, they were so focused on the sexual techniques they had learned that they lost the emotional connection to their lovers.

Men will tend to see romance as something very physical, sexual and visual, such as making passionate love to a beautiful woman in an exotic locale. They will have no interest in receiving chocolates or flowers. More often than not, it is extremely difficult for males to express affection. They may worry that displaying emotion would be seen as a sign of weakness that opens them up to the possibility of rejection. Instead, they want to appear strong and manly.

Women are much more likely than men to show their love for a partner. They might see romance in such things as beautiful surroundings, affectionate words, cuddles and being made to feel that they occupy a special place in their man's heart. When there is romance, even mundane tasks that would be boring with anyone else—such as washing dishes—have a sexual zing that pervades everything you do together. It is a common story that a man may be very romantic during the courtship period, but no longer bothers to continue behaving that way once he is married. Some believe that romance is simply unsated sexual desire. However, what turns off that insatiable sexual desire once the "in-lust" stage is over?

When lust and romance become love and commitment, sexual passion tends to diminish. In *The Heart of Desire: Keys to the Pleasures of Love* (John Wiley & Sons, 2012), Stella Resnick refers to this as "the love-lust dilemma." Her book describes how long-term emotional attachment inhibits sexual excitement, both psychologically and in the brain's biochemistry. The playfulness that is a critical part of romance disappears. The partners no longer take pleasure in each other's body, and they are simply not in the mood for sex. That is why, for example, Resnick says that a passionate relationship can fizzle when a couple moves in together. His long, deep kiss becomes a peck on the cheek, and his sexual caress becomes a brotherly arm around her shoulder. The loss of desire in long-term marriages does not mean that the spouses no longer have sex drives. There may be a strong attraction towards others, but none towards the husband or wife. Spouses may seek the passion missing from their marriage in extramarital affairs.

Resnick's book is valuable to read, especially for couples trying to repair a relationship damaged by infidelity. The author offers many ways that long-term partners can reclaim their initial passion. These methods include bringing playful spontaneity back into the relationship and cultivating relaxed excitement, which sounds like a contradiction in terms, but is actually a recipe for great sex. Orgasmic lovemaking depends on being able to enjoy high levels of physiological activation (excitement) coupled with deep relaxation. If you are too tense you will not be able to come, but neither will you be able to do so if there is no tension at all.

For many married and long-term couples, sex is relegated to the occasional bout around 10:30 at night, once chores are completed and the kids are in bed, when the husband and wife are both pretty tired out from the day's work. It is done according to more or less the same playlist every time, and usually the same partner will be the initiator. This is not the recipe for exciting, passionate sex. One or both of you may be half-asleep and having sex on autopilot, in effect on autofuck. Putting the fun back in your lovemaking requires you and your husband to take a step back from your customary activity in the bedroom and inject some unpredictability and playfulness into it.

Reclaiming Your Sex Life After Infidelity

There is no doubt that your sex life with your husband will be dramatically affected by his adultery. It will shake your belief in the stability of a loving relationship. You may go through several stages as you process what has happened, work through all the emotions that arise and decide what you want to do with the marriage. There are many different ways that cheated-upon wives react. Some women become very needy and crave more physical affection from their spouse than before. Many are so disgusted by their partner's behavior that even the idea of sex with him becomes totally repellant. Some wives become indifferent to sex in general, some become depressed and withdrawn to everyone, and others go on the prowl, desperate to hook up with someone else. Some may have a strong desire to find a permanent replacement for a partner they no longer believe is the person with whom they want to spend the rest of their life. Many wives go through several of these stages.

Sabine and Herman had been married for 15 years and lived in Stuttgart, Germany. Sabine became desperate for sexual attention from her husband after she found out he was seeing a younger woman. But the *schweinhund* was turned off by his wife's neediness and shunned the poor woman in bed. However, once Sabine found herself a lover, her husband became sexually repellant to her. Herman began making sexual advances to her again, but this time he was the one being rejected. The couple divorced a year later.

Sex tends to be much more of an emotional experience for a woman than for a man, who may be satisfied by the physical act alone. A wife may feel that she has lost the emotional connection with her husband because of his infidelity. This alone may prevent her from enjoying sex with him, even if the lovemaking was great with him beforehand. It may be almost impossible to return to that state if the husband will not dump his mistress. However, if he gives the other woman up, the couple has a much better chance of reclaiming their sex life together.

If you and your husband want to reconcile, you need to analyze what has gone wrong in your relationship and try to deal with these issues. Then, possibly the hardest challenge will be to let these issues go and relax so that you are able to enjoy making love together. Sadly, the easiest path might be to no longer have a sexual relationship with each other or give up the marriage entirely.

You may have once had great orgasms with your husband, but now cannot seem to climax with him. It is understandable that this might happen. The thought of him having sex with the other woman may be a complete and utter turnoff. It just shows how much of the orgasm response for women is emotional rather than purely physical. It is the same man, and his sexual techniques are unlikely to have changed, but your attitude has. However, he may be putting put less effort into his lovemaking with you than he used to be before he had his floozy—or at least, before you called him out on his infidelity. Furthermore, you might worry that his philandering puts you at risk of getting an STD. Your position is an extremely reasonable reaction to his behavior.

There are only a few ways that this situation can change, some of them not very satisfying:

- Find a way to change your attitude despite his philandering, perhaps using some ideas from Chapters Two, Three and Four.

- Persuade your husband to be more rather than less attentive to your sexual needs.

- Find a lover to have great sex with, so you are not bothered about how it is with your husband.

- Learn to put up with non-orgasmic sex with your husband.

- Move toward having a celibate marriage. The danger of this is that it might make your relationship with your husband even worse than it is already, and drive him farther into the arms of his mistress.

- Divorce him and try to find someone else.

Why Continue to Have Sex with Him?

If you have chosen to stay with your husband despite his adultery, it is worth remembering that sex plays a beneficial role in marriage. Couples that continue to have regular sex even into old age tend to feel more content and have less conflict. A study presented at the Gerontological Society of America's Annual Scientific Meeting in 2011 concluded that the more frequently older couples engaged in sexual activity, the happier they reported their lives and marriages to be. A husband and wife often find that the best time for frank, intimate conversation that brings them closer together is when they are relaxed after making love. Furthermore, researchers from Princeton University have found that regular sex can increase the growth of brain cells. Anna Hodgekiss, in a *MailOnline* article, reports that sexual activity, as well as releasing a flood of hormones that can create a state of happiness, may even stave off dementia in older adults (http://www.dailymail.co.uk/health/article-2031498/Sex-Why-makes-women-fall-love--just-makes-men-want-MORE.html).

Scientific research has uncovered another fascinating reason why lovemaking can make a woman feel good. It appears that semen may have antidepressant qualities. A 2002 study at the State University of New York in Albany compared the moods of women who had sex without condoms, had sex with condoms and had no sex at all. The research demonstrated a significant reduction in the rate of depression in women not using condoms as compared to the two other groups. Semen contains substances such as endorphins, estrone, prolactin, oxytocin, thyrotropin-releasing hormone and serotonin, all of which can improve your mood. Perhaps in the future doctors might prescribe semen pills instead of Prozac for people suffering from depression, or maybe they will send women off to a therapeutic bonking clinic.

There is no question that, if you want to stay married, you are likely to get on better with your spouse if you continue to have sex with him, despite his infidelity. If you withhold sex, even if you feel it is perfectly justified by his adultery, it can make him angry and irritable, causing the two of you to grow further apart. Human beings are often not very fair, balanced or rational in their behavior as regards love, sex or infidelity. Sadly, it is a common trait in both men and women to expect someone else to put up with a great deal more than they are willing to tolerate themselves.

Edgar did not have a great desire for bedroom activities with his wife, Norma, when his young mistress was in town. However, when his floozy was not available, he would want to have sex with his wife. Understandably, Norma was not particularly interested. "Edgar told me I was cutting him off sexually and that it put him in a lousy mood. But I just didn't feel turned on as I was so obviously his second choice who would only do when nobody better was around." The couple stayed together, but it was very much a marriage of convenience for both parties.

The effect that sex or lack of it has in a relationship is viscerally clear in Lucy Irvine's candid and uncompromisingly blunt memoir, *Castaway* (Penguin Books, 1984), about answering an advertisement to be the "wife" of writer Gerald Kingsland for a year on a deserted tropical island. Irvine had to marry the man in order for the local authorities to give their permission for the couple to live on the island. Initially she had sex with him, but soon decided that she no longer wanted to do so. Kingsland was 25 years her senior and she did not find him attractive. Kingsland was in love with Irvine, and he found it hard to understand why she denied him sex. This led up to huge build-ups of tension, bitterness and anger, occasionally exploding into venomous exchanges. Yet on the level of working together for their mutual survival and physical well-being, they got along very well.

After Irvine finally decided to have sex again with Kingsland, it was as if a switch had been turned on inside him. His mood changed profoundly and he was full of pure joy.

It takes a lot of work to reclaim good sex after you find out your husband has been philandering. If you expect an adulterer to be understanding and compassionate towards you just because he is the guilty party, you are likely to be sorely disappointed. Life is not always fair, and relationships can be complicated. If he wants the marriage to continue, he will have a strong incentive to step up to the plate to try to repair the relationship. However, that does not mean it will be easy for him to change from a chauvinistic ass, for example, to a considerate helpmate.

Where Is Your Orgasm?

It is seriously tragic that a significant number of women go through life never having experienced an orgasm. This is a major reason why many women do not enjoy sex at all. They may put up with it early on in the marriage but become celibate later on, especially after having children.

A woman may be non-orgasmic simply because she has a partner who comes too fast and does not take the time to give her pleasure. According to sex researcher Alfred Kinsey's book *Sexual Behavior in the Human Male* (W.B. Saunders Co., 1948), three-quarters of the men he surveyed would ejaculate within two minutes of vaginal penetration at least 50 percent of the time. It is a rare woman who can achieve orgasm in two minutes.

"Wham-bam-thank-you-ma'am" husbands are still exceedingly common. Eileen was a farmer's daughter who lived in Devon, England. She married young, and her husband's idea of lovemaking was to return home from the pub at night drunk and thrust away for five minutes or so until he came. Then he would clamber off her and go to sleep. Needless to say, Eileen found sex boring and distasteful. However, after divorcing him she had a wild, secret affair with a married TV celebrity and discovered that when a guy was good in bed, she absolutely loved sex.

According to a 2015 online survey by *Cosmopolitan* magazine of more than 2,300 women aged between 18 and 40, only 15 percent of women reached orgasm from vaginal intercourse alone, compared with 39 percent from masturbation. A whopping 67 percent reported faking an orgasm during sex. It is widely believed that about 10 percent of women never achieve orgasms under any conditions. The Cosmo survey came up with a lower figure for non-orgasmic women—6 percent of those over 30. However, some might say that there was some self-selection in the poll's participants. For example, women who have given up on sex and orgasms in general would not be very likely to choose to respond to a survey on those subjects. Similar studies by other research groups and magazines may disagree on the percentages but still come to the same conclusion—a majority of women do not experience orgasm from vaginal intercourse.

Sometimes it is a matter of how well your physical bodies fit together. When your genitals meet, are your heads in the right place for you to be able to kiss each other comfortably? Can your hands reach all the right places? I remember once seeing a 6-foot tall, heavyset American fellow with his tiny new mail-order wife from Thailand—just under 5 feet tall and impossibly thin—and wondering how they would be able to have sex without him causing her damage.

Jo's ex-boyfriend Charlie was tall and skinny, while she was very short, "The sex was terrible with Charlie—I just couldn't have orgasms with him. Just kissing him would strain my neck, and whether I lay on top of him or he lay on top of me, it was really uncomfortable. Then I met Rob, who was only a few inches taller than me and we fit together perfectly, like two jigsaw pieces. He was wonderful to cuddle, and the lovemaking was terrific."

Just as the lack of orgasms can make for an unhappy marriage, orgasmic sex may bring unsuited people to the altar. Gabriella wed an ill-mannered man, Julian, whom none of her friends liked. She later divorced him because she found out that he had been unfaithful throughout the marriage. Her previous boyfriend Edward nailed the reason why Gabriella had chosen to marry a clearly unsuitable partner, "I tried so hard to give you an orgasm and never managed to succeed," he lamented, "I knew Julian had succeeded where I had failed. There was no other justification for you to marry someone with so few redeeming features."

Often women do not even know what turns them on. Many expect their mates to be more than telepathic. It is rare that a woman will tell a man what she would like him to do in bed. She will tend to expect him to work out how to give her an orgasm that she herself may not have a clue about how to achieve. If wives have lukewarm attitudes towards lovemaking, it is not surprising that their spouses might consider extramarital exploration. There are many reasons a woman may be non-orgasmic. These include the following:

- Her body may hold a lot of physical tension, so that she cannot relax enough.

- She may have emotional or psychological issues around sex that prevent her reaching orgasm. These can be as dramatic as having been molested or raped, or as mundane as simply feeling embarrassed about revealing her body. Perhaps she believes that she is ugly down there. She may have somewhat Victorian views on sex, harking back to the days when women were told to "lie back and think of England" and any girl who enjoyed fucking was clearly an ill-bred nymphomaniac and not a lady of quality.

- Her partner may not use effective techniques in bed or spend enough time on foreplay for her to be sufficiently turned on to climax.

This last point is emphasized by the popularity of the method described in the bestselling book by Nicole Daedone, *Slow Sex: The Art and Craft of the Female Orgasm* (Grand Central Life and Style, 2011). The exercise the book advocates to bring non-orgasmic women to orgasm is for the woman to lie back (and neither think of England nor of sex) in a comfortable and relaxed position, with only the lower clothing removed. Then the man gently touches her genitals for 15 minutes. The fact that this technique is so successful in making non-orgasmic women reach climax demonstrates two important points:

- Many women do not take the time to relax and let go around sex.

- Many men do not bother to do enough foreplay on their women before penetration.

Mastering Masturbation

Sex for One: The Joy of Selfloving by Betty Dodson (Three Rivers Press, 1996) was first published in 1974 and is still extremely relevant today. This seminal book teaches women about the physical properties of their vaginas and how to masturbate without shame. At this point, I think it is appropriate to mention a wonderful quote from comedian Sheng Wang and also used by veteran actress, Betty White, "Why do people say 'grow some balls?' Balls are weak and sensitive. If you wanna be tough, grow a vagina. Those things can take a pounding."

Alternatively, if *Sex for One: The Joy of Selfloving* does not float your boat, you can use Nicole Daedone's approach and pay to go to a *Slow Sex* workshop to learn and experience the wonders of OM—Orgasmic Meditation—as her technique is called, and either bring your husband or have some obliging male participant stroke your nether regions for 15 minutes at a time. I have to ask, however, if you have a partner who is willing to try to please you, why not just do all this foreplay stuff for free in the comfort and privacy of your own bedroom?

If you have no trusty male to do the work, you can always try masturbation. If you have not done it yet, you will discover why many women masturbate. However, some women are afraid of or repelled by the idea of touching themselves. In various ways, females have been conditioned not to do it. This activity is seen as something dirty and forbidden. Throughout history, males have always masturbated, despite claims that such "self-abuse" will make them blind, insane, weak, and lead them to an early grave. So what are some of the benefits females can gain from masturbating?

- You become comfortable and familiar with your own genitalia—this will make you more relaxed about sex.

- You learn exactly what you need to do to turn yourself on—then you can let a partner know what he can do.

- For older women, masturbating keeps your genital area from becoming too tense and dry, particularly if you are not having sexual intercourse very often. It also gives you opportunity to lubricate the area and keep it moisturized.

- Having orgasms tends to improve your mood.

Try to practice mindfulness when you are masturbating. Focus intensely on the sensations you are feeling, and how they change according to what you are doing and where you are touching yourself. If your mind wanders off to thinking about making dinner or what you need to do for the kids, you are giving yourself short shrift. The more mindful and present you are to what you are experiencing as you masturbate, the more pleasurable it will become.

Seeing a woman masturbate turns on some men. Watching the process can show them how to bring her to a climax. Aside from attending to the necessary hygiene issues, there are no aesthetic standards for vaginas—everyone is slightly different. Some guys prefer the pubic hair to be shaved, some do not. Generally, younger men expect a woman to prune her pubes, while older men tend not to care so much. Many women do not like to shave or wax their pubic area, as the process can be quite painful and damage the sensitive skin there.

However, why take the trouble to masturbate by yourself when you can get your doctor to do it for you? From the time of the ancient Greeks through the Victorian era all the way up to the mid-20th century, doctors would give women "pelvic massage" therapy as a cure for hysteria. What they were really doing was giving orgasms to those frustrated females. Mary Roach writes about this treatment for hysteria in her often hysterically humorous book *Bonk: The Curious Coupling of Science and Sex* (W. W Norton, 2008). Physicians looked for solutions to save their hands from all that hard work to create those "female paroxysms" for which women were very happy to pay as a cure for their hysteria. Roach describes how, in 1869, an American doctor, George Taylor went one step further. He invented a vibrator powered by steam, which he dubbed the Manipulator. Then, about a decade later, Joseph Granville created an electromechanical version. These pre-dated the invention of the electric toaster. A home-use electric model of the vibrator became available in 1902—a "plug in and play" version, so to speak. This trusty tool was a valued and veteran home appliance, coming on the scene before vacuum cleaners and electric irons. Rather than relying on a machine to give you orgasms, however, you may prefer to get them from making love.

Sex as an Art and a Science

How do you and your husband learn how to make lovemaking a more satisfying experience, especially after your relationship has been rocked by adultery? Alex Comfort's seminal sex manual, *The Joy of Sex* (Crown Publishers, 2009), updated several times since it was first written more than 50 years ago, has helped many couples to improve their sex lives.

However, rather than seeking solutions close to home, you can try taking a look at what people do in Asia. The East has a thing or two to teach the

West about lovemaking. In ancient China, sex was considered to be both an art and a science. Married couples would have a "pillow book" describing techniques that could be used not only to increase pleasure for both the man and the woman, but also to enhance their health and even develop spirituality. Over the past 2,000 years, intrepid Taoists researched every bit of the human body and its energy fields to find all the erogenous zones. They worked out precisely how sex between a man and a woman could develop the body, mind and spirit, using what the Chinese call *qi* and the Indians refer to as *prana*—internal life-force energy. Thus, a couple that really knew what they were doing could bonk their way not only to orgasmic ecstasy but also to merge with the Tao.

Traditional Indian Tantra also incorporated spiritual shagging. However, many of these techniques, both Chinese and Indian, were quite complex and required a lot of training, rather than being something you could learn in a New Age weekend workshop, even if it took place in California.

Who Does All the Work in Bed?

The more mindful and present couples are to each other's needs and desires, the more pleasurable lovemaking will be. You or he will often know right away whether the other person is in the bedroom or somewhere else— worrying about work, where the keys are or what to have for dinner. If either spouse is not present to the other, what is the point of bothering to have sex?

In the best sexual relationships, the man and the woman share the work and do not consider it to be work at all. You will generally enjoy sex more if you feel that your partner is making love to your whole body and you are doing the same for him. You may discover some erogenous zones that you never knew existed. Spontaneous mutual enjoyment of each other's body is the best approach, where the more one partner is turned on, the more the other is too. The worst way to go is the exact opposite of this—where one partner does not get turned on because he or she is unable to turn on the other person—a vicious cycle.

When a husband has been unmasked as a cheater, it often causes that vicious cycle of neither partner turning on the other, even if everything has been fine before. The wife may find that all kinds of negative thoughts arise during sex that prevent her relaxing and going with the flow. She may:

- Feel inhibited with her husband, because she does not feel she can trust him.
- Worry that he neither really loves her nor finds her attractive.
- Wonder if he is giving her a mercy fuck out of guilt.
- No longer enjoy doing things to turn him on, as his body has been someone else's playground.
- Suspect that he has been more sexually attentive towards the other woman than with her.
- Start analyzing and criticizing his performance in bed when she has never done so before.
- Feel revulsion towards him because of his sex acts with the other woman.

It is a cruel truth that the repercussions of being discovered are likely to be a real turn-off for your wayward husband also. All the following are passion-killers for post-adultery marital sex:

- He feels guilty.
- He thinks he has to walk on eggshells to avoid his wife blowing up or getting upset.
- His wife acts needy, tearful, depressed, accusatory and/or angry around him.
- Neither spouse is in the mood to laugh or have fun together.
- The wife is tired all the time (maybe she should just put those pesky kids into suspended animation or quit her job).
- It is all sweetness and light with the other woman, as he has built up no baggage with her yet.

If you want to reclaim your sex life together, you and your husband must both be willing to make an effort to achieve this. Many couples have found that seeing a marital guidance counselor or sex therapist has helped them get the physical and emotional aspects of their relationship back on track. Many women find themselves turned off in the bedroom after discovering infidelity, even if they liked sex and enjoyed lovemaking with their husband before they knew he had someone else on the go. Thus, it may be helpful for the wife to talk to her husband about timeouts from sex. Then if she chooses to make love with him, she can lay down some ground rules about what he should do to turn her on and what he should avoid to prevent turning her off. Then the husband can see if she is willing to do the same for him.

In Western culture, perhaps stemming from that Victorian "lie back and think of England" approach I mentioned earlier, many women expect the man to do most of the work. Of course, it generally takes less time for a man to reach orgasm before a woman, so a gentlemanly mate should put some effort into bringing his lady to a climax before he ejaculates. However, in Asia and the Far East, there is a culture where women are expected to know how to please a man, and as young girls they will be taught specific techniques to do so. In those cultures, it may be the man who expects the woman to do most of the work. A mismatch between the expectations of the husband and the wife as to who should do what in bed often leads to dissatisfaction once the initial lust phase has dissipated. Couples rarely discuss this issue and may not even realize exactly why their lovemaking has become unsatisfying. This can lead to a celibate marriage, extramarital affairs and/or divorce.

Arnie was the son of American expats in Thailand, where he had spent much of his life. He had had many girlfriends there and got used to receiving a huge amount of sexual attention from them. After he moved to the United States, he met Harriet. They fell in love and got married. At first, they were so much in lust with each other that Harriet was happy to give him the long massages he liked to have as a prequel to lovemaking. He liked her to spend a lot of time turning him on with her hands and with her mouth. However, after a year or two, the sparkle wore off. She started to feel resentful that he was not spending anywhere near the same amount of time pleasuring her as she was on him. Then as Arnie reached middle age and was taking prescription drugs for various health problems, his ability to have an erection became increasingly impaired. She found it a thankless, endless task just getting him to have a boner. For both husband and wife, bedroom activities began to feel like a chore rather than something to be enjoyed. The couple would have sex less and less frequently. Both ended up having affairs, his enhanced by those little blue pills that had only recently become available. Harriet was amazed to find a lover who actually seemed to be enjoying her body in bed. The more turned on he made her, the more turned on he became himself. At last, she did not feel like she was doing all the work.

Passion Killers

The previous section covered some of the mental and emotional issues that can prevent a couple from enjoying sex when a wife has discovered a husband's affair. Infidelity aside, it does not take much to kill a woman's mood for passion. I asked some of the women I interviewed about their pet peeves. Men take note—here are the top twelve turn-offs:

1. He is smelly and cannot be bothered to take a shower, or if he does, he will not use any soap.

2. He does not cut his fingernails or toenails, giving you razorblade sex.

3. He slobbers when he kisses.

4. He has eaten garlic or has other bad breath issues.

5. He will not turn off the TV.

6. He criticizes you or acts impatient.

7. He is drunk—not just a bit tipsy.

8. He smokes in bed.

9. He starts talking about work or some other dreary unromantic subject.

10. He gets you into a physically uncomfortable position in bed.

11. He plays music you do not like.

12. He has become extremely overweight.

If the woman is doing these things, they can equally be passion-killers for a man too. These complaints may sound cruel and uncharitable, but they stop many from being in the mood for sex.

A critical part of couples preparing for sex is what has been dubbed the "tart wash"—showering in the bathroom to ensure that the nether regions, armpits, hands, feet and mouth are clean and fresh. This preparation is especially important for oral sex. I am certain you do not need me to explain why.

Desperate Acts to Keep Him Interested

After discovering that a husband has been unfaithful, some wives become willing to indulge in sexual acts with their partners that they would not have tolerated before. Whether this is coming from the sheer desperation of trying anything to hang on to their wandering mate, or a genuine loosening of inhibitions and enjoyment of new sexual frontiers, is a matter of debate.

Some modern couples claim that infidelity can spice up their relationship. The husband and wife may find that they discover new ways of enjoying lovemaking together from having sex outside the marriage. Some choose to have threesomes. It is a common male fantasy to bed two girls at once, but does the couple draw lots to decide whether the third person is male or female? The wife might even be willing to have the husband's mistress be the third person. Alternatively, the husband and wife could find themselves having foursomes or swinging with other couples. This all makes good fodder for adult cable TV reality shows, but nonetheless, the majority of women tend to find such kinky set-ups rather repugnant.

I am sure that there are some wives who love threesomes with their husband and another woman, but from the numerous people I interviewed for this book, I heard of only one case where group sex was genuinely enjoyed by all. It involved no married couples and only lasted a few months. During the hippy-style free love era of the 1970s, Jerry shared an apartment with three bisexual women. They were all good friends and group sex organically developed between them, sometimes with only three people, but more often with all four. They especially loved trying to have everyone achieve orgasms at the same time. Jerry knew of several other people indulging in threesomes at that time, but none of them worked out well. There would always be one of the three who got jealous and felt left out of the proceedings.

Damian was heavily involved with an S&M (sadomasochistic) group and loved playing the master, breaking in young girls to act as submissive sex slaves. Whips, bondage, domination—he was into it all. His wife was not interested in any of this stuff, but after many years, she finally got fed up with him seeing all these other women and asked him to stop. Damian insisted that indulging in S&M was what made him happy and told his wife he would stop seeing other women only if she would take their place and be his submissive. Amazingly, she agreed. Unlike Christian Grey, the S&M-loving protagonist in the bestselling book by E. L. James, *Fifty Shades of Grey* (Vintage Books, 2012), Damian was no young, handsome and impossibly rich guy. Instead, he was a balding, pudgy geezer in his 70s, and his long-suffering wife was in her late 60s.

STDs: Is He Damaging Your Health as Well as Your Self-esteem?

"What the hell? I've been faithful for 25 years. How did I get a sexually transmitted disease (STD)?" It frequently happens that the first time the wife becomes aware of her husband's extramarital exploits is when she gets an STD. A smorgasbord of viruses, bacteria and other problems can visit the sexually promiscuous. Once you find out about your husband's affair, you need to get yourself checked out by your gynecologist as soon as possible to make sure that the fucker has not given you a gift that keeps on giving. It is no laughing matter. There are several sexual diseases—human immunodeficiency virus (HIV) and herpes in particular—for which, at the time of writing, no cures exist. Perhaps infidelity should carry a government health warning, just like cigarettes. Similar to secondhand smoke, the wife who has not indulged in any infidelity is at risk too.

If you ask your husband for specifics about the woman or women he is seeing on the side, he might tell you it is none of your business. But apart from the unlikely event that whenever he fucks a floozy he is wearing a condom on his dick—putting a raincoat on Mr. Happy—and even that will not protect him 100 percent against STDs—whom he has sex with is absolutely your business.

You are at the mercy of not only your husband's sexual choices, but also the sexual choices of the women he is bonking. Some are likely to be promiscuous and have multiple partners if they are comfortable fucking a married man who may be available only part of the time. It is as if you are bonking not only your husband's bitches, but everyone else they have slept with too. Wow, all that sex without getting any of the enjoyment!

Jack was a well-liked news editor in a local radio station. Middle-aged and balding, he appeared to be a devoted husband. His wife, Courtney, only realized that Jack had a girlfriend on the side—one of the newsroom secretaries—once she developed the symptoms of an STD. Courtney was devastated but did not want a divorce. She was savvy enough not to go harpy on her husband but instead made sure that she used the situation to get exactly what she wanted out of him. Ashamed and contrite, Jack dumped the secretary, working hard at becoming more attentive and loving towards his wife. The couple managed to salvage their marriage.

Actor Michael Douglas claimed to have a sex addiction problem. Most likely, he was just highly sexed and, as is true for many celebs, had no shortage of willing babes to fuck. When he was diagnosed with throat cancer, he blamed it on having indulged in too much oral sex. Whoever thought that cunnilingus could kill? Human papilloma virus (HPV) strains 16 and 18 have indeed been linked to throat cancer in men, but the main danger of these particular STDs is cervical cancer in women. There are various other forms of HPV, but 16 and 18 account for about 70 percent of all the virus-induced cancers. Generally, the risk to men is much smaller than the risk women face from HPV. Therefore, even though males can be carriers and infect their partners, at the time of writing this book, there is only an HPV test for women, not for men.

Over the years, Phillip had affairs with various women. When his wife, Amelia, found out, off she went to the gynecologist and found that he had given her HPV, but fortunately not the worst strain. It was something that Phillip's latest floozy, Zelda, had contracted in the past but had now managed to clear. Whether Zelda had given it to her through Phillip, or whether Phillip was already a carrier, Amelia did not know. So she went out and bought Phillip several packs of condoms and put them in his suitcase whenever he went on trips. The packs always returned unopened. When she asked Phillip why he was not using them, he declared that sex with a condom was not worth having. "It just doesn't feel anywhere near as good," he explained. He told his wife that she was welcome to have an affair of her own, claiming that he would not mind at all. But what was sauce for the goose definitely was not sauce for the gander. "Just make sure you have protection," Phillip warned. Amelia eventually found a way to get rid of her HPV. She stayed with her asshole husband but stopped having sex with him, as she was unable to trust him not to infect her again. Definitely a sad situation.

When Delia found out that her horndog husband, Eric, was seeing multiple sexual partners, she immediately went to her doctor to get checked for STDs and tested positive for an infection. Her proudly polyamorous partner had the gall to tell her, "I never promised you that I wouldn't give you an STD." She stayed married to the rotten ratbag for a couple of years, but would only have sex with him if he wore a condom. However, eventually Eric's outrageous philandering took its toll and she left him.

If your husband happens to be fucking various men on the side, there is much more likelihood of him transmitting an STD to you than if he were only bonking babes. His extramarital activities now raise the specter of possibly giving you HIV. The more promiscuous he is, the greater the risk to you. So if the bugger's out there having anal sex with men, he and all his partners damn well better be wearing condoms on their dicks.

Sadly, the free love era of the 1960s is over. Gone are those days when we did not have to think about HIV, herpes or HPV, and all women needed to be concerned about was to go on the contraceptive pill to avoid pregnancy. Aside from the emotional minefield of combining adultery with marital relations, when you consider all these potential sexual diseases and what sex actually involves, it is remarkable that fornication actually happens at all. Sex is a messy, sweaty, smelly business, what with all those body fluids and that groaning and grunting. Nevertheless, people spend so much time and energy thinking about it and indulging in it. It can be wonderful when you are in lust; dreadful, especially when you have found out that he has another woman; or just ho-hum, particularly after decades of married life.

Nevertheless, we should be grateful that human sexual intercourse is not as unpleasant as that of a flatworm called *Pseudobiceros hancockanus*. Cock, anus? Whoever chose that name must have had quite a sense of humor. These flatworms are hermaphrodites with both male and female sexual organs, but have not been graced with vaginas. Two mating flatworms will engage in very aggressive fencing with their sharp dagger-like penises, each trying to stab the skin of the other and inject sperm into it. Whichever one wins the fight is the male, and the loser is the female, who suffers deep wounds in the process. I have to thank Lynn Saxon for bringing this bizarrely violent mating ritual to my attention in her book, *Sex at Dusk: Lifting the Shiny Wrapping from Sex at Dawn* (CreateSpace Independent Publishing, 2012). It certainly makes celibacy seem like a good option.

CHAPTER TEN

SHOULD YOU FIND A LOVER TOO?

If you are a woman who has been married and monogamous for many years, having an affair can almost feel like losing your virginity for a second time. You may have the idea in your head that it would be a good thing to participate in exactly the same kind of extramarital frolics as your husband is engaging in, but if the chemistry is not there—and more often than not, it isn't—you may find your prospective lovers to be sexually repellant.

Over decades of monogamy, you can become very used to one particular male body and his way of making love, and another guy's *modus operandi* may feel very weird indeed to you. Having sex with someone other than your husband can be similar to visiting another country. His touch, his sounds, his smell and the taste of his kisses will all be different. You might find that certain things you took for granted as being cast in stone at home are not that way at all in the place you are visiting. This can be liberating and invigorating or weird and unsettling.

To have truly enjoyable lovemaking, everything has to feel right. A man may be good in bed with one woman, but terrible with another. A great lover will have a sixth sense about how to turn you on. He will be sensitive and caring enough to really listen to your body, gauging your reaction to every little thing he is doing and adjusting accordingly. He is like a cross between a choreographer and an airplane pilot, moving himself and you around the bed effortlessly, always leaving you in a comfortable position. However, with a poor lover everything will seem fumbling and uncomfortable. He just will not be "cliterate" in bed.

If you do end up jumping into the pool of sexual infidelity, it can be both wonderful—at the very least, a huge boost to your self-esteem—and terrible, creating a whole new can of worms. To use another well-worn metaphor, once that Pandora's Box has been opened, you can never go back to where you were before. It can be like leaping off a precipice—exhilarating while you are in the air, but you never know what kind of landing you will have.

If you find someone else to whom you are attracted, take a hedonistic approach to the new relationship. Try to avoid having any expectations about what is going to happen and go for having as much fun with that person as possible. For example, find ways that you can laugh together and play at being wanton in bed with him. You can make the sex totally different from the way it has been with your husband.

When Geraldine found out her husband had recently acquired a mistress, he bluntly told his wife, "She's just so much more inherently joyful than you." Geraldine realized that her marriage to a very demanding man and raising their four children had indeed ground her down and diminished her capacity for joy. When Geraldine began having an affair with her easygoing, fun-loving tennis coach, her best friend remarked, "It's like we have the old Geraldine back—you're happy with life again."

You will always be comparing. Camilla was married to Donald, a high school wrestling coach. After discovering his affair, she decided to date a sculptor who had been a platonic friend for many years. Isaac had always fancied her. Camilla had liked him too, but had wanted to remain faithful to her husband. She had enjoyed boisterous sex with Donald, but realized that Isaac's gentle approach was much more of a turn on. When Donald nuzzled her it felt a little uncomfortable, as if he had her in a headlock. He also did not always trim his nails, so sometimes she actually felt quite sore following sexual activity. This was never the case with Isaac.

Bear in mind that just having a revenge fuck to get back at your husband is a recipe for disaster. It is neither beneficial for you nor good for the other man. If you do choose to have a lover, it is important that the two of you are genuinely attracted to each other and that the relationship is not coming from an emotionally reactive place. Here are five points to consider:

- Is there chemistry between you?

- Do you enjoy his company?

- Does he make you laugh?

- Can you truly be yourself with him rather than having to put on a bit of an act?

- Most importantly—does he treat you well?

You might want to ask yourself the same questions about your husband in order to decide if you still want to stay with him.

Are You Ready to Try a Tryst?

Are you ready to start the hunt for another sex partner or flirt with other guys? Or maybe you have decided to have a marriage of convenience and find a lover. Here are some telltale signs that could also apply if you are considering splitting with your husband rather than just interested in having an affair:

- You no longer feel comfortable wearing your wedding ring. You may have taken it off in disgust after hearing about your husband's affair, but one of the reasons you want to leave that ring finger bare is that it shows other guys you might be available.

- When talking about yourself with other people, you find yourself switching from first person plural to first person singular—changing from "we" to "I."

- You take much more care over your appearance than you used to, especially when going to social events.

- We know that BCE stands for Before Common Era. Now you start thinking and talking to others about your life BHE—Before Husband Era—or, at the very least, about what you are doing with your life outside the marriage.

- You decide to start using your maiden name rather than your married name in some social or even business situations.

- You take your married last name off your voicemail greeting, and only use your first name.

- You change your title from Mrs. to Ms. because you do not want to specify whether you are married or single. Ironically, as originally used in the 17th century, Ms. was derived from the word "mistress." After falling into disuse, the title was revived in the 20th century. Although there is still disagreement as to whether Ms. is appropriate to use, many etiquette writers now consider it the default form of address for a woman.

The kind of relationship you will be looking for will be strongly affected by your age, financial status and whether your children are still dependent upon you or already grown. An important question to ask yourself is, "Do I want an affair or another long-term relationship?" A woman in her 20s and early 30s might dump her cheating spouse, feeling that she has plenty of time to find a replacement. A wife in her 50s or 60s might want to hang on to what she has and just have an affair on the side. Someone married to a man with few assets might decide to leave him to find a better provider. A wife who wants to have children might decide to leave to find someone better to father her kids. Someone with young children might choose to stay with her husband and find a lover whom she only sees when the kids are at school. A financially secure woman past childbearing age may be looking for someone who is fun to be with rather than expecting him to support her, and will have fewer restrictions on the amount of time she can spend with him. A woman who can have a good standard of living only by staying married might decide upon a marriage of convenience and seek emotional support elsewhere. A wife may initially want to have an affair while retaining the security of her marriage, but she may eventually decide to leave her husband to be with her new man.

Older women may feel that they want to get into another relationship as soon as possible before time runs out and they lose whatever looks they have left. Some women who have been cheated upon may want to jump ship from their marriage, but not until they have another man on the go to move in with, without having to deal with any time on their own. Unfortunately, life is rarely that convenient.

It is important to note that women dealing with adultery and/or divorce are very emotionally vulnerable and may be prime targets for men to take advantage of. Many guys are out looking for women to leech onto not only for sex but also a comfortable place to live, financial support and domestic services.

Jenna had divorced her husband after discovering that he had had numerous affairs. The divorce settlement left her with an ocean-view condo in Waikiki, Hawaii. She tried online dating and had no end of men wanting to come to visit her. She knew that they were just interested in a free vacation to Hawaii. When she took the condo location off her profile, hardly anyone bothered to contact her. Zoe was recently divorced and owned a gorgeous home in the Florida Keys. She had a whirlwind romance with a hot Brazilian guy, considerably younger than her, who was very eager to move in. Once that happened, Zoe found that he was expecting her to do all the cooking and cleaning, as well as pay all the bills. He put a lot of emotional pressure on her to try to stay as long as possible, and she had a devil of a job getting him to move out.

Conventional wisdom says that rebound affairs are a bad idea and do not end well. If you are still an emotional mess from your husband's infidelity, you may be operating from a position of desperation and neediness. This is likely to be a recipe for disaster rather than a way to find a stable, fulfilling relationship with another man. It is best to wait until you feel less raw and wounded before leaping into dating. Your low self-esteem and loneliness may make you think that you have fallen in love with the first man that bonks you. Your expectations about how the affair should turn out may set you up for a hell of a fall. You will be much better prepared for a balanced relationship if you first get a handle on your negative emotions and work on becoming more independent rather than needing a man to feel complete. Chapters Two, Three and Four discussed various ways to achieve this.

What Do You Gain from Male Attention?

When is male attention sexual harassment and when is it flattering flirtation? Apart from a crass brute who will not take an obvious "No!" for an answer, usually there is only one difference—the woman either enjoys the attention or she does not.

Female visitors to Third World countries such as India and the Middle East are likely to know all too well what constitutes genuine sexual harassment. Andrea was traveling on crowded buses in Pakistan and her breasts and bottom would always be groped by male passengers, sometimes so hard that she would be left with bruises. She finally devised a solution that was extremely successful: wearing a bra and underpants studded with thumbtacks, so that groping would be a painful experience for the man before it became one for her.

Aside from this kind of extreme example, in most cases the critical issue is whether the woman is sexually attracted to the man. The same touch that you would find wonderful from someone you like may make you cringe and recoil if it comes from a guy you consider unattractive. However, what if you have been in a long-term marriage to a rogue who has a mistress who is younger/prettier/more successful or whatever, while you have been totally faithful? In that case, it may do wonders to your self-esteem to find out that another man actually fancies you, even if you do not want to have sex with him. Being married gives you a perfect out to turn down his advances without offending him—"Sorry, I'm married. I just can't do this, even though I really like you." This opens the door to being able to cultivate platonic male friendships without being burdened by unwanted sexual advances.

Someone whose self-esteem has been smashed by a husband's affair will have a more positive attitude towards sexual attention from other men than would a stunning hot babe who is fed up with having to constantly fend off male advances. Joanna was in the former category. She had been out of the dating pool for decades, feeling rather rusty in that department and not particularly attractive. Here is her story:

"I was swimming in the ocean in Florida, when one of the lifeguards came up to me on a paddleboard. A few weeks prior, someone had been attacked by a tiger shark in the area, so I thought he was going to warn me about that. He talked to me briefly about the water conditions and then proceeded to chat me up. He was tanned, fit and buff, maybe late 30s or early 40s—much younger than me. I was wearing a mask and snorkel, so unless he had been checking me out before I entered the water, he would have had little idea what my face looked like. Despite the fact that I wasn't really interested in pursuing anything, I still found the attention very satisfying; he was a handsome guy and fun to flirt with. I'd rather have a sexy stud prowling around me than a tiger shark any day!"

When Sherry, an attractive woman in her mid-fifties, found out that her husband was cheating on her with a much younger woman, it was a huge blow to her self-esteem. Not one to give his wife much in the way of compliments about her appearance, when Sherry confronted him about the affair, by way of an explanation, the slimy rat mentioned the fine tits and ass of his nubile babe on the side, Sherry's best friend Linda recommended salsa dancing. "It's like a whole series of three-minute love affairs," she said. Sherry went and had a blast. Even though initially she had no clue about how to do the steps, she had no shortage of men asking her to dance. Sherry was hooked. Several of her dance partners asked her for dates. Although Sherry had initially thought that the best therapy to deal with her husband's infidelity would be to have an affair herself, when push came to shove—metaphorically, at least—she could not quite stomach the idea of sexual contact with any of these other men. If they tried to kiss her, she would feel totally repelled, just like the repulsion between the sides of two magnets of the same polarity. Nonetheless, the male attention she received did wonders for her self-esteem and made her realize that she was still an attractive woman, despite her husband's behavior towards her. Amazingly, she stayed with her spouse and continued to have a good sex life with him—at least he was good in bed. She also did a lot of salsa dancing, developing a whole new circle of friends.

Dating After Infidelity

Have an affair, and you will find that your life will be full of irony. Your relationship with your new lover is likely to be similar to your husband's relationship with his mistress—all shiny and new, uncluttered by the baggage that always accrues in a long-term relationship. You are both on best behavior with your extramarital partners, without the warts-and-all face revealed to your spouse. If your husband asks you to do something for him, you may well want to tell him to fuck off, because his demand comes on top of everything else he has expected you to do in the past, plus the fact that you are pissed off with him for cheating on you. If your new lover gives you a similar request, off you trot joyfully to do it for him.

Everyone has their own unique collection of anecdotes and quirky opinions that sound fascinating when heard for the first time, but to hear your spouse telling one of those stories for the hundredth time commands as much interest as being put on hold by tech support. Once the sparkly passionate stage of your affair is over, you have no guarantees that it will last or that in the long run, the man would be any more suitable for you than your wandering husband. For example, if he is willing to go out with a married woman, what does that say about his views on monogamy? Is he seeing other women besides you, and if so, how does that make you feel? Some might say, "Better the devil you know..."

Still on the subject of the devil you know, having an affair with a former lover has some advantages over dating someone brand new. You will have shared history together. He will be more of a known quantity rather than a complete stranger—at the very least, he is unlikely to be an ax murderer. However, if you have not seen each other for a long time, a previous boyfriend is unlikely to be quite the same person he was years ago, and neither are you. In addition, you should also remember why your relationship did not last in the first place. The two of you may have incompatibilities you have forgotten about that begin to surface once you spend more time together.

If you are having an affair, resist the urge to blab too much about your husband or your marital problems. Your new beau will not want to deal with all the baggage. Try to make the relationship about you and your lover, not about the state of your marriage. If you show him your whole life too early in the relationship, the bad side as well as the good, it is rather like when Dorothy peers behind the curtain and discovers that the Wizard of Oz is just an ordinary little man and not a wizard at all. To put it bluntly, maybe that fascinating sex goddess you might have seemed to your new boyfriend now becomes just another screwed-up, neurotic female.

Joanne began an affair with Evan shortly after discovering her husband's various infidelities. Everything seemed to be going swimmingly, until she decided to share some very specific details of her marital problems with her lover. Evan had seemed very supportive of the difficulties that she was going through and appeared to be much more critical of her husband than she was herself, to the extent that, without thinking of the consequences, Joanne found herself defending her shitbag spouse. It was all just too much for Evan and too early in their relationship. Much to her great sadness, the affair ended.

Just as things may be absolutely wonderful when your affair is going well, do not forget that if the relationship falters, you may feel like hell. You have most likely already been there and done that, haven't you? Isn't that how you felt when you first found out that you were not the only woman that your husband was sleeping with? If your lover dumps you, it will be yet another blow to your fragile ego. If you are no longer happy with your extramarital fling and want to ditch your lover, that will not make you feel too peachy either. Then off you may want to go to find yourself a replacement, and the cycle will begin all over again.

The STD Jungle of Dating

As you venture forth to seek a lover, bear in mind that it is an STD jungle out there. For example, HIV is far more common in older people than is generally believed. According to the Centers for Disease Control (CDC), in 2012 about a quarter of the estimated 1.2 million people infected with HIV living in the United States were aged 55 and older (http://www.cdc.gov/hiv/group/age/olderamericans/index.html). An editorial published in the *Student British Medical Journal* in 2012 reported that more than 80 percent of people in the 50 to 90 age range were sexually active and over the past decade cases of STDs had more than doubled in this age group (http://student.bmj.com/student/view-article.html?id=sbmj.e688). According to both the CDC in the United States and government sources in the United Kingdom, cases of HIV, syphilis, chlamydia, and gonorrhea have risen dramatically among 45 to 64 year-olds.

There are numerous reasons for this. Older people are less likely than the young to discuss sexual habits with their doctors. Seniors also tend to be less aware of the risks of HIV (or any other STDs) and do not know how to protect themselves. They are less likely to get tested as the symptoms can be confused with the signs of normal aging. Women past menopause are unlikely to have their partners use condoms since there is no danger of pregnancy. ED drugs make older married men much more likely to indulge in philandering. Having an unfaithful husband and/or getting divorced can put a long-monogamous woman back into the dating game quite unaware of the STDs to which she might be exposed.

Andrew was married but wanted to see other women. He told his wife she could find a lover too. After doing so, she found herself infected with herpes. As a result, Andrew refused to have sex with her even with a condom, and the couple separated.

If you are a baby boomer, you cannot have any more children. So you do not need to use contraceptives to prevent getting pregnant. Yet if you want to have sex with anyone these days, it is safest to ask the man to use a condom. Bummer! Maybe the last time a guy used one with you was when you were a teenager and it felt like you were having sex with a plastic bag. Thankfully, now the things are much thinner.

I went to my local drugstore to check condoms out. I got sticker shock—more than a buck a fuck! Those ultrathin condoms are really expensive. And then what is the difference between the thin, the ultrathin and the microthin? I assumed that since microthin was the most expensive it must be the thinnest. I noticed the condoms that were thin rather than ultrathin were on a clearance sale. People obviously were not interested in having sex using the thicker condoms. Of course, they never label a condom as thick because if they did, nobody would buy it in the first place. I chuckled when I saw that the large ultrathin condoms were also on clearance. Obviously, there were not enough big dicks in the area for large condoms to sell well at the drugstore. These days, they seem to be one size fits all. This prevents men from the embarrassment of being seen buying small or large condoms.

Online Dating: Communication Breakdown?

Many relationships with the opposite sex these days begin online via dating websites, instant messaging, emails, Facebook, tweeting, and so on. In many ways it can be a cold and abbreviated way to communicate, at times too formal, at other times too loose and careless. Talking on the phone is a little better because there is more back-and-forth chatting. You can hear the nuance and tone behind what is being said. However, there is no substitute for face-to-face communication. You cannot see how a guy is feeling or read between the lines of what he says unless you can see his face. If your relationship has become physical, online or over the phone you cannot give him a hug or a kiss, always a good way to clear up any potential misunderstandings right away that can fester if you are not getting enough face time together.

Most people are unaware of exactly how much information they subconsciously glean from the micro-expressions on another person's face. These are very difficult to fake and are more or less standard across cultures. Malcolm Gladwell wrote a fascinating article on this subject entitled "The Naked Face" for *The New Yorker* magazine (http://gladwell.com/the-naked-face/). It explains why there is no substitute for face-to-face communication to understand someone. It is not the words being said that you or he may be reacting to. Body language and facial expressions can take place in microseconds, yet convey on the subconscious level a wealth of information about affection, impatience, contempt, happiness, sadness or fear.

In addition, there are many things you might be willing to say in person that you would not want to put in writing online. You may only be comfortable expressing your feelings verbally when the other person is right there next to you. You can receive immediate feedback to what you are saying so that you do not put your foot in your mouth and blunder into the abyss. In terms of privacy, the only form of communication for which you can be sure there is no electronic evidence is face-to-face conversation, provided that there are no recording devices nearby.

There are numerous success stories of people finding their husbands and wives through online dating. These sites are certainly convenient—you can list exactly what you are looking for and man shop from your laptop. For those seeking extramarital affairs, there are numerous websites such as ashleymadison.com and illicitencounters.com. For these two sites, aside from viewing profiles, for which there is no charge, men have to pay to play but women do not. What does that remind you of? It might cost about the same for a guy to get himself a call girl, and then sex would be guaranteed.

At their best, dating websites can find you great companions or even true love; at their worst they can be a minefield of deception and humiliation. It is important to be cautious and protect your personal safety. Avoid publishing very specific details about your life online, such as information that someone could use to track you down in person. It is always best to meet only in public places until you are sure that you want to take things further. You have no references on the guy from trusted friends, and no way to be sure he is being truthful in his online profile. Even if he is not an out-and-out liar, he still has to do a sales job, promoting the hell out of his good points and brushing anything negative under the carpet. You have most likely have done the same with your own online persona.

Rachel and David were married in a traditional Jewish ceremony. They had a beautiful house in an expensive part of London and three fine children. For two decades, everything appeared to be perfect until David dropped a bombshell—he was leaving Rachel to move in with his secretary. After the divorce, Rachel tried online dating and found Chris, a working-class London cab driver from the East End. Despite the fact that they came from very different cultural and religious backgrounds, they hit it off well right from the start, and after dating for a while decided to tie the knot.

Rupert had a very different experience with online dating. He was in his mid-50s and his wife had left him for another man. The women he met seemed sad and desperate. He found the whole process of online dating to be rather meaningless and depressing. Sometimes a woman would have sex with him on the first or second date, "I didn't feel good about it. I didn't feel that I had a right to be there. She was throwing away her ace card on the first night. If she was willing to do this with me when she hardly knew me, she'd do it with anyone. That's not the basis of a long-term relationship. A girl having sex with a guy right away shows him that she doesn't really value herself. She's fearful that she needs to do it to get another date, but if that's the only reason he will see her again, he's a pretty worthless prospect."

If you are seeking to hook up with another man while still married, are you going to admit that you have a husband? Many wives in your position pretend they are single. Obviously, it's much easier to do this through on-line dating rather than within your existing community, as in many ways you are completely anonymous online, whereas most people you normally mix with would already know that you are married. However, if you begin a relationship with someone on the basis of that big a lie, you are treating the new man badly and flirting with disaster. If you feel that your husband has deeply betrayed you by having an affair, why would you think it would be acceptable behavior to lie to a new lover about the fact that you are married? Many women, single or married, also underestimate their age in their on-line profile, especially because many men say they are looking for younger women. Nevertheless, if you find a man you really like online, sooner or later you will have to come clean about any fiction you have written to create your web persona and your deception may be a deal-breaker for him.

There are many other ways to meet guys apart from online dating sites. Some women go to bars and clubs, but a better way is to find an activity you enjoy and use it as a way to make new friends, whether it is a tango class or a hiking group. Bars and clubs can be highly sexual environments that are not conducive to taking the time to get to know someone before jumping into the sack with them. The next morning you may wake up with a stranger in your bed plus a hangover and wonder what the hell you were thinking.

Can't You Be a Cougar?

It is commonplace for a cheating husband to have an affair with a much younger woman. So what about the opposite situation, when the wife is much older than her lover? Dream on, would-be cougars—older women going out with much younger men are much rarer than old men with young women, especially in the Third World but also in developed nations. Nevertheless, this situation does happen. It may occur because the woman looks much younger than her chronological age. Sometimes a younger man will prey on a lonely older woman to gain financial benefit, perhaps even persuading her to rewrite her will and leave him all her assets. It is a common scenario that the older woman has status or money that outweighs the disadvantages of her age when trying to attract a younger man. Then she is likely to find plenty of suitors. In 2002, at the age of 69, actress Joan Collins married 37-year-old Percy Gibson. He was her sixth husband and 31 years younger. The actress Mae West, whose career spanned seven decades, had a relationship with a muscleman 30 years her junior that lasted 26 years till her death at the age of 87. She is famously misquoted as saying, "Why don't you come up and see me some time, big boy?" The actual quote was "Why don't you come up sometime and see me?" from Mae West's character, the scandalous Diamond Lil, in the 1933 film *She Done Him Wrong*. Its racy themes led to tough censorship of American movies. Mae West has also been credited with the wonderful quote, "Is that a gun in your pocket, or are you just glad to see me?"

However, in many ways, Mae West and Joan Collins are anomalies. Women often lose interest in sex as they age (just as do many men) or after having kids. Reggie had two long-term marriages, one right after the other, to women who were considerably older. Both of these relationships ended with several years of celibacy. Declared Reggie, "Of course I wasn't happy with that, but I still stayed faithful. Let's just say I masturbated a lot. But now I'm only going to date girls who are younger than me or at the very least the same age."

Nevertheless, many elderly women remain sexually active, or want to be so, if they can find themselves suitable partners. Hence the following comment from an older gentleman who was very leery of moving to a re-tirement community. With an alarmed expression on his face, he declared, "No man is safe in an old folk's home!"

Men—single and married—may like to have affairs with married women who are older than them because that it enables these guys to have uncommitted relationships without having to worry about her wanting to set up a home with him or make babies. Sometimes the relationship may be a rite of passage where a mature woman will teach a young man about sex and mentor him about how to behave in relationships. "I was 22 and ex-cruciatingly embarrassed to still be a virgin," said Malcolm. "An attractive local waitress in her 40s took pity on me and gently brought me to her bed. She was married and I knew that it was not going to be permanent, but I still feel eternally grateful to her all these years later."

In *The Graduate,* a comedy-drama from 1967, Dustin Hoffman plays a recent college graduate seduced by an older woman, Mrs. Robinson, played by Anne Bancroft. He then falls in love with her daughter, and Mrs. Robinson does whatever she can to keep them from being together. This is one of the most famous movies of all time about a cougar, and it is interesting to note that it paints her in an extremely negative light.

Ageism is alive and kicking in Western culture—movies show plenty of explicit sex involving nubile young women. While some of this fucking may involve older men, very few films will show older women bonking in the buff. No one wants to watch a middle-aged or elderly female making out. They are considered totally unattractive. It is similar to the way kids tend to be revolted by the idea of their parents making love, in the belief that it is only for the young and beautiful.

Saying the L Word

Do you expect your lover to express his love for you? The L word can press as many buttons as the F word. Many men will flee rather than say "I love you," even if they're very fond of the woman concerned, as the L word brings up all the pain, humiliation and rejection they may have suffered from earlier liaisons. In addition, if you are still married, particularly if you intend to stay that way, your lover may feel that his relationship with you can never go anywhere and thus he will not express any heartfelt emotions. A woman is much more likely to be willing to reveal feelings of love to someone. However, if she is not sure that he feels the same way, she is making herself very vulnerable to getting hurt by rejection, perhaps scaring him off by making the relationship seem more serious to her than it is to him. He may not be ready to make the emotional commitment she wants. So if you have followed your unfaithful husband's example and are having an affair yourself, however you might feel, avoid telling a new lover that you love him. It is likely to put too much pressure on him and make him want to bolt. How do you know that it is true love anyway? Most likely it is too soon to tell. Perhaps it is just lust or the romantic newness of the relationship that will wear off soon enough. Just because he is brilliant in bed and wonderful for your self-esteem does not make the guy your soul mate.

The connection between love and pain is not just a modern phenomenon. According to Buddhism, a religion that has been around for more than 2,000 years, attachment, which includes worldly love, causes suffering. This includes the pain of that love not being reciprocated, or if it is, the fear of losing that love. These sentiments permeate the 16th century Elizabethan Courtly Love tradition and the songs of the Baroque period. John Dowland's song from 1597, "Come Again: Sweet Love Doth Now Invite," includes these cheerful lyrics:

> *For now left and forlorn,*
> *I sit, I sigh, I weep, I faint, I die*
> *In deadly pain and endless misery.*

The phrase "I die" has a double meaning here—at that time it meant to have an orgasm, also referred to as *le petit mort,* a French phrase meaning "the little death." Modern folks might see the double meaning somewhere else—in the song's title "Come Again." A Baroque piece, "Per la Gloria D'Adorarvi" composed by Giovanni Battista Bononchini in 1722 includes the words *Amando penero, ma sempre v'amero* which roughly translated means "Loving you brings me pain, but I will still always love you." One

Group Sex

© 2016 C. J. Grace. Artwork by Aaron Austin, concepts by C. J. Grace.

reason they sang about all this melancholia over love at that time is that it was a relatively free and prosperous period. Earlier in history, people had to put all their energy into finding food, shelter, and keeping themselves from falling foul of the Church and secular leaders rather than musing about their relationship problems.

If you end up falling head over heels for your man on the side, you have a new issue to work out. Should you leave your husband for him? When you are still in the passionate, in-lust stage, it is very difficult to be sure if he will really be the right match for you once the initial sexual intensity has worn off. You may think it is true love, the best lovemaking you have ever experienced, the closest connection you have ever felt. But is it love or just short-term infatuation? The relationship may make you feel like a teenager again, with all the highs and lows, but most likely now you are in your 40s, 50s, 60s or even 70s! The safest way to navigate this situation might be to hold off walking into the sunset with lover boy until you have given yourself plenty of time to really get to know him well. You may ask, "What is plenty of time?" There is no definitive answer. Maybe six months, maybe a year, maybe two. The problem is that throughout your trial period with your lover, will you be able to keep your relationship going smoothly with your husband? Then if your lover wants you to leave your spouse, how long will he be willing to wait for you to make the decision?

Having an Affair When You Stay Married

On the surface, it may appear to be a perfect compromise: my husband is having an affair, so I will have one too. We can still stay together and have the same kind of intimacy we had before. Well, maybe yes, maybe no. After finding out about your husband's affair, when you and your husband are in bed together, you may be conscious of his lover in some way being there too, chipping away at the closeness and passion of your lovemaking. Once you take a new lover, he will also take up some of your mental space when you are in bed with your husband—in a much more detailed and concrete way than any thoughts you might have about your husband's mistress. You may imagine how your husband is when he is fucking the other woman. You will know exactly what sex is like with your new lover, and all kinds of comparisons between him and your spouse in bed will be hard to get out of your head. In effect, there are now four rather than three people in that bed. However, now it is an even number, and you are no longer the odd man—or rather woman—out.

You may be able to have one affair that does not seem to affect your sexual relationship with your spouse at all, but this may not be the case with your next lover. If you are not having much sex with your husband it may not be a concern, but if you are still enjoying a good sexual relationship with him despite his philandering, it most certainly does matter. So having affairs can be a slippery slope for women who want to stay with their husbands. You may have simply replaced one less-than-perfect scenario with another—instead of making love with your husband while wishing that he had not also been doing the same thing with someone else, you may end up in bed with your husband wishing that your lover was there instead.

Diane had decided to remain married to her husband, Earnest, despite his infidelity. He was not willing to give up his mistress, but Diane and Earnest still enjoyed lovemaking with each other. Diane then began an affair with an old flame, and found that he was so much better in bed than her husband that she no longer wanted to have sex with him. Earnest's body had grown foreign to her. She was now uncomfortable being naked around him, turning away from him when she was changing. He began to feel like a stranger. Divorce soon followed.

Emily's way to cope with finding out that her husband had a serious relationship going with someone else was to reconnect with someone she had dated when she was single. That affair ended up becoming more intense than she had expected, and it left her unable to really enjoy sex with her husband. He was an engineer who worked with a lot of heavy machinery, and now his sexual techniques felt heavy-handed in a way that they had never felt before. Her body just would not respond. This was a real quandary for her as she still had feelings for him and did not want a divorce. Her new clean-shaven, magic-tongued lover was amazingly good at oral sex. Previously, she had quite enjoyed it with her husband, but now his beard felt like sandpaper. Of course, he was not willing to shave off his beard. Ironically, her tactless twit of a husband let slip that he preferred oral sex with the other woman, as she had got rid of all her pubic hair with a "Brazilian" bikini wax job!

Mathilda's extramarital experimentations were more successful. She was able to have a no-strings-attached fling with an attractive younger man she met at the local supermarket, following joking and then increasingly flirtatious comments about the contents of each other's shopping cart. The affair was invigorating and fun, and best of all, did not affect her ability to enjoy lovemaking with her philandering husband. Will you be like Emily or Mathilda? You will not be able to know the answer to that question until you are actually having an extramarital affair.

Nonetheless, for older women, an affair may make you discover that your body is not as worn out you had thought. Kathy, in her late 50s, enjoyed a good sex life with her husband, Robert, but they always needed to use lubrication. Then Robert's affair spurred her to follow suit. Kathy had thought she was too old for someone to find her body attractive, but her new lover thought she was really sexy and had no qualms about telling her that she was beautiful. It was decades since she had heard anything like that from her husband. She needed no lubrication at all with her new lover, and realized she had been dry because Robert had simply not taken the time to turn her on enough.

If you are lucky enough to have found a man who is a better in bed than your husband, it is bad manners to talk about comparisons. Just tell your boyfriend that he is a great lover. Do not burden him with tales of how dreadful sex has been with your husband. Is that what you want your lover to look forward to if the relationship continues? Perhaps the sex was a lot better earlier in your marriage and went sour over time. Then, even if you are in the middle of a screaming row with your husband and you hate his guts, do not hit him below the belt by declaring that he is lousy in bed and that you have found someone else who is much better. He will neither forget nor forgive you for this insult. It might have serious repercussions later and make him much more difficult to deal with, whether you want to stay or you want a divorce.

Should You Tell Him You Are Having an Affair?

It sounds straightforward: he is seeing another woman and does not want to give her up; neither you nor your spouse wants a divorce, so you decide to have an affair too and let him know about it. You tell yourself: everything is out in the open; we can be perfectly honest with each other; and it will do wonders for the marriage. Unfortunately, this may not necessarily be the case. He might react very negatively to your affair, despite the fact that he wants you to put up with his. This is where a double standard is likely to surface—no matter what he tells you about being open-minded, generally a husband will not tolerate his wife bonking another man. So do not expect your husband to be consistent in putting up with behavior from you that he expects you to accept from him. If he finds out that you have a lover, he may react with rage and decide to end the marriage. You may not want to do that, especially not on his terms and within his time frame rather than yours. At the very least, your revelations may make him much more blatant in his philandering, claiming that you have given him carte blanche to do exactly what he wants. "Well, you're seeing someone else too," he might say. "So you're a hypocrite to complain about me."

When Penny found out about the mistress her husband, Frank, had been seeing for several years, he was not particularly contrite. He wanted to stay with Penny, but had no desire whatsoever to give up the other woman. "I don't believe that human beings are naturally monogamous," Frank declared gamely. "You're very welcome to have an affair too if you like. I don't mind at all." What he should have added was that he would not mind at all if he knew absolutely nothing about his wife's affair. When Penny took him up on the offer and openly began a passionate affair, Frank was consumed with jealousy and simply could not handle it. Perhaps he had initially thought that Penny was too monogamous by nature to have sex with someone else and would never take up his proposal; or once he knew about her lover, Frank might have thought that he would lose her to another man. Frank and Penny ended up splitting and neither of their extramarital relationships survived for very long. What was sauce for the goose was definitely not sauce for the gander. It was not clear whether the marriage would have lasted if Penny had kept her affair secret, or if she would have been happy to stay with Frank had she never learned about his mistress in the first place.

It is important to be sure of your motives if you do decide to come clean. Perhaps you hope to cultivate a more honest and balanced relationship with your husband, or you simply do not like lying. Alternatively, you may want to spill the beans out of revenge and in effect tell him "screw you!"

However, acting out of vengeance may bring you rapidly to an unpleasant, acrimonious parting with your husband that is not in your best interests.

Jenny began a torrid relationship with a former boyfriend after finding out that her husband, Ben, had a mistress whom he refused to stop seeing. Jenny's friends wanted her to tell him about her affair and rub it in his face. "That'll show the bastard—he'll be sorry he messed you around." But Jenny decided to keep quiet about her boyfriend as Ben had a strong personality and would not take it well. Until she was sure that she wanted to end the marriage, she knew that her husband would be much easier to deal with that way. Ben was being loving and conciliatory towards her because he knew that he was the guilty party. Jenny was convinced that his attitude would change dramatically if he knew she had a lover.

However, the lack of trust and betrayal you felt when you discovered his affair is what he may experience if he finds out about yours. He has not been honest with you, and now you are not being honest with him either. This is not the ideal foundation for a secure, loving marital relationship. If you do not tell your husband about your other man, it will put yet another wall between you and your husband. It may add to the things you no longer want to talk about together to avoid getting into arguments. You will not be able to communicate with each other as intimately as before.

You also should be aware that your lover might not be very discreet about your affair, even if you tell him not to reveal what is going on to anyone. He may discuss it with mutual friends, or publicly brag about it. If he is jealous of your husband and/or does not want to have to compete with him over you, he may even tell your husband about the affair or deliberately create a situation where he will find out in the hope that this will cause the breakup of your marriage. Mistresses play this game too.

Aside from hearing about it from a loose-lipped lover, is your husband likely to suspect that you are following in his adulterous footsteps? That depends on the kind of person he is. If he has a jealous nature, he will pick up every tiny clue and magnify its importance. However, many men are too oblivious and self-absorbed to even notice. "I dropped massive hints," said Cassandra, "I'd throw back at him some of the language he'd used to justify his affairs. But he had no clue. It was as if he could not imagine the boring old wife in the kitchen would be sexually appealing to another guy." You too may have been just as oblivious to his philandering. Daphne had her nose to the grindstone, taking care of the kids, looking after the house and running a home business too. "Everyone else seemed to know my husband had been womanizing for years. Apparently, it was perfectly obvious to all, but I just didn't notice until he told me he was going to leave me for his latest mistress."

If you are keeping your affair secret, you need to plan your cover-ups and alibis well, just as your husband was doing before he was aware that you knew about his extramarital activities—yet more irony. You may find out that you are a terrible liar. So, for example, you will need to work out ahead of time what to say if he walks in on you while you are emailing or talking on the phone with your lover. In addition, there are some telltale signs of being, as the Brits would say, well-rogered—having been thoroughly well fucked by your lover. You might need to damp down those signs a little if you do not want your husband to suspect what you are up to. They include:

- Breaking into song.
- Laughing or smiling for no apparent reason (because you are thinking about something funny that happened with your lover).
- Laughing or smiling when reading an email or text from your lover.
- Being in an irrepressibly good mood (when most likely previously, as a result of your husband's philandering, you were in either a grump or feeling really down).
- Bouncing with energy.

Of course, if you suspect your husband is having an affair, but you have no proof, you might want to see if he is exhibiting any of these signs of having indulged in some torrid sex.

Should You Have an Open Relationship?

According to Tibetan Buddhism, the root cause of suffering is ignorance. However, in the West we have ingrained conditioning and expectations about the ideal relationship being lifelong monogamy—living happily ever after and so on. It is a rare couple that can handle a completely open relationship. More often than not, ignorance is bliss. Most people, men and women alike, even if they themselves are straying, do not like the idea of their partner sharing a bed with another. What the eye does not see, the heart does not grieve over, so it might be better to kiss and not tell.

Often it is the husband who pushes what he describes as an open relationship onto the wife. He does not want to bother with all the hassle of having to see the other woman secretly. Maybe he will spin the situation to emphasize how honest he is being towards his wife, making out that he is such a nice guy to share what is going on rather than being deceitful. But if it is not completely consensual—and by that I mean that the wife is 100 percent OK with everything her husband is doing—it is not really an open relationship, and yes, he is a slime bucket rather than a nice guy. His unilateral, "like it or lump it" behavior that he just happens to have informed you about is by no stretch of the imagination consensual.

One of the women I interviewed told me a story about a Tibetan meditation teacher, with whom she had studied in the past. He and his Nepalese wife, both now deceased, had managed to maintain a very loving and respectful open relationship. The wife had traveled with him on all his trips until she became a very sought-after translator for other teachers from Tibet and had her own very busy travel schedule. So if she could not accompany her husband because she had other engagements, another woman who was a good friend of the wife would go with him instead, and they would be sexual partners during the trip. Nevertheless, the wife remained the husband's soul mate and the love of his life.

Patrick was a compulsive womanizer, yet when his wife, Arlene, complained about his other women, in his eyes she just became the jealous bitch. He claimed that he would never be jealous if Arlene had any lovers. Yet his actions belied his words. When at a party the couple happened to see a man whom she had dated before her marriage, Patrick got into a heated political argument with him. The true cause of the acrimony was not political differences—it was the fact that Patrick resented this guy for having had a sexual relationship with Arlene. It was the same story when one of Patrick's former mistresses came to visit their home with her new boyfriend in tow. Patrick's keen dislike of her current lover had a strong edge of sexual jealousy to it.

Sexual jealousy is indeed rampant among primates, creating aggressive, violent behavior. However, Richard Wrangham and Dale Peterson in their book, *Demonic Males: Apes and the Origins of Human Violence* (Hougton Mifflin, 1996), describe one rare pacifist primate among all the aggressors: the muriqui, a little-known monkey from Brazil that has an easygoing, friendly attitude towards sex. The females pick their partners at will and mate in full view of several males, bonking from six to eighteen minutes— about the same amount of time as many humans would spend doing the same activity. Sounds like those mellow monkeys know how to have a good time. So if you and your husband want to have a truly open relationship, to keep it peaceful and harmonious the pair of you need to be muriquis at heart rather than gorillas or chimpanzees.

Unless you want a messy, acrimonious parting of ways with your spouse, it is recommended that you do not—as they say in the vernacular—shit in your own backyard as regards your behavior if you have a lover of your own. If you are seeing him in the turf you share with your husband, the pair of you should be as discreet as possible, with no public displays of affection. Try to rise above any vengeful feelings you might have to stick it to your adulterous husband by making him lose face in this way, even if he is aware of your affair. However, if your spouse is very public about his mistress(es) and claims to be fine with you having other relationships, the rules of how you should behave may be quite different. Acceptable etiquette around the subject of spouses and their affairs is at best a continual work in progress and at worst a minefield. You are unlikely to find advice for this situation in any of Miss Manners' etiquette books.

Leo and Helena were married and had been in an open relationship for many years. They lived together in Helena's large house near the beach in Puerta Vallarta, Mexico. She took care of everything for him. Leo would have sexual relationships with women in other locations where he was traveling for his work. Then he met a younger woman, Lorraine, whom he got pregnant, and the three of them all lived together in Helena's house. Leo was the only one truly happy with this arrangement. Helena accepted Leo's other women by seeing them as a vehicle for her personal growth, declaring that so long as there was awareness, honesty and respect in her relationship with Leo, nothing else mattered. Yet the situation clearly gave Helena no joy. She was monogamous by nature and uninterested in having sex with other men. Helena had no desire to form a close friendship with Lorraine, with whom she felt she had nothing in common. Lorraine was laboring under the misapprehension that having Leo's child would make him leave Helena and be only with her. The household became increasingly unstable, and eventually Lorraine, desperately unhappy, moved out, taking her baby son with her.

Genuinely open long-term relationships tend to be more common among couples who are just living together rather than those who choose to get married. There is no need for that pesky marriage vow promising to be a loving and faithful husband or wife, and you do not have to wear a ring to show the world that you are already taken.

Are Human Beings Naturally Monogamous?

Open relationships work best if all parties involved are inherently non-monogamous. "Monogamy is a form of slavery if it doesn't arise naturally," one adulterous male declared to me. Of course, a woman having to put up with an adulterous husband might feel that she too is in servitude. She is stuck in the unenviable position of wanting to stay married but hating that her dearly beloved is fucking others.

Another polyamorous partner put it this way: "I'm happily married, but I don't subscribe to the idea that my wife has exclusive ownership over me or my body. I don't own her either. I don't believe that a lover is just an object to be possessed." Noble-sounding sentiments, but only if that wife unreservedly and wholeheartedly feels the same way. Problems will almost always arise if one partner in a relationship believes in monogamy, and the other does not.

In *Religions of Star Trek* (Westview Press, 2001)—I kid you not, this book exists—the authors describe how sexual morality and the treatment of women evolve in the later incarnations of this franchise. Everyone praises Gene Rodenberry, the show's creator, for his farsightedness in casting a black female as Lieutenant Uhuru, the Communications Officer on the Enterprise. Nevertheless, in the original 1960s *Star Trek* TV series the red-blooded Captain Kirk had a "love 'em and leave 'em" attitude towards women, and nobody expected him to be monogamous. The YouTube clip "How to kiss a woman by Captain Kirk" (https://www.youtube.com/watch?v=iip1viwCfLg) shows him giving a green-haired girl a long, deep-throated kiss, and then he knocks her out. Yes, he only punches her in the face to escape a jail cell, but even so, today the scene seems wonderfully politically incorrect. Broadcast on network television more than 20 years later than the original series, *Star Trek: The Next Generation* tended to portray relationships between a man and a woman as much more monogamous, stable and egalitarian to suit modern Western sensibilities. For example, *Religions of Star Trek* describes an episode from 1993 entitled "The Inner Light" where Captain Picard experiences living as a faithful, loving husband and father on a dying planet. Unlike his virile predecessor, Jean-Luc Picard does not tend to boldly go from blonde to blonde (or even from one green-haired girl to another).

It may not be politically correct to say this in the West, but women are inherently more monogamous than men. Many Western women feel that exclusivity is necessary for intimacy. To feel comfortable naked with someone and surrender to orgasm usually requires that you can truly open up to and trust your partner. You need to feel safe rather than vulnerable. If you are aware that he is also having sex with someone else, particularly if he has a strong emotional connection to that person, it puts those feelings of safety and trust in serious jeopardy. The total security of knowing that he has chosen you as his one and only true love is lost.

There is no doubt that far more men than women use extramarital dating sites to solicit uncommitted sex outside wedlock. The best known— some might say the most notorious—is ashleymadison.com. At the time of writing, it was operating in more than 30 countries, with the slogan, "Life is short. Have an affair." The company fell from grace when hackers leaked the personal data of more than 30 million users in August 2015, allegedly resulting in blackmail threats and suicides. Numerous men in various public positions have resigned from their posts because their emails appeared on the hacked list. A massive class action lawsuit is pending against the website's parent company, AvidLife Media. Ashley Madison's CEO, Noel Biderman, had claimed that the site's users were 30 percent women to 70 percent men overall, with equal numbers of males and females in the under 30 age range. However, the hacked data seemed to show that only 15 percent of users were women, adding fuel to long-standing allegations about the site using fake female profiles to lure men in. Caitlin Dewey reported on this story in *The Washington Post* on August 25, 2015 (https://www.washingtonpost.com/news/the-intersect/wp/2015/08/25/ashley-madison-faked-female-profiles-to-lure-men-in-hacked-data-suggest).

As a result, Ashley Madison has faced additional class action litigation over "fembot" fraud claims.

No doubt polyamory groups may exist with hordes of sexy female members. Nevertheless, this was not the case for a polyamory meetup group I found on the internet. The organization touted the benefits of a sex- and body-positive lifestyle in a supportive, open environment. Sadly, the most recent discussion meeting they had organized attracted only five people looking to develop a polyamory network—all male, apart from the organizer's +1 participant who I assumed was female. Women were not flocking in to expand their horizons of love.

The bestseller, *Sex at Dawn*, by Christopher Ryan and Cacilda Jetha (Harper Perennial, 2010), posits that both sexes are naturally prone to wanting multiple partners. The book claims that when a hunter-gatherer society became an agricultural one, individual property and inheritance issues became important and led to an imposition of monogamy, particularly as regards women. However, Lynn Saxton's book, *Sex at Dusk* (CreateSpace Independent Publishing, 2012), a book written purely to refute the claims in *Sex at Dawn*, makes a convincing case of that book having cherry-picked information. Saxton explains in detail how biologically, a male is driven to impregnate as many females as he can to spread his genes as far as possible, while females, in order to successfully rear their children, want to find one reliable male for support and protection. These are not compatible desires.

In many parts of the world today, women, as the physically weaker sex, are second-class citizens, in some cases having little more status than livestock. Throughout history, especially in the Middle and Far East, powerful men have had multiple wives and concubines. In ancient China, for example, Taoists saw monogamy as just one form of many ways that sexual relationships could be organized.

The few examples of polyandry tend to come from impoverished communities where there are either shortages of women or where brothers have to band together to be able to jointly afford to buy themselves a wife. Usually the woman has little choice in the matter. For example, in *The Good Women of China* (Pantheon Books, 2002), author Xinran describes the women of Shouting Hill, a poverty-stricken area in northwest China, where brothers from extremely poor families with no females to barter cannot get a wife of their own. Instead, they buy a common wife to continue the family line. Her life is exceedingly arduous.

Monogamy per se does not guarantee a good relationship. Florence left her philanderer husband, Andy, for James, who was loving and faithful but somewhat emotionally volatile. She had simply traded one set of problems for another. Every man comes with some kind of baggage, as do you. The problem arises when you think you can change him, rather than accepting him for the kind of person he is, and being able to live with that.

In 2014, gleeden.com, an extramarital dating website popular in France, commissioned an online poll on infidelity from the Institute Francais d'Opinion Publique. When looking at such surveys, the saying that tends to come to my mind is, "There are lies, damned lies and statistics." Vast numbers of surveys by commercial organizations are designed to come up with results that benefit them, drawing conclusions from thin or skewed data. Nevertheless, this poll came up with findings about Gallic infidelity that are entertaining to look at. Using a sample of about 800 people in France, it found that 55 percent of men and 32 percent of women admitted being unfaithful, a rate that has increased since the 1970s. More left-leaning than right-wing voters acknowledged their infidelity. Were lefties really more likely to stray or were they simply more honest in admitting to it? It was possible to love their partner while being unfaithful to that person, said 63 percent of French couples surveyed, yet 68 percent of those polled believed it was possible to stay faithful to one person for one's entire life. So some of the same people must have answered "Yes" to both of these questions. However, "possible" is a very vague word. Does it mean "likely" or that "there is a chance, but only a small chance?" Were the participants talking about themselves or some arbitrary random person? Perhaps the study shows that in France there is hope for monogamy as well as simultaneously being in love with two people at once; or maybe the study does not show that at all. I will leave you to decide.

So are you naturally and inherently monogamous? If you experiment by having an affair, you may find the answer to that question is viscerally obvious. Can you really like or even love more than one man at a time? Can you enjoy sex equally with each one? Do you find that nobody can compare to what you had (or maybe still have) with your spouse? If you are in lust with the lover, are you no longer interested in making love with your husband because you want to be monogamous with the new guy? You may be surprised and shocked by your answers to these questions.

Ashley began an affair after she found out about her husband's long-time mistress. Although the couple stayed married, they stopped having sex with each other and instead were monogamous with their other partners. Ashley found that she was no longer bothered at all by the fact that her spouse had a mistress. She found her boyfriend much more appealing than her husband in bed.

There are infinite ways that your affair might play out. At worst, you could be setting yourself up for more heartbreak and disappointment. At best, your extramarital relationship could open new horizons and bring joy into your life. It might make you happy to stay in your marriage or make it obvious that you should leave. Just as your marriage was never the same after you found out about your husband's infidelity, once you start seeing another man, nothing will be quite the same as it was.

EPILOGUE

Fucker, fat cat fucker, philandering fucker, deceitful dog, lousy cheat, lousy shit, untrustworthy shit, total and utter shit, shitbag, douchebag, scumbag, sleazebag, two-timing sleazebag, horribly horny, humping husband, horndog, scoundrel, shabby scoundrel, dolt, callous cad, asshole, bugger, slippery SOB, slime bucket, tosser, tosspot, slimy rat, rotten ratbag, rogue, silly sod, schweinhund, chauvinistic ass, contemptible creature, loathsome pain in the ass, old plonker, old codger, old goat, horny goat, jerk, bastard, selfish bastard, tactless twit. Throughout this book, I have used terms like these to describe an adulterous husband. How could I hurl all this abuse at him, while still advising you to take the higher ground and not take revenge on your spouse? How could I paint such a pejorative picture of your promiscuous partner (wouldn't that phrase make a wonderful tongue twister?), yet at the same time say I am trying to show you how to find contentment if you decide to stay married to him? Even if you want to divorce him, is it a good idea to think about him in such negative terms?

Some of what I have written is meant to be tongue-in-cheek. After all, if you cannot laugh at the cosmic joke that your life may be, then you may end up crying. However, many of these insults may reflect the way you feel about him when you first hear about his infidelity. It can be therapeutic to let out some of the anger and negativity you feel by reading those insults, rather than blowing your relationship by actually throwing those terms at him. The fact is that you can still "kinda sorta" love your unfaithful man and want to stay with him, yet some of the time also think that he is a scoundrel or some of the other choice epithets I have used.

My writing background was as a journalist for BBC Radio, more years ago than I would care to admit. At that time, scripts had to be as objective as possible and based on facts rather than opinions (very different from what you will find in American current affairs programs nowadays). Overly emotive language was frowned upon, and you would only use expletives if you had a strong desire to be fired. In this book, I have found it very refreshing to be edgy, sarcastic and opinionated at times, and to be able to use the vernacular and plenty of swearwords. Though fairly Americanized from many years of living in the United States, I am still a Brit at heart. At this point, I will mention a 2013 survey by globalvisas.com on foreigners' attitudes towards the United Kingdom, which was widely reported in the British national press at the time. The survey found that the top three things that foreigners disliked about living in Britain were:

- Sarcasm—guilty as charged.
- Heavy drinking—not guilty, but I have British friends who, if they invite you for dinner, do not believe they have done a proper job of entertaining you unless you have a serious hangover the next day.
- The weather—not my fault.

I have had no qualms about being irreverent, as I have no interest at all in bowing to the constraints of current political correctness. One of my favorite examples of the nuttiness of this was the banning of a hilarious British advertisement for Marmite, a popular food spread, where spoof welfare teams rescue neglected pots of the stuff (https://www.youtube.com/watch?v=79-sFaeLVJg). This 2013 ad was deemed to be insulting to animal rescue officers.

Nevertheless, despite my political incorrectness and sarcasm, my hope is that you have found this book to be helpful and therapeutic, as well as giving you plenty of food for thought. In all the topics I have covered, you have to strike a balance between going with your initial gut feeling and giving yourself sufficient time to consider your options as rationally (rather than emotionally) as you can. Do not underestimate the validity of your initial opinions, whether they concern your husband, his mistress, a man with whom you are considering having an affair, and/or what you should do with your marriage and your life in general. Josh Waitzkin, author of *The Art of Learning: An Inner Journey to Optimal Performance* (Free Press, 2008), asserts that intuition is our most valuable compass, bridging the unconscious and the conscious mind. Human beings have a remarkable ability to come up with correct conclusions about various situations facing them, sometimes in a fraction of a second, frequently using subconscious cues outside their conscious awareness. Malcolm Gladwell eloquently describes this process as "thin-slicing" in his book *Blink* (Little, Brown & Co, 2005). Of course, bear in mind that some people are much better at thin-slicing than others.

Perhaps many people who read this book will find themselves saying, "That's me she's talking about." This is because so much of what adulterers and their wives undergo is universal.

I hope I do not share the fate of a writer friend of mine who lived in a small town in the Midwest. He once wrote a wonderful article about the natural progression of extramarital affairs from beginning to end. He included all the expressions that people involved in illicit relationships would tend to use to describe what they were going though. Published in a local magazine, the article was eagerly read by practically everyone in the whole town. People were fascinated by the piece, but the writer was shocked by the backlash. Numerous friends, relatives and acquaintances were furious. All were convinced that he was writing about their own affairs. How dare he break their confidences? How dare he publicize something that was so private and that could be so damaging to their marriages and their reputations? Some folks cut him off entirely and refused to have anything more to do with him. In fact, apart from just a few of them who were close friends, he was totally unaware that all these people were bonking on the side. He had taken great pains to ensure that he included nothing specific that might link anything he wrote to the few friends in the town whom he knew were having illicit relationships, but it was all to no avail. The adulterous townsfolk were convinced that features common to so many affairs applied to them alone.

It is still all too common for women to keep silent about physical abuse from their husbands. Wives also tend to stay silent about their husband's adultery, especially if they choose to stay in the marriage. Instead of marital infidelity being an embarrassing secret to keep hidden, I hope that this book will help bring the subject more out into the open, so that women no longer suffer in silence but instead are able to take charge of their circumstances as best they can.

I have endeavored to take as pragmatic an approach as possible on how to deal with adultery, rather than playing the blame game. The aim has been to provide some useful tools for wives with unfaithful husbands, so that these women can truly thrive rather than be crushed by the experience, whether or not they choose to stay in the marriage.

Did I Get It Right?

Adultery is a vast subject with many different aspects. Perhaps as you were reading this book, you felt that something important was missed out, or that a particular situation was not described in a way that you found relevant or accurate. If so, I would like to hear from you. Perhaps your suggestions will appear in a later edition of this book or a sequel—*Daughter of Adulterer's Wife*, perhaps.

If there were things I wrote about that really resonated with you, or that had a strong impact on how you were able to cope with your own relationship with an unfaithful man, please let me know. You may also want to expand on some of the points I have raised. The chapters you have read here cover a lot of ground. It is valuable for me to know what has worked and what has not.

A cousin of mine, in his mid-20s at the time of writing this, with the wonderful arrogance of youth, told me that he had had a lot of experience in relationships (yes, I can remember some of the doozies!) and that he would be very happy to help me write a sequel. To his credit, he did give me some good points that I have included in this edition. In the past, he has been to some extent a follower of "PUA" or "pickup-artist" techniques to attract women. He claims that *The Blueprint DECODED,* available in

DVD and CD format from Real Social Dynamics, has provided him with some very helpful information (see http://www.blueprintdecoded.com). In large red type, the company's website modestly proclaims that "Like a Syringe of Adrenaline Punched Straight Into Your Heart" you will "Tap The Seething Power Of Your Masculine Essence." You will begin "a whole new life where your very being there reduces women to dripping puddles of lust." Even though it is geared towards men, my cousin claims that many of his female friends have liked the material too. So if you have several hundred dollars to spare, you too can gain "Invincible Confidence That Will Make You The Uncontested Center Of Your Social Universe." Just make sure that your wayward husband does not get hold of the program, or his affairs could really get out of hand.

Share Your Story

This book would be severely diminished—and considerably shorter—without all the stories in it describing how women have dealt with adulterous husbands. If you are going through such circumstances, do you have a story that you would like other women to hear? Perhaps it can help them to cope with similar situations. If it makes you feel more comfortable, you can do so anonymously, without having to give me your real name. Living with adultery can be a very sensitive issue that many women prefer to keep private. As a matter of course, I tend to change names and certain details of people's stories in order to protect their identities. I believe that a good journalist should never reveal the sources of confidential information. If you would like to tell me your story or add comments to my blogs, please visit my website, **adultererswife.com.**

BIBLIOGRAPHY

Books

Alkon, Amy, *Good Manners for Nice People Who Sometimes Say F*ck*. New York: St. Martin's Griffin, 2014. I thought this book was just going to be a sarky bit of fluff—fun and shallow. However, it is both insightful and hilarious. Give a copy to your cad of a husband (or ex-husband), and if he bothers to read it, he might treat you better.

Breggin, MD, Peter R., *The Antidepressant Fact Book: What Your Doctor Won't Tell You About Prozac, Zoloft, Paxil, Celexa and Luvox*. Cambridge, Massachusetts: Da Capo Press, 2001.

Bryson, Bill, *At Home: A Short History of Private Life*. New York: Doubleday, 2010.

Buss, David M., *The Evolution of Desire: Strategies of Human Mating*, rev. ed. New York: Basic Books, 1994, rev. ed. 2003.

Chapman, Gary D., *The 5 Love Languages: The Secret to Love that Lasts.* Chicago: Northfield Publishing, 2010.

Chaucer, Geoffrey, *The Canterbury Tales,* Trans. David Wright, rev.ed. Oxford, England: Oxford University Press, 2011.

Comfort, Dr., Alex, *The Joy of Sex.* New York: Crown Publishers, 2002. However, there is a newer version published in 2009. Alternatively, if you want an antique, get the original edition from 1972.

Daedone, Nicole, *Slow Sex: The Art and Craft of the Female Orgasm.* New York: Grand Central Life and Style, 2011.

Davis, MD, William, *Wheat Belly: Lose the Wheat, Lose the Weight, and Find Your Path Back to Health.* New York: Rodale, 2011.

Dickens, Charles, *A Tale of Two Cities.* Mineola, New York: Dover Publications, 1999.

Dodson, PhD, Betty, *Sex for One: The Joy of Selfloving.* New York: Three Rivers Press, 1996.

Druckerman, Pamela, *Lust in Translation: Infidelity from Tokyo to Tennessee.* New York: Penguin Books, 2007.

Dweck, Carol, *Mindset: The New Psychology of Success.* New York: Random House, 2007.

Gladwell, Malcolm, *Blink.* New York: Little, Brown and Company, 2005. I have read many of Malcolm Gladwell's books and New Yorker articles and they are all absolutely brilliant—highly recommended. He is a master at showing how a totally counterintuitive position actually makes sense.

Gladwell, Malcolm, *David and Goliath: Underdogs, Misfits and the Art of Battling Giants.* New York: Little, Brown and Company, 2013.

Halifax, Joan, *Being with Dying: Cultivating Compassion and Fearlessness in the Presence of Death.* Boston, Massachusetts: Shambhala Publications, Inc., 2008.

HMH Publishing Co. Inc. *Why Do I Get an Irresistible Urge to Laugh Every Time I Make Love?* Chicago, Illinois: Playboy Press, 1971.

I Ching or *Book of Changes.* The Richard Wilhelm Translation rendered into English by Cary F. Baynes. Bollingen Foundation, 1950.

Irvine, Lucy, *Castaway.* Harmondsworth, England: Penguin Books, 1984.

James, E. L., *Fifty Shades of Grey.* New York: Vintage Books, 2012.

Kinsey, Alfred, *Sexual Behavior in the Human Male.* Philadelphia: W.B. Saunders Co., 1948.

Kraemer, Ross S., Cassidy William and Schwartz, Susan L., *Religions of Star Trek.* Boulder, Colorado: Westview Press, 2001.

Kubler-Ross, Elisabeth, *On Death and Dying: What the Dying Have to Teach Doctors, Nurses, Clergy and Their Own Families,* 40th Anniversary Edition. London: Routledge, 2008.

Levin, Ira, *The Stepford Wives.* New York: Random House 1972.

Lipton, Bruce H., *The Biology of Belief: Unleashing the Power of Consciousness, Matter and Miracles.* Fulton, California: Mountain of Love Productions and Elite Press, 2005.

McCall Smith, Alexander, *The No. 1 Ladies' Detective Agency (Book 1).* New York: Anchor Books, 2003. There are several books in this series, and all the ones I have read so far have been delightfully entertaining, perfect for dealing with long periods in waiting rooms.

Niven, David, *Bring on the Empty Horses.* Sevenoaks, Kent, United Kingdom: Coronet Books, 1976.

Nogales, Ana, *Parents Who Cheat: How Children & Adults Are Affected When Their Parents Are Unfaithful.* Deerfield Beach, Florida: Health Communications Inc., 2009.

Patrul Rimpoche, *Kunzang Lama'I Shelung: The Words of My Perfect Teacher.* San Francisco: HarperCollins Publishers, 1994.

Pedro-Carrol, JoAnne, *Putting Children First: Proven Parenting Strategies for Helping Children Thrive Through Divorce*. New York: Penguin Group, 2010.

Pollan, Michael, *In Defense of Food*. New York: The Penguin Press, 2008.

Power, Dale, *Fancy Coffins to Make Yourself: A Schiffer Book for Woodworkers*. Atglen, Pennsylvania: Schiffer Publishing, 2001.

Resnick, Stella, *The Heart of Desire: Keys to the Pleasures of Love*. Hoboken, New Jersey: John Wiley & Sons, Inc., 2012.

Resnick, Stella, *The Pleasure Zone: Why We Resist Good Feelings & How to Let Go and Be Happy*. Berkeley, California: Conari Press, 1997.

Roach, Mary, *Bonk: The Curious Coupling of Science and Sex*. New York: W. W. Norton, 2008.

Rosenberg, Marshall, *Nonviolent Communication: A Language of Life*. Encinitas, California: PuddleDancer Press, 2003.

Ryan, Christopher and Jetha, Cacilda, *Sex at Dawn: How We Mate, Why We Stray, and What It Means for Modern Relationships*. New York: Harper Perennial, 2010.

Sacks, Oliver, *The Man Who Mistook His Wife for a Hat and other Clinical Tales*. New York: Summit Books, 1985. This author must win the prize for one of the best book titles ever. He has written numerous fascinating books about bizarre neurological conditions.

Saxon, Lynn, *Sex at Dusk: Lifting the Shiny Wrapping from Sex at Dawn*. CreateSpace Independent Publishing, 2012.

Shakespeare, William, Nicholas, Nick, Strader, Andrew, *The Klingon Hamlet: The Restored Klingon Version,* prepared by the Klingon Language Institute. New York: Pocket Books/Star Trek, 2000.

Stanley, Christopher S., *Highlights in the History of Concrete*. London: British Cement Association, 1979. I believe that the first edition of this book was written by Jimmy Hoffa.

Sun Tzu (Sunzi), *The Art of War.* Trans. Ralph D. Sawyer. Boulder, Colorado: Westview Press, 1994. Interestingly, the same publisher also produced *Religions of Star Trek.* Obviously, Westview Press goes for both ancient and modern philosophical treatises.

Waitzkin, Josh, *The Art of Learning: An Inner Journey to Optimal Performance.* New York: Free Press, 2008.

Wansink, PhD, Brian, *Mindless Eating: Why We Eat More than We Think.* New York: Bantam Books, 2006.

Willan, Derek, *Greek Rural Postmen and Their Cancellation Numbers.* London: Hellenic Philatelic Society of Great Britain, Publication Number 4. 1994.

Willis, Resa, *FDR and Lucy: Lovers and Friends.* New York: Routledge, 2004.

Winkler, Allan M., *Franklin D. Roosevelt and the Making of Modern America.* New York: Longman Publishing, 2006.

Wrangham, Richard, and Peterson, Dale, *Demonic Males: Apes and the Origins of Human Violence.* New York: Houghton Mifflin, 1996. I had to include this book just for its great title, but it is also a fascinating investigation into the biological reasons why males are more violent than females. You already knew that was the case, didn't you?

Xinran, *The Good Women of China: Hidden Voices.* Translated by Esther Tyldesley. New York: Pantheon Books, 2002.

Yudkin, John, *Pure, White and Deadly: How Sugar is Killing Us and What We Can Do to Stop It.* New York: Penguin Books, 2013.

Articles and Research

Bernstein, Elizabeth, "After Ashley Madison, How to Cope with Infidelity." *The Wall Street Journal,* September 7, 2014. http://www.wsj.com/articles/after-ashley-madison-how-to-cope-with-infidelity-1441652059.

Bingham, John, "Two thirds of today's babies may celebrate 100th birthday." *The Daily Telegraph,* London, December 12, 2013. http://www.telegraph.co.uk/news/health/news/10511865/Two-thirds-of-todays-babies-could-live-to-100.html.

Boyes, Alice, PhD, "50 Characteristics of Healthy Relationships." *Psychology Today* website, January 22, 2013. https://www.psychologytoday.com/blog/in-practice/201301/50-characteristics-healthy-relationships.

Bloomfield, B., Silk, J., "More kisses, cuddles and affection." *Mature Times,* February 3, 2014. http://www.maturetimes.co.uk/more-kisses-cuddles-and-affection/.

Dewey, Caitlin, "Ashley Madison faked female profiles to lure men in, hacked data suggest." *The Washington Post,* August 25, 2015. https://www.washingtonpost.com/news/the-intersect/wp/2015/08/25/ashley-madison-faked-female-profiles-to-lure-men-in-hacked-data-suggest.

Dunbar, R. I. M., Baron, R., Frangou, A., Pearce, E., van Leewen, E. J. C., Stow, J., Partridge. G.,MacDonald, I., Barra, V., van Vugt, M., "Social laughter is correlated with an elevated pain threshold." *Royal Society Publishing,* February 9, 2012. doi: 10.1098/rspb.2011.1373. http://rspb.royalsocietypublishing.org/content/279/1731/1161.

Ellis, B. J., Bates, J. E., Dodge, K. J., Fergusson, D. M., Horwood, L. J., Pettit, G. S., Woodward, L., "Does Father Absence Place Daughters at Special Risk for Early Sexual Activity and Teenage Pregnancy?" *Child Development,* Volume 74, Issue 3, pp. 801-21, May 2003.

Eady, Piers, "Marmite TV ad faces ban after complaints from animal welfare campaigners." *Mirror* website, August 7, 2013. http://www.mirror.co.uk/news/uk-news/marmite-tv-ad-faces-ban-2136148.

Gladwell, Malcolm, Annals of Psychology, "The Naked Face." *The New Yorker,* August 5, 2002, pp. 38-49. http://gladwell.com/the-naked-face/.

Gallup, G. G., Jr, Burch, R. L., Platek, S. M., "Does Semen have Antidepressant Properties?" *Archives of Sexual Behavior,* 2002 Jun; 31(3): 289-93.

Galperin, A., Haselton, M. G., Frederick, D. A., Poore, J., Von Hippel, W., Buss, D. M., Gonzaga G. C., "Sexual Regret: Evidence for Evolved Sex Differences." *Archives of Sexual Behavior,* 2013 Oct; 42(7): 1145-61. doi: 10.1007/s10508-012-0019-3.

Goleman, Daniel, "A Feel-Good Theory: A Smile Affects Mood." *New York Times,* July 18, 1989. http://www.nytimes.com/1989/07/18/science/a-feel-good-theory-a-smile-affects-mood.html.

Gopnik, Adam, "A Point of View: Sex and the French." *BBC News Magazine* website, January 17, 2014. http://www.bbc.co.uk/news/magazine-25756961.

Hamilton, R., Vohs, K., Sellier, A., Meyvis, T., "Being of Two Minds: Switching Mindsets Exhausts Self-regulatory Resources." *Organizational Behavior and Human Decision Processes,* December 2010. Available at the Social Science Research Network (SSRN) website: http://ssrn.com/abstract=1147689.

Harper, C. C., McLanahan, S. S., "Father Absence and Youth Incarceration." *Journal of Research on Adolescence,* 14(3), 2004, pp. 369-97. http://www.ncbi.nlm.nih.gov/pmc/articles/PMC2764264/

"The health benefits of tai chi." *Harvard Women's Health Watch, Harvard Health Publications,* Harvard Medical School, May 1, 2009. http://www.health.harvard.edu/staying-healthy/the-health-benefits-of-tai-chi.

"HIV Among People Aged 50 and Over." CDC website. http://www.cdc.gov/hiv/group/age/olderamericans/index.html.

Hodgekiss, Anna, "Sex: Why it makes women fall in love - but just makes men want MORE!" *MailOnline,* 29 August, 2011. http://www.dailymail.co.uk/health/article-2031498/Sex-Why-makes-women-fall-love--just-makes-men-want-MORE.html.

Ishigami, Y., Klein, R. M., "Is a hands-free phone safer than a handheld phone?" *Journal of Safety Research,* Vol. 40, Issue 2, 2009, pp. 157-64. doi: 10.1016/j.jsr.2009.02.006.

Morris, J. N., Heady, J. A., Raffle, P. A. B., Roberts, C. G., and Parks, J. W., 1953. "Coronary heart disease and physical activity of work." *The Lancet*, 21 November 1953, Vol. 262(6795) pp. 1053-57.

Odone, Cristina, "Sexually we haven't moved on since the fifties." *The Daily Telegraph*, October 5, 2013, p. 12. http://www.telegraph.co.uk/culture/tvandradio/bbc/10357341/Mariella-Frostrup-interview-Sexually-we-havent-moved-on-since-the-Fifties.html.

Ringback Weitoft, G., Hjern, A., Haglund, B., Rosen, M., "Mortality, severe morbidity, and injury in children living with single parents in Sweden: a population-based study." *The Lancet*, Volume 361, Issue 9354, pp. 289-295, 25 January 2003. http://www.thelancet.com/journals/lancet/article/PIIS0140-6736(03)12324-0/abstract.

Rosen, Christine, "The Myth of Multitasking." *The New Atlantis*, Spring 2008, pp. 105-110.

Sharma, A., MD, Madaan, V., MD, Petty, F. D., MD, PhD, "Exercise for Mental Health." *Primary Care Companion to the Journal of Clinical Psychiatry*, *Physicians* Postgraduate Press, Inc. 2006, 8(2), 106. http://www.ncbi.nlm.nih.gov/pmc/articles/PMC1470658/

"Study Finds Sex a Significant Predictor of Happiness Among Married Seniors." *The Gerontological Society of America*, November 20, 2011. http://prod.geron.org/About%20Us/press-room/Archived%20Press%20Releases/77-2011-press-releases/1182-study-finds-sex-a-significant-predictor-of-happiness-among-married-seniors.

Tomlinson, Simon, "You didn't have an abortion and now you come here with your big stomach: Extraordinary catfight between bride and new husband's pregnant mistress at wedding reception." *Daily Mail*, November 27, 2013. http://www.dailymail.co.uk/news/article-2514350/Extraordinary-video-catfight-bride-husbands-pregnant-mistress.html.

Von Simson, R., Kulasegaram, R., "Sexual health and the older adult: Trends show that doctors must be more vigilant." *Student British Medical Journal*, February 2, 2012. http://student.bmj.com/student/view-article.html?id=sbmj.e688.

Wallace, Benjamin, "Bikram Feels the Heat." *Vanity Fair,* January 2014. http://www.vanityfair.com/society/2014/01/bikram-choudhury-yoga-sexual-harassment.

Wike, Richard, "French more accepting of infidelity than people in other countries." Pew Research Center website, January 14, 2014. http://www.pewresearch.org/fact-tank/2014/01/14/french-more-accepting-of-infidelity-than-people-in-other-countries/.

"Yoga for anxiety and depression." Harvard Mental Health Letter, *Harvard Health Publications, Harvard Medical School.* April 1, 2009. http://www.health.harvard.edu/mind-and-mood/yoga-for-anxiety- and-depression.

Zimbardo, Philip, Stanford Prison Experiment, 1971. http://www.prisonexp.org/.